TREKKING IN LADAKH

About the Author

Radek Kucharski was born in Poland. After graduating in Geography from the University of Warsaw he worked for a small GIS (geographic information system) company for over ten years, during which time he embarked on several months-long trekking trips in Nepal, Iran, Pakistan and India, getting to know the landscapes, the people, their cultures – and himself. After his first visit in 2004, Ladakh instantly became his favourite destination, and he promised himself he would return with the aim of collecting information for a guidebook. A few years later he began this work.

Since that first visit to Ladakh he has also changed profession and has now been working as a tourist guide for a couple of years. Radek lives in Warsaw and guides groups to India, Nepal and Scandinavia for one of Poland's leading adventure travel agencies. Check out Radek's website at www.radekkucharski.com.

TREKKING IN LADAKH

by Radek Kucharski

2 POLICE SQUARE, MILNTHORPE, CUMBRIA LA7 7PY
www.cicerone.co.uk

© Radek Kucharski
Second edition 2015
ISBN: 978 1 85284 830 9

First edition 2012
ISBN: 978 1 85284 675 6

Printed in China on behalf of Latitude Press Ltd.
A catalogue record for this book is available from the British Library.

All photographs are by the author with the exception of the author photograph
on page 2, which is by Magdalena Zaborowska.

Relief data courtesy of NASA, USGS, JPL, Caltech and CIAT.

Dedication

*To the people of Ladakh who face the hardships of life in a harsh environment
with joy, and who willingly share their high spirits and rich culture with
guests from the wider world; and to those trekkers who wish to
enrich themselves through travel.*

Updates to this Guide

While every effort is made by our authors to ensure the accuracy of guidebooks
as they go to print, changes can occur during the lifetime of an edition. Any
updates that we know of for this guide will be on the Cicerone website (www.
cicerone.co.uk/830/updates), so please check before planning your trip. We
also advise that you check information about such things as transport,
accommodation and shops locally. Even rights of way can be altered over
time. We are always grateful for information about any discrepancies between
a guidebook and the facts on the ground, sent by email to info@cicerone.co.uk
or by post to Cicerone, 2 Police Square, Milnthorpe LA7 7PY, United Kingdom.

Front cover: Pidmo village in the Zanskar Valley

CONTENTS

Warning

Mountain walking can be a dangerous activity carrying a risk of personal injury or death. It should be undertaken only by those with a full understanding of the risks and with the training and/or experience to evaluate them. While every care and effort has been taken in the preparation of this guide, the user should be aware that conditions can be highly variable and can change quickly, materially affecting the seriousness of a mountain walk.

Therefore, except for any liability which cannot be excluded by law, neither Cicerone nor the author accept liability for damage of any nature (including damage to property, personal injury or death) arising directly or indirectly from the information in this book.

Readers are warned that there is no organised mountain rescue service in Ladakh, such as exists in some other mountain regions. Furthermore, there is no mobile phone coverage in most of the places along trekking routes. In case of emergency self-help may be the only option. Any helicopter rescue would be expensive and payment guarantee required, so be insured.

Map key

————	asphalt road	■	habitation (not permanent)
••••••••	route on road	□	abandoned village
————	unpaved road	○	village
= = = = = :	pathway	▲	monastery
Ⓢ	start point	☾*	mosque
Ⓕ	finish point	☺	shelter (very basic)
⑤Ⓕ	start/finish point	Ⓑ	bridge
————	Trek 1	⚕	area where you can camp
————	Trek 2	▲	peak
————	Trek 3	⤢	pass
————	Trek 4	•	ridge
————	Trek 5	⚕	campsite
————	Trek 6	⊕	airport
————	Trek 7	◎	town
————	Trek 8	⬭	lake
————	stream		glacier
————	river	➡	route direction (various colours)
═══	main river	→	direction arrow

The view from the Sengge La (4954m) (Trek 5 Stage 6)

Acknowledgements

My parents and my girlfriend waited patiently for news during the long weeks I was away in the mountains, and also supported me while I was writing this guidebook. My high school friend, Marcin, was my companion for some time on each of my trips to India. My friends Edyta and Bartek were always ready to give advice and discuss my ideas about the book, and helped me with the maps. The Tatra Mountains guide, Justyna, was the first person to use this book in Ladakh, and gave me some useful suggestions and corrections.

I am grateful to Siân Pritchard-Jones and Bob Gibbons, who helped to polish up some of my Polish/English grammar. They have also provided much of the information about the historical, cultural and religious features of Ladakh, which fascinate all visitors to the region. Their contributions appear in parts of the main introduction and in the glossary and are abbreviated details from their book *Ladakh: Land of Magical Monasteries*. They have also shared some of their experience of trekking over the Kanji La in the early season and some of their vast knowledge on the effects of high altitude on trekkers' health. Great thanks also go to Sue Viccars for editing this book. She worked patiently to discuss issues with me and resolve any doubt over my meaning, and also suggested some important additions.

Last but not least, I am very grateful to Jonathan Williams of Cicerone Press who decided to publish the book in spite of my imperfect English, which needed additional editing. His understanding and appreciation of the book is a great honour to me. In addition I would like to thank Lois Sparling, Clare Crooke and Neil Simpson at Cicerone Press, who have guided me through the preparation stages.

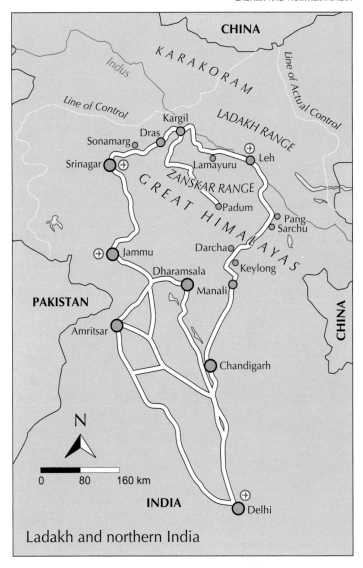

Ladakh and northern India

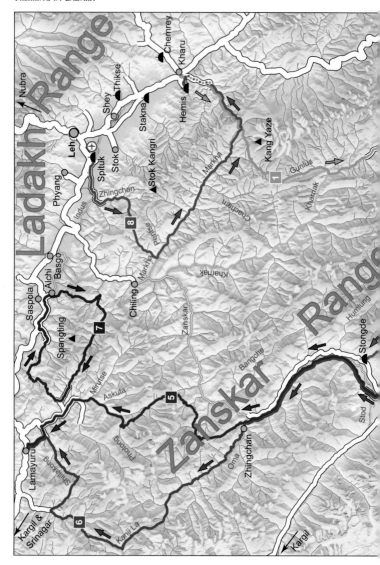

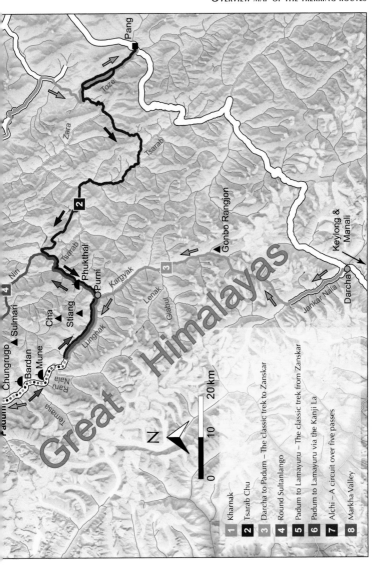

1 Kharnak
2 Tsarab Chu
3 Darcha to Padum – The classic trek to Zanskar
4 Round Sultanlango
5 Padum to Lamayuru – The classic trek from Zanskar
6 Padum to Lamayuru via the Kanji La
7 Alchi – A circuit over five passes
8 Markha Valley

Ursi village, and the Tar La high above (Trek 7 Stages 5–6)

PREFACE

My initial foray to the Himalayas was in 2000, to India and Nepal, where the Annapurna region gave me my first taste of the fascinating Himalayan Buddhist culture. I also visited the Karakoram of Pakistan. However, it was the mountains of Ladakh that drew me back to India in 2004. I was bewitched by the place, enchanted as much by the friendly, kind, hard-working and joyful people as by the tranquil landscapes and stunning vistas. Just being in Ladakh seems to bring a special peace of mind and calmness not easily found elsewhere.

I knew I would have to return again and again to experience the fabulous trekking trails, enchanting villages and magical monasteries. Trekking in the wild gorges, climbing to a high pass dusted with pristine snow, hiking under crystal-clear skies, enjoying a freshly brewed cup of tea with a stranger – these are the special qualities of Ladakh that stay in the memory forever.

To satisfy my newfound addiction I spent four months there in 2009, exploring the landscapes on foot, and covering more than 1000 kilometres. And still Ladakh draws me back! I remember leaving the region in late October 2009, at the approach of winter. As the plane took off, we flew over Spituk Gompa and then turned towards the southeast. I looked down at the passes I had and had not yet crossed, dreaming of re-walking the first and exploring the latter.

I am lucky to have had the chance to visit Ladakh a few more times since this guidebook was first published. I've re-trekked major parts of some routes and tested a few new options. There are some changes in the book based on this experience. January 2014 found me trying to trek in Ladakh in winter; and now, here I am again, getting ready for another winter trek!

Ladakh is changing. Roads are expanding along old trails and trekking routes. They make some places easily accessible, but they also reduce some treks or make them less enjoyable, particularly the classic Darcha–Padum and Padum–Lamayuru treks. There has also been a large increase in the number of visitors. There are more guesthouses in Leh, more cars, and a bigger impact on the environment. It is more important now than ever that we leave as few traces on the trail as possible, consume minimal resources and – in general – prepare our trip with consideration for the environment.

I hope this book will help you to find your own Ladakh story. I'm quite sure that once you have had one, you will want to have more. And my wish is that you will experience as much pleasure, enjoyment and fulfilment as I have in this incredible part of the world.

Radek Kucharski
December 2014
Leh, Ladakh

The impressive Shillakong canyon (Trek 6 Stage 10)

INTRODUCTION

Author's rucksack and walking poles on the Gotunta La (Trek 2)

Situated in the far north of India, Ladakh is far more culturally and environmentally linked to Tibet than to the plains of India, Kashmir or the Indian Himalayas. But Ladakh is certainly much more than just 'Little Tibet', as it is frequently called. Located in the shadow of the Great Himalaya Range it is isolated from the summer monsoon rains. Like western Tibet and the adjacent former Guge Kingdom, its high elevation and low precipitation combine to create a high-altitude cold desert environment, with limited vegetation. The ethnic origin of the majority of the people is Tibetan; their language is similar to Tibetan, and their religion is Tibetan Buddhism. However – unlike Tibet – being at the crossroads of major trading routes between the Indian plains, Kashmir, Central Asia and Tibet, Ladakh has always had strong connections with the outside world. These interactions over the centuries have changed, enhanced and enriched the region's heritage.

The Tibetan roots of the land and its people are not the only magnet for visitors seduced by the far-reaching Ladakhi landscapes and Tibetan Buddhist culture. Outdoor activities such as cycling and rafting are on offer, but trekking in the mountains is a major draw: from deep gorges to glaciated peaks, from wide valleys to narrow, high mountain passes, from alpine meadows to arid plateaux. There are popular routes where accommodation is in village 'homestays' with local hosts, others where fixed campsites with good facilities provide overnight comforts, as well as remote, exciting wilderness treks where you will not see anyone for days and will be totally dependent on yourself and your team. With its magnificent landscape, hospitable and charming people, rich heritage – and still limited numbers of tourists – Ladakh is a desirable destination for every trekker.

From a practical point of view, however, trekking in Ladakh is not always easy. The paths are not waymarked, and the number of villages limited. Food supplies must usually be carried from the starting point, and there are long stretches where water is unavailable. Additionally, the effects of high altitude make increased physical demands on the trekker. Creature comforts are few (although there may be a surfeit of spiritual diversions for those who engage the culture!). However, Ladakh is a perfect place for trekkers with a lust for adventure and sound knowledge of mountain walking.

Good pre-trek preparation is essential. Assess your experience and condition; check the available routes and choose a suitable one (a range of treks with different requirements are described in this book). An independent trek will give you much freedom, but is the most demanding choice; a fully organised group trip will provide

more comfort and security, but you will need to compromise on flexibility. Hiring a horseman and a few pack animals independently is yet another option. Whatever you decide, this book will help with your preparations and give you sufficient information to follow the routes safely, and thus to make the most of your visit to this extraordinary land.

GEOLOGY

We are looking upon the inexhaustibly rich rock formations. We note where and how were conceived the examples of symbolic images. Nature, having no outlet, inscribed epics with their wealth of ornamentation, on the rocks. One perceives how the forms of imagery blend with the mountain atmosphere.
Altai Himalaya Nicholas Roerich

Ladakh is located at the boundary zone between the Eurasian continent and the Indian subcontinent. The Indus Valley, regarded frequently as the spine of the region, is located just north of the so-called suture zone, where the two continental plates collided some 50 million years ago. North and south of the Indus are a series of mountain ranges, more or less parallel to the valley. These are the Great Himalaya Range that forms the southwestern boundary; the Zanskar Range – mountains formed of oceanic sediments – between the Great Himalayas and the Indus; the

The Great Himalayas: the Nun Kun massif on Ladakh's southwest boundary

Ladakh Range – mountains formed of plutonic rocks – north of the Indus; and the Karakoram that marks the northern boundary.

LANDSCAPE

Ladakh has a very clear physical identity, which can be instantly appreciated by anybody approaching by road, either via the Zoji La (from Srinagar) or the Baralacha La (from Keylong and Manali). However, it would be a gross over-simplification to say that Ladakh constitutes only one type of landscape. It is a huge area of nearly 60,000sq km (according to the official statistics of Kargil and Leh districts), similar in size to Croatia or Latvia. Its highest point stands at 7672m (Saser Kangri in the Ladakhi part of the Karakoram);

the lowest at about 2650m. Human habitation is found within an altitude range of some 2000m.

Officially the region consists of two districts: Leh and Kargil, both within the State of Jammu and Kashmir. The sub-regions of Ladakh are usually defined as follows:

- **Central Ladakh** is the region along the Indus River between Upshi and Khalatse.
- **Nubra** consists of the valley of the Shayok River between its sharp turn towards the northwest, down through the confluence with the Nubra River, to its narrow section at the Line of Control (the Indian/Pakistani border and the boundary of Ladakh), together with the Nubra Valley.
- **Changtang** is considered to be the high-altitude plains of Eastern

17

Ladakh, with Rupshu to the south and Pangong, Changchenmo and Aksai Chin (under Chinese control) to the north. This is a continuation of the Changtang of Western Tibet, where the mountain ranges are less pronounced and a number of vast lakes are situated.

- **Zanskar** is the southwestern part of Ladakh, north of the Great Himalayas, made up of the area around the tributary rivers that form the Zanskar River and the early part of the Zanskar River valley.
- **Western** or **Lower Ladakh** consists of the relatively lower-altitude Suru, Mulbekh, Bodhkarbu and Kargil areas, where the climate is correspondingly more moderate and the growing season longer.

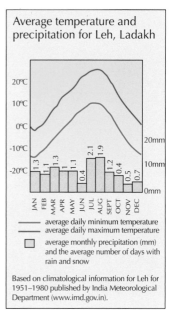

Average temperature and precipitation for Leh, Ladakh

—— average daily minimum temperature
—— average daily maximum temperature
▢ average monthly precipitation (mm) and the average number of days with rain and snow

Based on climatological information for Leh for 1951–1980 published by India Meteorological Department (www.imd.gov.in).

CLIMATE

High altitude, isolation from the rains of the summer monsoon and the vast altitude range within the region are the main factors dictating the nature of the Ladakhi climate. Precipitation is almost totally limited to snow, which falls mostly in the high mountains. The gradual melting of glaciers and snow throughout the year is the main source of water, enabling agriculture and human habitation. It is generally sunny, but clear skies lead to a rapid loss of ground warmth via thermal radiation during the night.

There is therefore a great range in temperature throughout the day all year round, and even between a place in the shade and one in direct sunlight. The combination of high mountains, deep valleys and vast temperature differences creates wind that, although not usually strong, is a constant feature.

PLANTS AND ANIMALS

At first glance, the mountains seem to be completely barren. However, even the driest slopes are covered by sparse grasses, perennials and small shrubs. Meadows are found in the

A poplar tree in Zanskar in autumn

wide high-altitude valleys, of which Nyimaling is probably one of the most beautiful. Bigger shrubs, like seabuckthorn or willow, grow only on the valley floors, by rivers. Trees are limited to riverbanks or irrigated places at elevations around 3000m or lower. Agriculture is restricted to land where irrigation is possible; the main crops are barley, wheat and peas.

Surprisingly, despite the scarce resources, the wildlife of the region is quite diverse: there are about 250 species of birds and 30 of mammals. These include the black-necked crane, Himalayan snowcock, golden eagle, bharal (Himalayan blue sheep), Tibetan wild ass, marmot and snow leopard. It is not uncommon to see many of these during a trek; you will certainly see a good number of birds, bharals and marmots. Although snow leopards are extremely shy and very rare, there is always a chance of spotting one (the author once saw one on the way from the Kungski La, just west of Hemis National Park).

HISTORY

The main aspects of the culture of Ladakh are its fascinating history and Buddhist heritage. For many centuries, its history has been inextricably connected with events on the Tibetan plateau, and culturally it has closer links with Tibet than with other parts of India. Ladakh existed as a separate

An autumn evening near Hanamur village (Treks 5 and 6): the moon is rising over the peak, which is lit by the warm rays of the setting sun

kingdom for nine centuries, from the middle of the 10th to the 19th when the borders changed: a turbulent period, with the region as a buffer state between Muslim empires in the west and Buddhist Tibet in the east.

The Mon were probably the earliest inhabitants of Ladakh and Zanskar, possibly migrating by way of Manali before the third century BC. Another group, the Dards, also migrated into Ladakh; their descendants still live along the Indus River in the villages of Domkhar and Skurbuchan. They could have originated from Afghanistan or even have descended from the Aryans, who migrated to India from Eastern Europe. The adventurer AH Francke, who explored Ladakh in the early 20th century, discovered what he thought were royal graves close to modern-day Leh. The

Likir Gompa, situated in a tranquil valley off the main road, is famous for its huge statue of the Buddha Maitreya

Dards worshipped fire, earth, sun, moon, water, animals and the like, similar to the Bon of early Tibet.

The earliest Buddhists probably came to Ladakh in the third century BC. Later the Ghandaran civilisation from Taxila in northwest Pakistan influenced Ladakh with its links to the ancient Buddhas of Bamiyan. Buddhism spread all along the Silk Route into China, and superseded the old Tibetan Bon faith on the plateau itself. In the second century AD, the Kushana kings of the Kashmir region ruled over the predominantly Buddhist region that extended into Ladakh; King Kanishka probably

21

constructed a *chorten* in Zanskar. As early as the fifth century AD, the cult of Maitreya Buddha was found in Ladakh, according to the celebrated Chinese monk explorer Fa Hsien.

During the eighth century the spread of Tantric ideas – emanating from an inter-religious spiritual movement that arose in medieval India in the fifth century – began to influence Buddhist traditions, heralding Buddhism's eventual decline across India, as Hinduism gained in popularity.

However, Tantric ideas remained in Tibet and Ladakh. Srongtsen Gampo of Tibet had adopted Buddhism as the state religion in the seventh century. Later King Trisong Detsen invited a series of Indian masters, including Padma Sambhava, to teach Buddhism in Tibet. Ironically, it was the assassination of King Langdarma, a strident Bon practitioner and anti-Buddhist ruler, that prompted a revival on the high plateaux of Ladakh, Guge and Tibet. His great-grandson Nyima Gon established firm rule over Ladakh and Western Tibet, and it was his descendants, Yeshe O and Changchub O, who invited Atisa to Toling in the 10th–11th centuries.

The great translator Rinchen Zangpo helped to establish 108 monasteries across Ladakh, Western Tibet and Spiti, visiting the fledgling monastic centre at Spituk around AD1050. However, the first of the great Ladakhi monasteries was built in the early 12th century at Likir. During the 12th–15th centuries the various kings of Ladakh loosely concentrated their power and constructed bridges, palaces and *chortens*. However, they remained under the influence of Central Tibet.

Stok Palace, on the bank of the Indus River near Leh

After the 15th century many of the Ladakhi monasteries, including Spituk and Likir, transferred to the new Gelug-pa sect of reformer Tsong Khapa. Under King Grags Bum-lde, a prolific builder, Thikse was founded and images of Buddha Maitreya constructed at Tingmosgang and Tsemo above Leh. Surprisingly, the Sakya-pa *gompa* at Matho was also consecrated at this time. The lineage of King Grags Bum-lde ended, allowing the Namgyal dynasty to take power. The first king was Tashi Namgyal, but despite his despotic rule the Drigung philosophy flourished across Ladakh. Tsewang Namgyal (approximately 1530–60) managed to hold power in Ladakh and even extend rule towards Turkic Yarkand. Jamyang Namgyal became ruler of Ladakh from 1560 to 1590, facing opposition from the Muslim Baltis.

Perhaps the most successful ruler was King Sengge Namgyal (approximately 1590–1620). With the assistance of the Buddhist master Stagsang Raspa he founded many new monasteries, including Basgo, Hemis and Chemrey. He was a follower of the Druk-pa Kagyu-pa order, and also built the nine-storied palace at Leh that remains today. Deldan Namgyal (1620–40) followed; he was a wise and socially adroit ruler. It was during his rule that the Portuguese Jesuit, Antonio de Andrade, travelled to Tsaparang, which gave rise to the decline of the adjacent Guge Kingdom.

When the Mongol hordes took Tibet, the new Ladakhi King Delegs Namgyal retreated to Basgo. He asked Kashmir, then under the great Moghul emperor Shah Jahan, for help. He became a Muslim and the

The fleeces of pashmina goats have been an important part of the Ladakhi economy for hundreds of years

first mosques appeared in Leh (30–50 per cent of the population now follow Islam).

From around 1680 to 1780 there was a great quarrel for power between two branches of family heirs. Rigzin Tsewang Norbu, an emissary of the Dalai Lama, came to Ladakh and resolved matters, with the kings of Zanskar keeping separate power. King Tsestan Namgyal was another wise ruler who played polo and kept the peace. With no heir his brother Tsepal took power, having spent his youthful years in Hemis Gompa, and ruled until 1841. William Moorcroft, the first British subject to explore the land, visited Ladakh from 1820 to 1822. Later the second son of Tsepal took over, but his rule was doomed by the rising power of the Sikhs, Ranjit Singh of Lahore, the Dogras of Jammu and the British East India Company.

The Dogra army of Zorawar entered Ladakh from the south, because the Sikhs held Kashmir at the time, but little changed. The Dogras made a brief advance to the north against Muslim Baltistan. In order to cross the rivers, they used ingenious ice and wood bridges constructed by the Dards of the Indus River. King Tsepal's grandson Jigsmed inherited the throne. Zorawar next set his armies, including Ladakhis, towards Tibet with 6000–7000 men. After his death on the battlefield, peace ensued between Tibet and Ladakh and Jigsmed retired to his palace in Stok.

Under the British, Ladakh remained under Jammu, with monasteries retaining their land and status. The descendants of the royal family continued to live at Stok, but all power resided in Srinagar. In 1947 Ladakh formally became part of the Indian State of Jammu and Kashmir. The Indian army retains a strong presence, because of the continuing border disputes with Pakistan and China. Tibet ceased to exercise any sovereign powers after 1959. With political turmoil in Kashmir, Ladakh has gained more independence, with direct air links to Delhi. Tourism has become a major new contributor to the economy.

TRADE ROUTES AND TOURISM

Trading caravans have crossed Ladakh for many centuries, only ceasing in the early 1950s (see below). On the east/west route between Tibet and Kashmir *pashm* – the raw material used in shawls produced in Kashmir from pashmina goats bred in western Tibet – as well as sheep wool were traded. Gold, saffron and textiles were sent to the high *lamas* of Tibet. Tea was imported from Lhasa via Ladakh – the only source of tea for consumption in the Kashmiri Valley until the early 19th century. Salt, grains and dried fruits were traded too.

The north/south trade route between the Indian Punjab, south of the Himalayas, and the town of Yarkand in Sinkiang, Central Asia, passed through Manali to Leh, much as the modern road does. From Leh it crossed the rugged Khardung La, then went north over the treacherous Karakoram Pass. Luxury goods, like fabrics, carpets, precious stones, jewellery, spices and narcotics, were traded.

These ancient trading routes have all remained closed since just after India's independence in 1947. To this day, Ladakh's borders are disputed between India and Pakistan, as is the Aksai Chin region, east of the Pangong Lake area, between India and China. With the building of the airport in Leh and roads into the countryside, Ladakh opened for foreign tourists in the mid-1970s, and numbers have grown rapidly since then. Between 50,000 and 78,000 visitors (Indian and foreign) annually travelled to the region by the end of the first decade of this century, and exceeded 100,000 in 2011. This creates big opportunities for the people of Ladakh, but also poses a danger to the last stronghold of the unique, ancient Tibetan Buddhist culture, that has declined in Tibet itself. Its survival is the responsibility of all visitors into whose hands it is entrusted.

CURRENT POPULATION

Some 290,000 people live in Ladakh, a population comparable to a medium-size European city, similar to that of Utrecht in the Netherlands, Bradford in England or Bialystok in Poland. Their ethnic roots are found in the Dards, the Tibetans and some other groups. The Dards are an Indo-Iranian group, but the Tibetans who migrated to the region during the 8th–10th centuries belong to Burmo-Mongolian stock. Other different groups from the south, west and north of Ladakh continually passed through the region over the centuries along old trading routes.

Ladakhi people are predominantly Buddhist, but Muslims (both Shia and Sunni) are an important part of the community too, forming the majority of the population in Kargil District, in the western part of the region. Hindus, Sikhs, Bonpo and Christians are also represented, although not in significant numbers.

BUDDHISM IN LADAKH

The nature of Buddhism in Ladakh is closely enmeshed with the Vajrayana Buddhism of ancient Tibet. It has all the accoutrements that Tantra has brought to Tibetan Buddhism; some of its aspects can be traced far back to the Bon faith of the earliest periods of Tibetan history. Look in any Ladakhi *gompa* and you will be dazzled by the proliferation of Buddhist artistry and iconography. The sheer number of Buddha figures, *bodhisattvas* and idols, whether as paintings or statues, is astonishing. Even the most confirmed atheist will surely find something uplifting about Ladakh's rich and colourful Buddhist heritage.

Mala (Buddhist prayer beads)

The philosophy of Buddhism is based on the four noble truths and the eight noble paths. The four noble truths are the truth of suffering, which occurs through the cycle of rebirth. The second truth is the desire for things that lead to dissatisfaction. Nirvana, or the cessation of desire, is the third truth, and the fourth is the way of the middle path as a solution. The eight ways to attain the path to Nirvana are: right understanding, right thought, right speech, right action, right livelihood, right effort, right mind and right concentration.

The impermanent nature which is being taught in the 'Four Noble Truths' refers to the more subtle aspect of impermanence, which is the transitory nature of existence.
Daily Advice from the Heart Dalai Lama

Although Buddhism is considered to be a religion, much of its practice is a philosophy for life. Prince Gautama Siddhartha, the earthly Buddha, was born in southern Nepal and first initiated the ideas of Buddhism. The son of a king, his early life was one of luxury and he married the daughter of a neighbouring *raja*. At the age of 29 he realised that other life existed beyond his palatial confines and, leaving behind his wife and newborn son, he took up the life of an ascetic. He wandered far listening to wise men and Hindu Brahmin priests, but found no solace. After much meditation he found the path to enlightenment around 600BC, choosing to accept that life meant suffering.

Principal Buddhist Sects

Across Ladakh each monastery has close associations with the different Tibetan Buddhist schools. The main sects are as follows.

Nyingma-pa

The Nyingma-pa is the oldest Buddhist sect originating in Tibet, known as the Red Hat sect. It developed when the Indian master Santarakshita, and later Padma Sambhava, the Tantric sage, were invited to Tibet to teach Indian Buddhism. The Nyingma-pa postulates that a person can find their own path to enlightenment without the

The statue of Maitreya in Likir, Central Ladakh

aid of teachers, collective meditations and the reading of scriptures. Padma Sambhava, later known as Guru Rinpoche, is considered to be the founder of Lamaism in Tibet. His consort Yeshe Tsogyal recorded many of the scriptures of her mentor and these were concealed, to be revealed to future masters when appropriate. Today the Nyingma-pa sect is found in Ladakh, Tibet and the Khumbu region of Nepal around Mount Everest.

Kadam-pa

The Kadam-pa developed in the 11th century after a Bon rebellion. Atisa, another intellectual Indian teacher from the Buddhist university of Nalanda in India, conceived it. He held the view that Tantric methods to enlightenment should only follow on after in-depth reflection on the philosophy of the religion. These austere practices probably led to it being eclipsed by the powerful Sakya-pa sect. The Kadam-pa doctrines later became the basis of the Gelug-pa.

Kagyu-pa

The Kagyu-pa sect is attributed to the Indian mystic translator (Lotsawa) Marpa (1012–97), a disciple of Atisa. He followed other famous Indian sages, Tilopa and Naropa, who are also considered masters of Kagyu-pa. The Kagyu-pa concentrate their meditations on inner mental and spiritual matters. They choose to be close to their teachers. The Kagyu-pa sect has a number of sub-groups, such as Dagpo, Drigung-pa, Druk-pa, Taglung-pa and the Karma-pa.

Karma-pa (Karmarpa)

The Karma-pa (Karmarpa) is a sub-sect that has descended from the master, Gampopa (1079–1153), whose life was reputedly foretold by Buddha Sakyamuni. The Black Hat Karmarpas are just one influential body within the sect, but are famous for their festival dances.

Drigung-pa

The Drigung sect has its founding monastery of Drigung Til about 125km northeast of Lhasa. Its founder was Jigten Sumgon (1143–1217). In Ladakh he is called Skyoba Jigjen.

Druk-pa

The northern Druk-pa are found in Tibet and Ladakh, while the southern Druk-pa are found in Bhutan. The sect originated in the 12th century in Ralung, near Gyangtse in southern Tibet. Many Druk-pa *lamas* left Ralung because of persecution by Gelug-pa followers. The Shabdrung, the spiritual leader of the Druk-pa sect, was a descendant of the founder of the Ralung Gompa, and in 1616 he also left for Bhutan.

Sakya-pa

The Sakya-pa began in the 11th century south of modern-day Lhatse, west of Xigatse. This sect stresses the need for study of the existing Buddhist scriptures. Under the Sakya-pa the two great Tibetan Buddhist bibles, the Tangyur and Kangyur, were compiled. The Sakya-pa flourished under Mongolian patronage, but later declined.

Gelug-pa

The Gelug-pa is the Yellow Hat sect of the Dalai Lama, initiated by Tsong Khapa, who reformed and developed Atisa's original ideas. This form of Buddhism reverted to a purist format, bringing greater morality and discipline to the monks. It sought to remove some Tantric aspects and to cleanse the religion. The first monastery was established at Ganden, near Lhasa. The Dalai Lamas are the spiritual leaders of the Gelug-pa sect. In the early 15th century, the Gelug-pa schools came to Ladakh from Tibet and established the majority of the monasteries that exist today.

When to go?

Putting aside winter treks, the recommended trekking season runs from late spring (mid-June) throughout the summer to late autumn (mid-October). The peak season, both for sightseeing and for trekking, is much shorter and lasts from mid-July to the end of August. Late August or September is therefore probably the best time for trekking in Ladakh. In spring and early summer many routes are inaccessible due to snow on the passes. In late June and July the rivers are high, making some of the crossings impossible. In August there are many big tour groups – not a

Wildflowers flourishing on the wide plains of Zanskar, near Padum, in summer (Treks 3–6)

good time for those who seek a quiet mountain adventure.

By September autumnal colour starts to appear. Rivers, grey with melted glacier water in summer, become clear and incredibly turquoise in colour. Wild animals, having spent the summer on high pastures, come to the lower elevations and are more easily spotted. People have finished their work in the fields and have more time to talk and to host you in their homes; and it is still warm enough for a pleasant trekking experience.

October is cold but trekking is not impossible. It is a good idea to stay in the villages at night, avoid river

Local women with donkeys in the upper Markha Valley, with the Kang Yaze peaks beyond (Trek 8)

crossings and high passes, and take extra clothes. Snow can fall in mid-October, even in Leh!

Which route?
The choice of route depends on the season, your experience, the available time and the preferred style of trekking. No trek is easy in Ladakh, but some are hard, others less demanding. If you are not an experienced trekker and want to trek on your own (see How to trek?), choose one of the classics: Markha Valley (Trek 8), Darcha to Padum (Trek 3) or Padum to Lamayuru (Trek 5). The Alchi circuit (Trek 7) is a little more physically demanding than the Markha Valley trek, but is generally easier than other treks. It is a good alternative to the latter, which is much more popular and crowded in the high season.

The Kharnak trek (Trek 1) is the longest, most diverse, remotest and most demanding trek in this guidebook. The Tsarab Chu trek (Trek 2) is a demanding route to Zanskar, a great alternative to the classic Darcha to Padum. The Kanji La route (Trek 6) is a beautiful although tough alternative to the classic trek from Zanskar (Trek 5). Needless to say, these three are the best in the book. None of them, however, can be done throughout the whole season.

The beautiful Round Sultanlango trek (Trek 4) is taxing with precipitous, narrow paths, river crossings and a long ascent to the pass. However, the time spent in remote areas is relatively short, hence the amount of supplies to be carried is reduced. It is a less popular trek in Zanskar, accessible only in late summer and autumn.

The treks overview table (see Appendix A) will help you decide which trek is most suitable for you.

How long to stay?
You need to allow at least two weeks in Ladakh if you want to trek. Remember that acclimatisation takes time, that even shorter treks require about seven days, and that getting to the starting points on most of the routes also takes time.

Additional time must be built in for getting to and from Ladakh. You can't be sure about flights and roads, because of the weather, snowfalls and landslides that may cause delays and closures at any time during the season. It normally takes two days to get to Leh by road from either Manali or Srinagar (**check the security issues if contemplating a route via Srinagar in the Kashmir Valley**). Getting to Manali by road from Delhi takes at least a day, and getting to Srinagar from Delhi takes one to three days, but this cannot be recommended at the time of writing due to political unrest.

Flying is the preferred way for many travellers and most groups. It is much faster (under two hours from Delhi), but allow for possible delays due to inclement weather conditions and remember that you will need to build in more time to acclimatise (see How to get there).

How to trek?
All the treks described in this guide have been covered independently by the author, mostly alone. This style of trekking in Ladakh, however, is hard work and is considered by many as either madness or masochism! Luckily there are other options available.

Any of the styles of trekking described below can be tailored to the routes in this book. Your choice should depend on which trail appeals, the fitness and experience of the trek members, and the time you want to spend trekking. Judge your capabilities honestly before you go.

Trekking alone or in a small, independent group
Ladakh is basically a wild mountain desert. Trekking independently

Author's camp below the Kanda La (Trek 8); if trekking independently you will need to carry all your camping equipment as well as food for most of the trek

to remoter areas and thus increasing the level of risk should not be the first choice for most people – far better to do a shorter trek on the first visit. Obviously walking alone (or as a couple) gives great flexibility; there are no disputes with others in the party about route options, where to camp and how long to trek each day. However, it should be remembered that there is no emergency evacuation from almost the entire region, and so being self-sufficient, fit and strong is vital.

Trekking without a guide or a horseman is possible, but is a demanding choice. It is both physically and mentally hard. If trekking alone in remote areas you will usually need to carry much more than 20kg on your back, and it will be a tough routine of early wake-ups, packing, cooking and so on. You will depend on no one, but also there will be no one there to help you. Finding the way is not always easy; the path will be precipitous; rivers will be cold and hard to cross.

Carrying your rucksack all day gets tiring. You will need to learn your physical limits and find the strength to keep going. You will be alone for hours at night and sometimes even for a few long days. You will be totally cut off from the modern world. However, no other style of trek will teach you so much about yourself, give you so much experience and probably so much satisfaction!

Because Ladakh is such a demanding place it is not a good idea to trek independently if you have not done it elsewhere. Choose a popular route, where you will meet people and pass villages where you can sleep and eat. If you are an inexperienced trekker take a companion with you – two heads are better than one.

Trekking alone requires skills that cannot be learned from a book and must be gained through experience. The author is convinced that, despite the obvious risks, trekking alone can be enjoyed by those with the right attitude and ability.

Village-to-village trekking

Such trekking is based on local accommodation and food (homestay) and is the easiest form of independent trekking. It gives a glimpse into local life and you learn infinitely more about the culture than when travelling with an organised trekking group. Although no route in this book can be done entirely in this way, the number of camping nights can be limited. You can also modify some of the routes to make a wonderful village-to-village trek. This mode of trekking will lessen the load you need to carry, yet will let you retain your independence. Some commercial trekking companies now offer this style of trip.

Arranged locally

Hiring a horseman and ponies makes the trekking easier; it is a fantastic

Testha village on the Kargyak River, Zanskar (Trek 3); staying in villages is a great opportunity to learn about local culture

experience and may herald the beginning of long friendships. You may arrange your trek directly, simply by going to the starting point and trying to find animals and a horseman. This is usually possible during the peak season on the popular routes; horsemen who have finished their last trek wait for a new job for a few days before starting for home. The price depends on the route; it should be about Rs400 for a day for one horse, but remember that not only your own luggage has to be carried, but also the horseman's equipment and the animals' food. You can arrange to use the horseman's stove or other gear. Usually, he can also cook for you and will be your guide, translator and companion. Good places to try this are: Lamayuru, Phanjila, Martselang (near Hemis), Shang Sumdo, Padum

and Darcha. Be prepared, however, to take a few days to find someone. For other destinations it is better to arrange everything in advance, and the agencies in Leh will be happy to help. For treks in Zanskar, try contacts at www.trekzanskar.org.

It is also possible to arrange a fully organised trek directly with a reputable agent in Ladakh. You can find a list of agents based in Leh in advance, but it is best to arrange the trek on the spot in order to ascertain exactly what is (and what is not) included. There are dozens, if not hundreds, of companies there (most offices are only open in high season), and your guesthouse staff can certainly help. If you plan to start the trek in Darcha or in Zanskar check out www.trekzanskar.org. The price depends on the service you buy (staff, equipment, food, pack animals),

Overnight camp on a commercial trek: Purni village (Treks 2–4)

the route, the season and number of people in your group. Be prepared to pay at least £33 per day per person for a full package. Be aware that it may take a few days to arrange, so if you have little time organise as much as you can in advance. (Agents offering treks in Ladakh are easily found on the Internet; try to choose one run by local Ladakhi people. Check the agents on the official website of Leh District – www.leh.nic.in (under Tourism) – and on www.trekzanskar.org). Note that there will be no liability insurance cover in the event of any accident so make sure to buy a policy before leaving your home country. Double check that enough time has been allowed for acclimatisation – if you are not sure, discuss the issue with the agent. Make sure to talk about planned stages and the route before you leave, and discuss the price for an extra day in case you need one.

If you have time and are willing to forego some security and comfort arranging the trek on your own will save you some money, but usually only those who have already been to and experienced Ladakh are comfortable with this option.

Commercial trek

The vast majority of trekkers to Ladakh select this option for their first visit. Most of those with a limited time period choose to book in their own country with an established trekking outfit. Going for a fully organised trek will give you much comfort and security. Because the trekking company will supply much of the necessary camping equipment, you will not need to invest in a lot of expensive gear. There is usually a guide and a cook, as well as one or more horsemen to take care of the pack animals and do the work in camp. Horses or donkeys carry all the equipment and luggage, but you will need a medium-sized rucksack to carry your water and anything you need during the day.

One disadvantage of group trekking is that you may be hiking with fellow travellers who have underestimated the challenges and may not be in the best of spirits. However, most hikers enjoy the conviviality of like-minded fellow walkers. One other serious danger of group trekking is the possible effect of 'peer pressure'. At its worst this can overrule common sense, with some members ignoring symptoms of altitude sickness in the unacknowledged race to compete. Do not fall into this lethal trap.

The following checklist may help you decide which company to go for:
- Check what is included in the price when comparing different companies, and balance that against what equipment you will need to buy if trekking independently.
- Many fully organised groups fly to Leh, although you might find a trek that starts in Darcha or even in Padum, getting there by bus or jeep.

THE IMPACT OF GROUP TREKKING

Many trekking companies tend to organise perhaps overly 'luxurious' trips and take items that may seem a nice treat, but that are not essential for the success of the trip. Think about your impact on the environment. The more items there are to be carried, the more animals are needed. More animals mean more grass to be eaten on the way, which in some cases means less grass for local villagers' livestock. It also means more excrement on the pathway, which becomes a real problem on the most popular routes. Conversely, bigger groups mean more employment for the local people – it's always a trade-off between economic benefit and environmental concerns.

You might want to check the items to be taken by your trekking agent; some may be unnecessary. The chairs and tables that most of the companies carry are comfortable. However, do you really need such comfort on a trek to 5000m-high passes? Discuss your menu too. The more factory-made food, the more rubbish. It might be nice to receive a juice carton or chocolate bar in your lunchbox every day, but wouldn't you be fine with fresh stream water and dried fruits from a local organic food shop?

Do not litter. Arrange with the company to bring back all the rubbish that will be produced. Try to be a part of the team, not just a customer. Try to help with pitching tents and packing them, loading the pack animals and with food preparation. It will certainly enrich your experience and you will get to know more about the region and the locals.

Loaded horses at one of the many passes along the Tsarab Chu on a commercial trek (Trek 2)

- Make sure that there would be enough time for acclimatisation; beware of trips that are very short and at high altitude.
- Ask for details of the company's insurance cover, and make sure that is broad enough.
- Examine the scheduled stages, the distances and altitudes.
- Note the number of people taken: the trek will probably be less enjoyable in a big group.
- Compare prices, bearing in mind all these points.
- Try to keep fit before the trip and follow any preparatory advice given by the tour operator.

No list of tour operators has been given in this guidebook. You may find useful advice in travel magazines and via reliable travel websites. Most of the reputable international trekking companies have trek options in Ladakh available.

WHAT TO BRING FROM HOME

Leh has excellent shops, offering good quality trekking equipment and clothes, usually made in China. Many of the tourist agencies in the city have equipment for rent. However, some things are hard to obtain, or for other reasons it is better to bring them from home. You may also not want to spend your time shopping!

Trekking boots, socks and rucksack are going to be your closest companions on the trek – you will wear them all for hours each day – and so they should not be obtained in a rush. Buy boots and rucksack some time before the trip and test them on

Setting up camp in the Kargyak Valley on an independent trek (Trek 3)

37

a few long walks at home; they must fit properly.

On the trek take care of your feet and avoid blisters! Take off your boots and socks whenever you stop; change wet, sweaty socks for a clean pair during the day. Do not ignore the smallest stone in your boot – stop and take it out as soon as it disturbs you. Examine your feet every evening; treat irritated areas with soothing ointment and apply a plaster if necessary. Before you leave for the trip buy gel plasters designed for blister protection and healing as well as a suitable ointment for treating blisters and small cuts. Ask your doctor or chemist for advice.

Trekking socks may save you from blisters – it is worth making an effort to find good ones and to pay for them. Two pairs should do; washed socks left out overnight will usually be dry by morning. You need strong, leather **trekking boots** that support your ankles, not light hiking boots or sandals.

The type of **rucksack** you need depends on the style of trekking you plan to do. On a supported trek a day-pack of around 30l will be sufficient (you will need to carry an extra jacket, water and probably a camera). If you are going to carry everything yourself, the back system is most important. A strong and comfortable hip-belt is vital if carrying heavy loads. All the straps must be easily adjustable; carrying the bag for hours necessitates changing the position of the load often. The size of bag required for an independent trek depends on how

much of the load you can share with your companion, on the time spent in the area where no food is available, and so on. A rucksack of around 80l capacity seems to be a minimum requirement. Remember to make use of the space and that it will be easier to carry the load if you pack everything inside the bag instead of attaching some items to the outside.

Electronic equipment

Although electrical devices are generally available in India, you will probably want to bring them from home. Bear in mind that unless you use a solar charger you will not be able to charge batteries during your trek. Good quality AA and AAA batteries are available in the cities (including Leh), but do not expect to buy them in villages. Proper recycling of used batteries is not popular in India, and so using rechargeable batteries is recommended. When buying them, consider their capacity, cycles of charging, durability and the time the charge will hold at low temperatures.

India uses a 220–240V/50Hz electric system. European plugs with two round pins fit most of the sockets used in the country.

If you still use a film camera, do not expect to buy your favourite film in Ladakh (although there are a few shops offering a range of film in Delhi) so bring all you expect to need. Processing at a Kodak Q-Lab certified laboratory is possible.

Medical supplies

Medicine is easily available in India, and is cheap; usually you can buy antibiotics without seeing a doctor. However, according to popular opinion, some pills available in the country are made of substances that are banned in the West, and medicine storage regulations are less strict than those in Europe. On the other hand, some local medicaments, antibiotics especially, are more effective in fighting local bacteria. This seems to be particularly true in the case of common gastric problems.

It is strongly recommended to visit a doctor before leaving your home country. Do this well in advance – at least one month – of your trip as you will probably be advised to have a course of vaccinations (hepatitis A, typhoid and tetanus). You don't need malaria prophylaxis for Ladakh, but it is quite possible to get infected on the way to Leh. However, unless you are spending some time in the lower parts of India, avoiding mosquito bites and using a strong mosquito repellent should be sufficient precaution. **Seek the correct medical advice concerning malaria.** MASTA (Medical Advisory Service for Travellers Abroad) is a useful source of information in advance of your trip. See www.masta-travel-health.com.

If you spend an adequate amount of time on acclimatisation you will not need any medications for altitude sickness. If you need to adjust rapidly, however, you may

Valley north of the Kanji La (Trek 6); shepherds spend the summers in the upper valleys and high mountain meadows, tending yaks, sheep and goats

39

want to use drugs that support the process. See below and consult your doctor, and go to the website of the International Society for Mountain Medicine at www.ismmed.org. Soluble multi-vitamin and **mineral tablets** are recommended; choose different flavours.

A light **space blanket** (mylar or first aid blanket) is very useful, not only for use in an emergency, but also for protection against the cold.

Water purification should be considered before the trip. You should never drink tap water in India, not even for cleaning teeth. In cities outside Ladakh you should use bottled water, available everywhere (make sure that it is sealed). The mass disposal of plastic bottles has become a serious problem in India (and Leh in particular), and it is strongly recommended to refill bottles with boiled or filtered water. This can be done in many shops and guesthouses in Leh.

Water filtration does not usually change the taste and is helpful in cleaning cloudy sediment-filled water and reducing chemicals. However, filters are ineffective in protecting against viruses.

Generally, water from small streams in Ladakh is clear, but will need chemical treatment for protection against bacteria and viruses. Buy an adequate quantity of solution or tablets before the trip. Use vitamin tablets (vitamin C is effective, particularly against iodine), powdered fruit-flavoured drinks or neutralising tablets to improve the taste of the treated water. Although you will use cloudy and turbid water from a big river at a few camps on some treks, filtering is not the most important gear you need for a trek in the region.

For more information on water treatment check www.high-altitude-medicine.com, www.katadyn.com and www.msrgear.com.

DRINKING WATER ON TREK

Opinions on water purification during the trek vary. Although water in small streams is generally clean, there is always a risk of bacterial or viral infection, especially if the stream passes a village or pasture. Boiling water is the most effective way of making it safe for drinking, even at high altitude. However, considering that you need to drink about 5 litres a day, it is not practical. Chemical methods are based on iodine, chlorine and silver. The simplest consists of dropping iodine into water and waiting for some time. This, however, does not kill all the bacteria and is sometimes considered unsafe for anyone with a thyroid problem. Advanced chemical methods (available as soluble tablets) are effective in treating bacteria and viruses, but these usually affect the taste and smell of the liquid.

Toze Chu: a braided river (Treks 1 and 2)

HEALTH AND FITNESS

You do not need to be extremely fit to go on a trekking trip, but you do need to choose the right option. The various styles of trek, the distance covered, flexibility of stages and diversity of routes make trekking possible for people of different physical strengths and age. Trekking is a matter of walking – you don't need any particular skills to do it! But it has to be said that the fitter you are, the easier the trekking will be, so some preparation in advance is essential. You can train for long walks in Ladakh anywhere: go for longer and tougher walks than usual, carrying on your back the sort of weight you expect to carry on trek. Ideally, of course, your preparation for Ladakh would take place in a mountainous area though this is rarely feasible.

Preparing for a trek at high altitude

A trip to any high altitude region requires acclimatisation. This is the process of adjusting the body to lower oxygen levels at high elevation. Most of us need a few days of acclimatisation to any altitude higher than 2500m. Inadequate adjustment to high altitude can lead to altitude sickness and, in its most severe forms, a quick death, so make sure you learn how to identify the symptoms.

Never ignore any symptoms of altitude sickness! If you have a headache combined with dizziness, sleep disturbance, loss of appetite, nausea or vomiting, do not ascend; descend or stay at the same altitude until you recover completely. If you have more severe symptoms that may include breathlessness at rest,

The rarely visited Langthang Valley leads to the Zalung Karpo La – one of the best viewpoints in Ladakh (Trek 1)

fast, shallow breathing, cough, chest tightness, drowsiness and loss of coordination while walking, descend immediately. If it happens at night do not wait until the morning – your life may depend on an immediate descent! If you have previously trekked at high altitude and been unaffected, do not assume that you will never suffer from altitude sickness; it is a fickle condition.

However, providing that you follow a few simple rules, you should not be seriously affected. Search for Altitude Sickness on the Internet, and check the following sites: www. ismmed.org; www.high-altitude-medicine.com; and www.merck manuals.com/professional.

Other possible ailments on trek

The air at high altitude is drier than at lower elevations, so greater water loss than normal occurs through breathing. Due to processes that take place in our bodies urination is more frequent. Another reason for greater fluid loss during trekking is the enhanced physical exertion at altitude. Therefore one needs to drink more than at lower elevations – you should drink about 5 litres of liquid (preferably water) a day (remember that consumption of coffee, tea and alcohol increases fluid loss). Observe your urine; if it is dark in colour, you must drink more.

Long exposure to direct sunlight may cause dizziness, headache, nausea, weakness or mental confusion. These are symptoms of sunstroke and

THE EFFECTS OF HIGH ALTITUDE

Learn as much as you can before you go, and check out the medicines on offer to aid acclimatisation: see below. Note the main symptoms above: these in themselves are not a reason to stop the trek, but are good indicators of problems that may be overcome by taking a rest. At altitude difficulty is often experienced with sleeping, breathing patterns may be erratic (Cheyne-Stokes breathing), and the heart might thump a bit disconcertingly; however, none of these is unusual. It is also dangerous to overexert yourself on arrival at any destination, thinking you have no symptoms. These often only begin to appear after an hour or more.

It is particularly important to walk very slowly at all times, especially when climbing any hill. Be sure to admit any problems (if only to yourself at first), and don't be pressured by your trekking peers. If you experience any serious effects before a pass, you should consider descending. Carrying on with mild symptoms, perhaps just a mild headache, is acceptable so long as it does not get worse or persist all day and night.

Continuing to ascend with any persistent symptoms can lead to the serious risk of pulmonary and cerebral oedema, or even death; sometimes complications from altitude sickness can strike very quickly. There are deaths each year in the Himalayas, where the criterion is 'Descending is the only ▶

Peaks of the Gyamshu massif as seen from the Zalung Karpo La (Trek 1)

safe cure, at any time of day or night.' However, in Ladakh descent is not an option in all locations. It is therefore of the utmost importance to acclimatise before going higher. For this reason, many groups spend a few days sightseeing in and around Leh before starting their trek.

What else can you do to ward off the effects of altitude? Many trekkers start a course of Diamox (Acetazolamide), a diuretic that thins the blood, makes you urinate more and is generally considered to be of some benefit, although it can have the disturbing side-effect of pins and needles in the fingers. Another option is to try coca. Not the smoking variety, but a version of the substance used by natives of Peru and Bolivia. Coca is available as homeopathic tablets that some trekkers swear by. It can be difficult to locate these in the UK, but French pharmacies stock them, should you be limbering up in the Alps before your trip. Also recommended by some are ginkgo biloba tablets, which appear to work for reasons not yet defined. It is suggested that these can be taken twice a day for five days before arrival and once a day during the trek, but consult your doctor beforehand as they can affect blood count and are not suitable for everyone.

Gamow bag and oxygen cylinders

A Gamow bag is a large plastic bag into which a person suffering from serious altitude sickness can be cocooned under higher air pressure to mimic a lower altitude for a limited period. Mountaineers have, of course, used oxygen for years at altitude. If you are with a commercial trekking group, your staff might have one of these and know how to use them.

may lead to severe medical disorders. To avoid it, protect your body, especially the head, from the direct sun. Always wear a hat or head covering. Consider taking your noon breaks in a shady place during the hot days of summer. If you experience any symptoms, stay indoors or in a cool, shady place and drink a lot of water. If your body temperature rises to about 40°C you must be cooled off. If possible take a moderately cool bath or splash water over yourself repeatedly.

Any traveller to India risks an infection or disease that probably does not exist or is rare in their home country. The majority of diseases are transmitted by contaminated food or water, and many by insect bites. Prevention consists of vaccinations as well as the avoidance of risky food and insect bites. Choose restaurants where dishes are prepared to order: avoid ready-prepared food. Drink bottled or hot drinks. Be cautious with fresh juices and *lassi* (made from yoghurt):

Lingshed village (and gompa just above) seen from the Hanamul La (Trek 5)

if you do drink one make sure that no ice or water has been added. Eat fresh salads only if you are sure the ingredients have been washed in clean water. Avoid unpeeled fruit.

Travellers' health is the topic of an annual report prepared by the World Health Organisation (WHO), available at www.who.int/ith. Information for travellers to India can also be found at www.cdc.gov (go to Travellers' Health, Destinations and then choose India). Read up on the subject before the trip, consult your doctor, discuss the medicines you need to take with you, and receive proper vaccinations. You should also visit your dentist, to make sure your teeth are in good condition.

A useful book to take with you is *Pocket First Aid and Wilderness* *Medicine* by Drs Jim Duff and Peter Gormly (Cicerone 2012).

VISAS AND PERMITS

Unless you are a citizen of Nepal or Bhutan, you will probably need a visa to go to India. If you can, you should apply for it in your home country. You can find contact information for Indian embassies at The National Portal of India website at www.india. gov.in. Usually the tourist visa is valid for six months (90 days in some countries) from the date of issue and it cannot usually be extended. Recently a rather strange rule has been introduced, insisting that visitors who leave India, despite having a six-month visa, cannot re-enter the country for at least two months.

No extra permits are necessary to enter Ladakh, but access to some parts of the region is limited or restricted. The latter refers to areas near the disputed borders with China and Pakistan. For some areas (Nubra Valley, Tso-Moriri Lake), permits are needed, and are easy to obtain in most of the tourist agencies in Leh. No permits are needed for any of the trekking routes described in this guidebook.

MONEY, INSURANCE AND DEALING WITH EMERGENCIES

Pounds sterling, euros and US dollars are easily exchanged for Indian currency in official places like banks as well as in private exchange offices. Changing other major currencies is usually possible too. The rates vary, so check in a few places first. Changing in small offices is usually easier, much less bureaucratic and faster than in banks. Exchange offices may be closed on Saturdays, Sundays and public holidays.

Visa and Mastercard debit and credit cards are accepted by most ATMs, operated by local banks such as the State Bank of India, or the Punjab National Bank. Other international banks like Citibank, Deutsche Bank and ABN Amro are found in the bigger cities. There are at least two ATMs in Leh, but none in Padum or Kargil.

Card payments are not popular. International money transfer service via agencies like Western Union is available both in Delhi and in Leh. Travellers' cheques, mainly American Express/Thomas Cook, are accepted in the cities. It is wise to have at least two different ways of accessing money during the trip.

If you stay in budget guesthouses, eat in simple restaurants and bars, and travel overland by public transport, an allowance of £12.50 per day should be sufficient. If your budget is very tight, you might get away with around £8 per day. Hiring a horseman with animals to carry your equipment on the trek, or an agent to arrange the trek for you, will increase the cost (see below).

The amount of money you will need depends on the mode of trek chosen. If you sleep in your own tent

EXCHANGE RATES

As exchange rates are subject to change, and have been particularly variable in recent years, it is strongly recommended that you keep an eye on them before your journey. The following list gives an indication of current rates but see the Reserve Bank of India website at www.rbi.org.in for the most up-to-date details.

- £1 Rs99
- €1 Rs70
- $1 Rs64

The kitchen of a typical Ladakhi house

and carry your own equipment, you will only need money for campsite fees in some places (around Rs150–200 per tent), for transport to and from the starting and finishing point, and for snacks in teashops and restaurants on the way. Home accommodation (homestay) costs range between Rs250 and Rs500 per person per night. Food is included (dinner and breakfast; sometimes a takeaway lunch too). It is always wise to have some extra money in cash, just in case. Credit and debit cards are useless anywhere outside Leh, and foreign exchange is hard to arrange outside the Ladakhi capital too. Try to have small change, because Rs1000 notes will not be accepted in many places and even Rs500 notes may sometimes cause a problem.

Note that in the last two years inflation (6–10 per cent annually) has had a notable impact on prices in India, so you should consider this when planning your budget.

The cost of getting to India, and travel insurance, also need to be considered. Your insurance should cover not only hospital treatment but also emergency evacuation costs. There is no mountain rescue service organisation in Ladakh. A seriously injured person would need to be transported to the hospital in Leh by Indian Army helicopter, but it will not take off unless your insurance has been confirmed. If trekking independently you will depend on yourself, villagers and their animals, and other trekkers, in case of emergency. If going on an organised trek leave your insurance details at your agent's office and discuss emergency scenarios there.

Mountain emergency operation is not usually covered by travel insurance, but most agents offer an extension of the standard package for an additional fee. Good insurance covering the costs of a rescue operation in the mountains is often combined with membership of a mountain club, such as the British Mountaineering Council (www.thebmc.co.uk) or the Oesterreichischer Alpenverein (Austrian Alpine Association). The latter has a few branches in other European countries: see www.alpenverein.at, www.aacuk.org.uk, www.alpenverein.com.pl and www.alpenverein.cz. For other countries, please check with your local mountaineering organisation; and make sure that the necessary insurance cover is in place before leaving home.

COMMUNICATION

In most of India, the Internet is widely accessible. There are hundreds of Internet cafés in Delhi and dozens in Leh. However, there is no Internet access along the trekking routes and you can't even rely on connecting to the net in Padum. Fees are generally low (Rs15–90 per hour), but in Leh they are much higher than elsewhere. Downloading photos from a camera or a memory card, and burning DVDs, is possible in almost every café, but watch out for computer viruses – it is quite common to lose the data from a card! Choose computers with anti-virus software installed. If you lose important data, stop using the card and try to restore the data using disk-recovery software when you get home. Skype is available in most cafés, but some of them charge extra for voice conversations.

A young monk at Thikse Gompa, near Leh

A man from Kalbok village (Treks 2–4)

Foreign SIM cards generally work in Delhi, Punjab and Himachal Pradesh but some do not enable you to make calls (you can receive calls and send/receive SMS messages). In the State of Jammu and Kashmir not only are foreign cards not accepted by the system, but neither do prepaid cards from all other Indian states work. To use your mobile phone in Ladakh you either need a contract phone from another Indian state (certainly not all of them will work) or a SIM card from one of the J&K state networks. The latter is not easy to arrange, even for a prepaid card.

There are two networks operating in Ladakh: BSNL (www.bsnl.in) and Airtel (www.airtel.in). The latter is said to have better quality service, but the first has better coverage. Regardless

of the company, do not expect to use your mobile phone outside Leh, Kargil, Padum and villages along the Indus between Upshi and Khalatse.

Landline phone service is widely available in India at special offices or kiosks, PCOs (public call offices), where international calls can usually be made. In Ladakh the service is available in Leh and Padum, and in some villages along major roads. Do not expect to make phone calls from villages on trekking routes. International connections are usually cheap; prices do not exceed Rs10 per minute for most destinations. Ask the price in a few offices before you choose one; Internet cafés often have a cheaper service.

Note that bringing a satellite phone to India and using one in the country is restricted by law; a licence (difficult to get) is required from the Department of Telecommunications.

There are post offices in Leh and Padum. If you need to receive a letter or parcel, use the guesthouse address or *poste restante*. Courier services are available as well; the major international courier companies have representatives in India and it is certainly possible to send a parcel from Leh.

LOCAL LANGUAGE

English is one of the official languages of India and is used in most official documents, on signs and announcements, and is spoken by many people. On the way to Ladakh, and in Leh, you can expect to hear at least basic English.

Ladakh has its own language. It is similar to Tibetan, but the two languages are said to be so different that Tibetans and Ladakhis living in India often prefer to use English or Hindi to communicate. Additionally, the Ladakhi language has regional differences.

In the villages on the most popular routes people who offer accommodation, run shops or manage campsites will speak some English. Guides and many horsemen are usually fluent; in remote villages, however, you will need to know a few words in Ladakhi to communicate.

Knowing a bit of the local language always helps in relations when travelling regardless of whether English

is also spoken. One word that you must learn is *julley*, meaning 'hello', 'goodbye', as well as 'thank you'. Some useful words and phrases are listed in Appendix C; try also Ladakhi Phrases on www.wondersofladakh.com. If you want to know more get hold of a copy of the Ladakhi phrasebook (see Appendix F) that was published a few years ago and is easily available in every bookshop in Leh.

TIPS ON TRAVELLING IN INDIA

India has been a popular destination for years. As with many places in the world, this means that, on one hand, tourist facilities of vastly different standards are easily available; and on the other, of those people who make their living through tourism, some will, unfortunately, behave dishonestly.

Accommodation options, for example, range from a plethora of simple guesthouses with varying facilities, starting at around Rs300 per night, to five-star hotels of the famous Taj group at over Rs10,000 for a room. Generally you do not need to book rooms in guesthouses or hostels in advance. Bus tickets for long journeys can usually be arranged one day in advance; short trips can be taken on the spot. Train and bus tickets may both be booked online.

Simple restaurants (*dhabas*) serving local food are found everywhere. Western food is available in big towns but less so elsewhere. Although the appearance of many food places is below the standard you would accept in your home country, the food is usually good and safe. A general rule regarding restaurants is that if it is popular with locals it is good; if there is nobody in sight, find another place. Don't eat if the food is not hot or fresh. Choose bottled or hot drinks.

Some simple precautions can save you from trouble. Use safety-pockets/moneybelts for your important documents, credit cards, and so on. Divide your money and keep it in a few different places; carry only a small amount of cash in your wallet. Never leave your luggage with a stranger, even for a moment. On a train, secure your big bag under a seat with a chain and lock, and keep a smaller bag, if you have one, with you at all times. Be wary on buses; avoid putting bags on the roof if possible. In the street or on public transport, hold your bag close and do not carry or wear anything that looks obviously valuable. Keep your camera in a bag and only get it out to take a photograph. Have your own padlock to secure your hotel room door.

Women should avoid being alone with a stranger. Try to dress a little more conservatively than you might in your home country. On a bus or train (especially an overnight journey) try to find a seat next to another woman. In the metro, choose a ladies' carriage.

Most travellers find it hard to cope with the poverty found in India's big cities. Every day you meet people who need help, and you will probably be tempted to do so. However, there are groups or even gangs who will try to play on your sympathy and generosity to extract money that does not always reach those in greatest need. It is not easy to deal with; and quite apart from the fact that any money you give may be diverted away from the needy, simply by giving it you will

DRESS CODE

No Ladakhi man or woman wears shorts or crop-tops. It goes without saying that tourists, out of respect for local customs, should not wear such clothes. Although a Ladakhi would rarely point out improper dress to anybody, wearing it is considered offensive. You should wear loose clothes covering your legs and shoulders; T-shirts are fine, but strapless tops are not! No head covering is necessary, but you should wear a hat or cap as protection against the strong sunlight.

Sadly many tourists, both in Leh and the villages, disrespect these rules. You will even see visitors to monasteries wearing shorts and strapless tops. Again, no one is likely to say anything, but just because Ladakhis dislike complaining it does not mean that they don't mind!

Shepherds of the Kong Togpo Valley (Trek 6)

encourage begging. It is much better to encourage working! Try to support those who do by using rickshaws and cycle-rickshaws, buying from tea-sellers and shopkeepers. Choose local restaurants rather than supporting big concerns.

In Ladakh do not distribute sweets, pens and money to children, and discourage them from asking for things. None of us would like our own children to behave in a similar fashion. If you do have things for children in a village find the teacher; he or she will distribute the items to those in need. If you want to give money, think about helping locals in building a school or support an NGO; there are dozens based in Leh, and talking with locals during your trek will give you an idea of the best way of helping, and which organisations you can trust.

WHAT TO TAKE ON TREK

Don't treat the following information as a checklist, but rather as a suggested list of items that are necessary for a trekker in Ladakh. On organised treks, where much of the equipment may be supplied (and you may be given a kit list in advance) some items could be unnecessary: you will not, for example, have to worry about what type of tent to take, but are still likely to supply your own sleeping bag and possibly sleeping mat. An independent trekker, however, must always consider the weight of equipment when purchasing and working out what is essential to take.

Clothing

Regardless of the season, you will probably experience nights with temperatures near or even below 0ºC. It usually gets chilly in the evenings and the mornings are cold. Days are often hot, but it will be windy and often cold or even freezing on passes. When you get out of your tent in the early morning, you will need to put on warm trousers, a pullover and a windproof jacket, but as soon as the sun's rays hit camp, you will want to take these off. Rain is very rare, but may last for a few hours when it comes. Snowfalls are more frequent in the higher mountains. These are not heavy in late spring, summer and autumn, but are often accompanied by wind which increases the chill factor.

This is what I took on all my treks in Ladakh between mid-June and late October.

- Cotton trousers
- Polar fleece trousers
- Thin, thermal T-shirt
- Polar fleece T-shirt
- Light polar fleece pullover
- Windstopper jacket
- Rain/windproof coat
- Two cotton T-shirts
- Underwear
- Head covering for sun protection
- One light and one thick polar fleece cap
- Balaclava
- Gloves (regardless of season)
- Trekking socks (two pairs) and pair of woolly socks

This is a minimal set of clothes. If you trek in the autumn, taking one more jacket that could be used as an extra layer is not a bad idea.

While walking, I wore cotton trousers, thermal T-shirt and polar fleece pullover. On cold days, although rarely, I added the polar fleece T-shirt under the pullover. Occasionally, on very hot days, I removed the thermal T-shirt and just wore the pullover. It may seem strange, but the pullover was fine. Even if it was a bit too hot while I was in the sun, it was just perfect in the shade and on ascents to passes. While resting on the way, I put on my jacket and, sometimes, especially on passes, my coat. At camps, I changed the cotton trousers for the pair of polar fleece ones, and the thermal T-shirt for a dry cotton one, then I put on all the remaining layers. I wore woolly Ladakhi socks while in camp and modern trekking socks for walking. Usually I slept in just my underwear and the cotton T-shirt. Additionally I used a piece of cloth to make a turban to protect my head and neck from the sun, a light cap for warmer evenings and colder days, a thick polar fleece cap for evenings, mornings and passes, and a balaclava for windy days and evenings.

Trekking boots and rucksack have already been mentioned. Sandals are necessary for crossing rivers and for giving your feet a rest in camp. Make sure they fit properly and that you can tighten them firmly.

Tents and cooking equipment

A summer tent is not enough even if you trek in the hottest part of the season. You need at least a three-season tent, and if you plan to trek in spring or autumn, a four-season tent.

Independent camp in the Langthang Valley (Trek 1)

Air-filled sleeping mats are recommended, as they generally give better insulation than simple foam mats. Your sleeping bag needs to have its lower limit a few degrees below 0°C. If you are not sure whether your sleeping bag will do, buy a polar fleece inner bag to augment warmth. These are available in Leh and are certainly a cheaper solution than buying a new sleeping bag.

Kerosene is the most commonly used fuel in Indian households and is easily available; sometimes it is even possible to buy it in a remote village, although you should not expect to do so. Kerosene stoves are therefore the most suitable on trek, and MSR products (www.msrgear.com) considered by many travellers to be the best. Primus (www.primus.eu) is another legendary stove manufacturer. Simple Indian stoves, even portable models,

are widely available, including in Leh, but they are heavier than the modern ones designed for outdoor activity. Trekking stoves are available in Leh, both for hire and to buy, but don't expect to have a choice. A lone trekker with a modern, good quality stove, will need around a litre of kerosene for a 10-day trek.

Gas cartridge camping stoves and cartridges are available in Leh. It is fine to use them (and they cook faster than petrol stoves), but you cannot buy the cartridges anywhere outside Leh. If you go on a trek where most nights will be spent in villages, you may want to use a solid fuel stove and fuel tablets. These are unsuitable for cooking full meals, but can be useful for boiling water and making instant soup and so on along the way.

Relying on a campfire for cooking is almost impossible, as you will

The camp in Nyimaling (Trek 8)

find hardly any wood, only dry shrubs and perennials. Dried horse and yak dung is also used for fuel by locals in the villages. Using this you can make a small fire and cook a meal, but it requires quite an effort and takes much time.

Don't forget a couple of boxes of matches; lighters are usually unreliable, especially at high elevations. A candle is useful too.

The cooking equipment that you need depends on the food you take for the trek; you will certainly need no more than two pots, a lid, a cup and a spoon.

Other personal items

The use of trekking poles is strongly recommended. They will help when crossing rivers, support your knees on descents, help you to balance when traversing sheer slopes and generally support your walking. The locking system must be strong; tips must be hard and quite sharp.

A pair of good quality sunglasses, reflecting or filtering 100 per cent of UVA and UVB light, with blinders at the sides, is essential as protection against both the sun and snow blindness.

Medicines have been already mentioned, but you must be prepared to deal with cuts, wounds, blisters, sprains, burns, fever, diarrhoea and pain. Carry antibiotics in case of serious infection.

You must have a sun cream with a high factor sunscreen, and a sun-blocking lipstick. You will also need suitable ointment to deal with the cracked skin that will certainly form on your fingers, toes and heels due to the cold, dry air and freezing water. Consult your doctor about the exact

A man from Zanskar posing for a group of trekkers in a village in the Kargyak Valley (Trek 3)

list of medicines, bearing in mind the region to which you are heading, the activities planned and your personal health record.

Don't forget a pocketknife, torch, sewing kit and photographic equipment, and spare batteries. A GPS receiver is not really necessary unless you have a digital map of the region or someone's GPS tracks uploaded to your unit. A compass is needed.

Food

Food needed for a trek, including high-energy, freeze-dried food as well as local organic produce, is available in Leh. On an organised trek food will be usually prepared for you. Expect breakfast, dinner and a packed lunch. Breakfast will probably consist of some kind of simple Indian bread like

EATING ON AN INDEPENDENT TREK

I eat twice a day during treks. The morning meal is based on milk prepared with milk powder. I make porridge, adding nuts and raisins, or just eat it with muesli or *tsampa*. The latter is a sort of porridge made of roasted barley. It is the most popular and the simplest local food, and needs no cooking. You can add *chur ship/churpe* (mild homemade granulated cheese, dried in the sun, made from the milk of a *dimo* (female yak) or *dzomo* (yak/cow hybrid)).

Evening meals almost always consist of rice. I eat it with tinned tuna or instant soup. When preparing the latter, I add chur ship and onion or garlic. Occasionally I eat two instant noodle soups, but I always add onion, garlic and some kind of dry yak cheese to make it more nutritious. Sometimes a plain noodle instant soup is the first plate for me, followed by rice. I also use bouillon cubes – they are great for making a warm drink – and tea, preferably green, sometimes with cardamom and cinnamon bark. During the day I eat nuts, raisins or dried fruit, and occasionally biscuits, when small shops are available on the way.

*A child from Kalbok village
(Treks 2–4)*

chapati or *parantha* and an omelette or porridge. For dinner expect rice with some sort of vegetable/lentil/meat sauce. As mentioned earlier, if you arrange the trek directly with the local agent, you can discuss the menu in advance. Try to use local products instead of manufactured food (see How to trek?).

USING THIS GUIDE

Route descriptions and maps
Eight trekking routes are described in this guide, each divided into day stages. You may want, however, to change the proposed schedule and shorten or prolong your trek, or alter stages. Where possible, information on alternative routes and places to camp is given to let you arrange your trek accordingly.

Each stage description consists of a detailed description of the trail, enabling you to find the way. It should be sufficient guidance for anybody with basic experience of independent trekking. Details of starting and finishing points are given, with their respective altitudes, and the altitude range.

Distance for each stage is given, and the approximate time required. These are based on the author's own experience of trekking independently with a heavy backpack. You may find yourself walking faster or slower – please treat the figures given for reference only and not as the exact time required. Individual hiking speeds are too variable to quantify.

Whenever the time given is shorter than one hour, it refers to the walking time; when it is longer, it includes stops. The time specified for

LEFT VS RIGHT BANK

Sides and banks of streams and rivers in route directions are understood according to geographical lore, and are related to direction of river flow. Whenever a *left side/bank* of a river is mentioned the *true left bank* (or the left side of the river as you face downstream) is implied. The same applies to tributaries: a *left* tributary is a tributary that joins the main river from the *left* as you face downstream (ditto *right* side/bank/tributary).

the entire stage also includes breaks. The author usually took about 20 minutes' rest after each hour of walking, but this was terrain-dependent.

Route directions are given according to those showing on a 16-point compass. The four cardinals, four ordinals and the eight compass points between these are abbreviated in the text as N, S, NW, NNW and so on. Where a direction is indicated that is *not* part of a route direction it is given in full: north, south, northwest, north-northwest.

The stage introductions also include crucial information about the availability of water. **Read these carefully and take note!** You will need to drink at least 4–5 litres of water a day, and in some places it takes a few hours to get from one source of water to another.

Route profiles give an overview of the altitude range you will have

A tiny footpath on the impressive traverse 300m above the Zara River (Trek 2)

Incredible autumn colour at the confluence
of the Niri and Tsarab rivers (Trek 2)

to tackle during each stage. More detailed information on ascent and descent will be found in the stage summary for every day.

There are generally two kinds of places where you can camp. 'A camp' or 'camping place' refers to a wild place where camping is possible (indicated by a white tent symbol on the maps). Whenever a campsite is mentioned, this means an organised fee-paying camping site (a yellow tent symbol) – usually you can expect to find a simple shop and a Ladakhi toilet there. Be aware that the exact location of some campsites may change slightly from season to season.

Shepherds' shelters are often mentioned in the text. Don't expect a hut; it is usually no more than a low wall of stones giving basic protection against wind. Don't rely on these, as they can change.

Maps supplement the text and route descriptions, most at 1:250,000 scale and based on the author's own GPS measurements as well as on NASA, USGS, JPL, Caltech and CIAT data. Treks 1, 2, 3, 5, 6 and 8 are each illustrated on a separate overview map, showing such information as the locations of stage starts, finishes and the major passes along the way. These treks are then further illustrated by more detailed stage maps placed alongside the route descriptions, which show a more in-depth level of detail including the heights of passes and significant camps. (Treks 4 and 7 are short enough that they do not require separate overviews and are therefore shown entirely on the stage maps.)

Note: even in a single village there can be a significant range of altitudes. Where a stage start or finish village height is given in the text and on the maps, it is the height of the author's chosen camp. Where a village has a different height on the profile, it is the height of the village centre.

The detailed route description, tables, elevation profiles and maps give sufficient information to trek independently in the region. However, you may want to have an additional map. The Trekking Map of Ladakh by Sonam Tsetan (easily available in Leh) is quite basic in scale (about 1:650,000) but (as far as it has been checked by the author) is accurate regarding the location of roads, trails, villages, rivers and bridges. In particular, the trail is marked on the correct side of the stream for most places, and bridges are shown where they really exist.

The Ladakh & Zanskar Trekking Map, sheets North, Centre and South, by Editions Olizane, is the most detailed map of the region (1:150,000). It is accurate regarding landforms and features, but has some important mistakes regarding trail location. It is quite expensive; unless you plan to make side treks or variants that are not described in the book, you don't need this map.

Maps by the US Army Map Service, produced in the 1950s and '60s, are good in scale (1:250,000), freely available on the Internet and certainly worth consideration.

A new map – Ladakh and Zanskar Trekking Map – has recently been published by Milestone Books. At a scale of 1:175,000, it covers the whole area described in this book.

In the UK the best places to search for maps of Asia in general are Stanfords in Long Acre, London (www.stanfords.co.uk), and The Map Shop at Upton-upon-Severn in Worcestershire (www.themapshop.co.uk). For worldwide delivery check www.amazon.com, where the most important maps of the region will be found.

Place names and altitude information

The spelling of local names in this book has been based primarily on the Trekking Map of Ladakh (Sonam Tsetan, Fifth Edition 2007) as this is a popular map produced by the Ladakhis. It uses the common spellings, which makes them quite easy to pronounce. One exception is Zanskar, which appears as 'Zangskar' on that map; Zanskar, however, is the spelling commonly used in literature.

The Trekking Map of Ladakh (edited by Hanish & Co, 2006) has been used as the secondary source for naming, and is based on Survey of India sources. It has been used in preference to the first map in the case of the Gotunta La (Gothurstar La), as this name is more common. Indian Himalaya Maps Sheets 2 and 3 (Leomann Map) and the Ladakh & Zanskar series (Editions Olizane) have been used as additional sources.

The altitude information for most of the places mentioned comes from the author's own GPS measurements. The Ladakh & Zanskar Trekking Map at 1:150,000 is the most detailed map available, and altitude is accurate at the places that have been checked. This map has been used as the source of information for places that the author did not measure personally. These should be accurate in places with an open aspect, like passes, and in camps where a series of measurements has been taken, but may be inaccurate at times along the route, particularly in narrow valleys. Treat the figures as a guide, not as exact altitudes.

The names and spellings of some of the remoter places and features have been taken from these printed maps, although variant names and spellings do exist in many cases. The second index at the end of this guide contains all the significant Ladakhi place names used in this guidebook, including some of the more common variants.

Unless you plan to see other places in India before your visit to Ladakh, Delhi will be the most likely starting point for your trip. The city has daily air connections with many major cities around the world.

Delhi
Arriving in Delhi
Delhi Indira Gandhi International Airport (www.newdelhiairport.in) has undergone a lot of expansion recently. International flights and many domestic flights now operate from the new Terminal 3, although some domestic flights still operate from Terminal 1.

Terminal 3 has a new metro connection with the city (Orange Line). Using it is the cheapest option to travel between the airport and the city, unless you arrive late at night.

State bus en route between Jammu and Srinagar

To take a taxi, use the regulated pre-paid service (easily found at the Arrivals hall). The fixed price depends on the destination and ranges between Rs400 and Rs500 for most places. You need to know the name of your particular destination (see Accommodation below). Many drivers will try to take you to a hotel on the way, so tell them that you have a reservation even if you don't. It is usually easy to find a room at the places mentioned below and reservations are not necessary. Taxi drivers get commissions from hotels, so beware of paying more and find a hotel on your own.

Interesting architectural styles in houses and the Khanqah (Mosque) of Shah Hamdan on the Jhelum River in the Old Town of Srinagar

There are regular buses from the airport to the city operated by the state-owned Delhi Transport Corporation (www.dtc.nic.in). Buses follow a few different routes. One passes Rajiv Chowk (previously known as Connaught Place), goes near New Delhi Railway Station (eastern side) and finishes at the Kashmiri Gate Inter State Bus Terminal (ISBT). The service is available around the clock and there are usually two buses per hour. The buses do not stop at Terminal 3, but opposite the Centaur Hotel; airport buses run between the two places.

An airport shuttle bus service runs between Terminal 3 and Terminal 1.

Getting around

This has become easier as the fast-growing network of the Delhi Metro

COPING WITH DELHI

Delhi may come as a bit of shock to those on their first visit to the developing world. The sights and scenes are initially overwhelming: pollution and noise, heat and humidity, colours, dresses, religions, the mix of faces, some sad, some happy and welcoming. The huge number of people everywhere is astonishing, with vast differences between rich and poor, modern and undeveloped. The aggressive, chaotic traffic seems so outrageous as to be hilarious at times. There is no way to be prepared for Delhi.

Tourists have been providing a living for many Delhi citizens, hotel staff, restaurant owners, shopkeepers, taxi and rickshaw drivers, beggars and even hash-dealers for years. Some will try to benefit from your lack of experience. Double-check all the information; have limited trust in people you have met by chance. It often happens that someone who appears to be helping you for nothing actually works for a travel company. Many of the so-called 'free tourist information centres' are tour agencies, looking for business. Taxi and motor-rickshaw drivers, and cycle-rickshaw riders, will charge you double the normal price (and tend to drive around further if the price was not pre-arranged).

You need to bargain for many items in shops and on the street. Restaurants and hotels usually have fixed prices, but check before you commit. Always arrange the price for transport before you set off. Bargain for taxis and rickshaws, whose drivers will try to take you to shops and emporiums. On arrival, allow yourself a day to adjust before making important decisions on travel arrangements or shopping.

Beware of pickpockets! Leave only your luggage in your hotel room; always lock the room. Conceal your valuables on your person; keep your cash in a few different places. Carry only a small amount of money and no important documents in your wallet. Have your hotel business card with you when going out – if you get lost, you will always be able to get back to your hotel.

opens new stations and lines (www.delhimetrorail.com). To travel by metro you need a token for a single journey to a particular destination. It must be bought at a station just before the journey, and costs no more than Rs25 for most routes. Security checks and queues for tokens make the trip slower than you would expect, so allow enough time.

Travelling by city buses is quite confusing, because there are hardly any signs with information on routes, but it is possible! The conductor who collects the fee (usually a few rupees) on each bus can help with advice about the route and tell you where to get off. Ask about bus routes at your hotel.

Taxis are relatively expensive and you will probably not use them except on the way from and to the airport; usually you will use motor- or cycle-rickshaws. The latter are not allowed in many parts of New Delhi, being limited to Old Delhi and Paharganj. Always arrange the price before the trip; and bargain.

The majority of trains leave from and arrive at New Delhi Railway Station (NDLS). Others leave from Delhi Station (DLI). The stations are quite far apart and most trains do not stop at both. Double-check from which station your train is leaving.

New Delhi Railway Station is located just east of Paharganj and 1km north of Rajiv Chowk/Connaught Place. It is easily accessible by metro – take the Yellow or the Orange (Airport Express) Line to New Delhi Metro Station. New Delhi Railway Station has a reservation office for foreign tourists upstairs on the first floor of the main station building, clearly signed. Beware of touts here. It is the easiest place to get information and buy a ticket, and has an extra quota of seats/berths that are not available elsewhere. It's normally possible to get tickets for busy trains here.

Delhi Station (also called Old Delhi or Delhi Junction) is located in Old Delhi, near the Red Fort and Chandni Chowk Street. Chandni Chowk Station (Yellow Line) is the nearest metro station.

To buy a train ticket in India, you usually need to fill in a form (available at any reservation office). The key feature is the code of the train. See the timetable book *Trains at a Glance* that is available at some ticket offices and at www.indianrailways.gov.in; see also www.indiarail.gov.in. You also need to determine the class of the coach you want to travel in – most backpackers take Sleeper Class (SL) for long-distance trips – and the position of the berth, whether upper, middle or bottom (for comfort and safety, take the upper one). Online reservation is possible at www.irctc.co.in and www.makemytrip.com.

Accommodation

Those arriving in India on a pre-arranged group tour will probably spend one night in Delhi en route to Leh, because the flights across the Himalayas go early in the morning. Generally groups use well-appointed, modern, comfortable hotels that are quiet and relaxing, and usually spend a day or two sightseeing in Delhi at the end of their trek.

Accommodation can be found easily in Delhi. There are three areas where most independent travellers stay. **Paharganj**, the most popular, is a big bazaar west of New Delhi Railway Station. There are dozens of cheap guesthouses and hotels, as well as some mid-range accommodation;

prices start at about Rs400 for a double room. Full of restaurants, shops and travel agencies, it is a noisy and rather dirty area, but central and easily accessible. To get there, take a metro to Rama Krishna Ashram Marg (RK Ashram Marg) Station, take the exit that leads to the *ashram* (N) and go ahead. Shortly, you reach Main Bazaar – the main street of Paharganj – that is more-or-less parallel to the metro track, and turn right. The street leads to New Delhi Railway Station (about 1km) and another metro station.

Hotels and guesthouses here include the Metropolis (www.metropolisguestouse.com, expensive), Cottage Yes Please (www.cottageyesplease.com), Ajay (www.ajayguesthouse.com), Prince Palace (www.hotelprincepalace.in), Hotel Vivek (www.vivekhotel.com, with a good roof-top restaurant) and Vishal Guesthouse. This last one (no website) is quite centrally located, so if you have no reservation it is a good starting point; all taxi drivers should know it. Cafés in this part of Paharganj include the Madan Café (also offering travel services) and Malhotra Restaurant. There are more accommodation options towards New Delhi Railway Station, such as Hotel Down Town (quite basic but relatively cheap, popular and signed from the main street), Hotel Star Paradise and Hotel Star Palace (www.stargroupofhotels.com). The Everest Café (Momo Cave), a nice Nepali restaurant, is nearby. Outside December, January or February (the high season for non-Himalayan India), you generally do not need to book accommodation in this area.

Prayer flags, the minaret of Jama Masjid and Leh Palace

Rajiv Chowk (Connaught Place) is one of the main business and commercial centres in New Delhi with a major metro station. It is quieter than Paharganj, has good access to public transport and is central. Hotels here are more expensive and harder to find. Ringo Guesthouse (17 Scindia House, Connaught Lane) is an old favourite. Go along Janpath for 100m from Rajiv Chowk and turn left into Connaught Lane. The hotel is 50m further on your left.

The third budget area in Delhi is the **Tibetan Refugee Colony** at New Aruna Nagar, Majnu-Ka-Tilla. There are a few hotels, many restaurants, tourist offices and Internet cafés. It is the quietest of the three areas but is inconvenient for the city, being located about 3.5km north of Kashmiri Gate Inter State Bus Terminal (ISBT), by the Yamuna River (and just north of Gurudwara Majnu-Ka-Tilla Sikh temple). It is convenient, however, for anyone who wants to go to Manali by bus. Take the metro to Vidhan Sabha (Yellow Line) and a cycle-rickshaw (2km, about Rs15) to the Tibetan Colony (recognisable by prayer flags). From the Kashmiri Gate ISBT, take a motor-rickshaw (3.5km, Rs50). Vehicles are not allowed inside. For accommodation check www.majnukatilla.com (choose Services).

Guesthouses may be busy at certain times of the year (such as Tibetan New Year – a moveable holiday dependant on the Tibetan, lunisolar calendar – and occasional gatherings of the exiled community) so check before arriving.

Sightseeing

Delhi has plenty of sights worth visiting, some of which are unmissable UNESCO World Heritage Sites: the Red Fort, Qutab Minar and Humayun's Tomb. Add the Jama Masjid, Gurudwara Bangla Sahib, Safdarjang's Tomb and the Bahai'i House of Worship if you have a bit more time. The Taj Mahal in Agra is 200km south of New Delhi, and worth a day trip.

Getting to Leh from Delhi
By air or road?

Which of these options to go for is a question of balancing the advantages and disadvantages of each mode of travel. Your choice will largely be based on how much time you have, the current weather conditions and political situation.

Ladakh's only public airport is in Leh with regular flights to Jammu, Srinagar and Delhi operated by a few airlines including Air India (www.airindia.in), Jet Airways (www.jetairways.com) and GoAir (www.goair.com). Because of the prevailing weather conditions, most of the flights take off and land in the morning. Flights are often delayed and sometimes cancelled. If you fly in or out of Ladakh, never make your succeeding schedule tight. Prices vary according to season and time

The approach to the Zoji La from the Kashmir side

of booking, and may be as low as Rs3000 or over Rs20,000 in the high season (one way). According to some Indian travellers, www.makemytrip. com is the best online booking service in India and can be used from Europe; it also enables on-line transactions made from other countries.

But unless your trip is planned at a time when the roads are closed, my advice is *not to fly* into Ladakh. Of course, if your time is very limited, you have no other option. Leh is at an elevation of about 3500m, at which most people suffer some symptoms of altitude sickness. To let the body adjust you will need to dedicate a few days for rest, and for not-too-taxing sightseeing. Of course, the sights are fascinating and you will not get bored hanging around in Leh, but be aware that flying to Ladakh is

not necessarily the fastest way to the start of your trek.

Flying out of Ladakh at the end of your trek *is* a good idea and will avoid the uncomfortable trip by road. Seeing Ladakh from a bird's-eye perspective is a great experience, and you might see some of the places you trekked from the plane!

Another option is to fly to Srinagar and then continue by air or road, but this is not a safe option at the time of writing (see below).

For those with time taking a road route to Ladakh is an adventure itself and gives you the opportunity to observe the immense diversity and landscapes of the Himalayas. But when travelling on any roads in the Indian Himalayas, be prepared for delays. Have an extra jacket, hat, torch and bottle of water in your hand luggage. If you travel by bus, have a string or rope to fasten your bag to the roof (if there is no other option), as no one else will bother to do it.

There are two roads into Ladakh:
- From Manali, entering Ladakh from the south
- Passing through Srinagar in Kashmir from the west.

Both cross the Great Himalaya Range. There are passes exceeding 4000m on both routes and neither road is open all year round. The current status of roads may be checked at www.leh.nic.in. It takes three days at least to get to Leh from Delhi by either route.

The Manali road crosses higher passes and is more uncomfortable than the Srinagar road. It is more popular, however, as it passes through Manali, a famous destination, and because the Srinagar road through Kashmir is still regarded by most as unsafe, with the possibility of armed militant activity. That road also passes through Kargil, which is almost on the Line of Control with Pakistan. **Check the current situation before heading anywhere near Srinagar.**

Make sure you acclimatise properly en route: having left Delhi it is crucial to sleep at least one night at an elevation of around 3000m before going any higher. On the main route via Manali, Keylong (3100m) is the overnight stopping point for the Inter State buses. The Manali–Leh road is a hard test for your body, because it crosses a 5000m-high pass and you will spend many hours above 4500m. Stopping overnight beyond Keylong, in Sarchu (above 4000m), or going directly from Manali to Leh, which

The tiny pathway leading to the Stongde La (Trek 4)

some private buses do, is not a good option and may lead to altitude sickness. Check where the overnight stops are planned before committing yourself to travelling with a particular company.

If the Srinagar–Leh road is safe there are two places to stay, Sonamarg and Kargil – the latter being stopping point for most buses. Ideally, stop in both places.

Although the buses usually stop for the night, the tickets sold in Manali and Srinagar usually cover the entire journey to Leh. That is fine unless you want to spend more than a night in Keylong or Kargil, or want to make an intermediate stop in Sonamarg. Both Keylong and Kargil have bus depots, so arranging onward transport there should not cause any trouble unless the buses are packed. Sonamarg is just a small village without a bus reservation office, so if you stop here for a night or two, it's best to make arrangements for the onward journey in advance in Srinagar. If you cannot find a place on a bus leaving Kargil for Leh, try a shared taxi.

Getting to Leh via Manali and Keylong

There are various options for covering the distance between Delhi and Manali (approximately 600km): go by bus directly to Manali, or take a train to Chandigarh and then continue by bus.

Private companies have daily bus connections between Delhi and Manali (Rs600–1000+). For reservations, visit www.makemytrip. com or go to any tourist office in Delhi. These buses leave from different places in Delhi; make sure you check the exact boarding point. State-owned buses leave from Kashmiri (also spelt 'Kashmere') Gate Inter State Bus Terminal, and the route is operated by Himachal Road Transport Corporation (HRTC: www.hrtc.gov.in). Tickets cost about Rs500 for an ordinary bus and about Rs900+ for an air-conditioned deluxe bus. It takes about 16hrs for the ordinary bus to cover the distance. There are also direct buses to Keylong and to Leh (the latter makes an overnight stop at Keylong).

Otherwise take a train to Chandigarh (5hrs, Rs140/100 for Sleeper/Seat Class). Chandigarh was built in the 1950s as an experimental project planned by the French architect Le Corbusier. However, unless you are a lover of modern architecture, continue by bus to Manali; there are a few connections every day from the new Inter State Bus Terminus at sector number 43 (it is quite far from the railway station; a bus links the two places) in Chandigarh. It takes about 10hrs to Manali, and an ordinary bus ticket costs about Rs300.

Although Manali (at about 1900m) is not at a sufficiently high elevation for you to acclimatise fully to the altitude of Leh, staying a few days and taking day-long hikes will certainly help. The scenery is spectacular and there are plenty of trips to do, with a number of interesting temples.

View of the Lesser Himalayas around Manali

MANALI

Manali is located in the upper Beas River Valley, southeast of the Pir Panjal Range (part of the Lesser Himalayas) in the Kullu Valley region in Himachal Pradesh state. It is an important mountain resort for both Indian and foreign tourists. Hiking, trekking, cycling, skiing, white-water rafting, paragliding and rock climbing are popular here. The nearest airport is about 50km from the town.

The town has two parts, Manali and Old Manali, the latter being the main foreign tourist section. There are dozens of cheap hotels, restaurants and shops; Rockway Cottage is a quiet accommodation option. If you arrive by a private bus, you may be dropped at Old Manali; otherwise you will probably be dropped at or near the Manali bus station. As you stand at the bus station with the Beas River on your right, the main street – the Mall – is on your left. To get to Old Manali, follow it upwards until you arrive at a roundabout, about 150m further. Take the main street slightly to the left. Follow it for 1.5km with a spruce forest on your right (hotels and shops left). Reach a bridge over a side river, the Manalsu Nala. Old Manali is on the other side; to find the main part, cross the bridge and go left. There are number of guesthouses and restaurants by the main road, 250m from the bridge. To get to the author's favourite guesthouse – Rockway Cottage, off the road – look for a sign at the first loop in the road.

If you spend some time in Manali visit Hadimba Temple, temples in Vashisht and go for a trip to the Solang Nullah Valley.

Snow on the Rohtang and Baralacha passes dictates whether the road is open beyond Manali. The Rohtang is between Manali and Keylong, and the Baralacha is beyond Keylong. Generally, the road beyond Manali is accessible only between early June and late October and throughout the season may be closed at any time for a few hours or a few days due to heavy snowfalls, landslides or bridge damage. The planned Rohtang tunnel to link the upper Solang Nullah Valley with the Chandra Valley should improve the accessibility of Keylong.

Private minibuses operate on the route and start/end the service earlier/later in the season than the HRTC buses. Most leave Manali at night, about 2am, and go directly to Leh, taking 20–24hrs. There is often only one driver – this is sufficient reason not to take this option! – and if you don't stop overnight in Keylong, the risk of altitude sickness is high. However, if the HRTC buses do not run beyond Keylong, you do not have much choice. In this case, to aid acclimatisation, try to go to Keylong first by an ordinary HRTC bus (they should run between Manali and Keylong early in the season, at which time they do not operate beyond Keylong), sleep there at least one night, and continue by minibus the following day. Minibuses do not start in Keylong so you will need to book the ticket before leaving Manali and arrange to be picked up in Keylong. In this case you will probably have to pay the fee for the whole route from Manali to Leh (approximately Rs2000).

A Hindu temple in Old Manali

There are a few state-owned buses from Manali to Keylong each day, leaving in the morning. As the snow of the Rohtang Pass is a day attraction for Indian tourists, leaving Manali no later than 6am is crucial to avoid traffic jams on the pass. The ordinary bus costs Rs130 and takes 7hrs.

Crossing the Rohtang Pass (3970m) over the Pir Panjal Range you leave the Kullu Valley and enter the region of Lahaul. Beautiful forests give way to vast treeless areas of green meadows, bare slopes and glaciated peaks. From the pass you descend along the Chandra River as far as its confluence with the Bhaga at Tandi. Upstream along the Bhaga, the road reaches Keylong after a few kilometres.

The state-owned bus (Rs500 in an ordinary bus) leaves Keylong about 5am and arrives at Leh that evening.

There are hardly any permanently inhabited places beyond Darcha as far as the Gya Valley north of the last pass. Although there are shops and restaurants in temporary camps en route, where the bus will occasionally stop, take water and emergency clothing in your hand luggage.

Darcha is about 25km beyond Keylong, where various major valleys meet; there are a few restaurants and primitive hotels (foreigners have to register at a checkpoint here). The very popular trekking route to Zanskar starts here (see Trek 3). Beyond Darcha, the valley of the Bhaga River goes to the Baralacha La (4910m) over the Himalayas. Across the pass is the wide valley of the Yunam River surrounded by barren mountains – you have clearly entered a different land. This is Rupshu, a highly elevated sub-region of Ladakh. Agriculture is

KEYLONG

Situated high above the Bhaga River, on sheer slopes, Keylong is the capital of the Lahaul region of northern Himachal Pradesh. It is a predominantly Buddhist area with a few monasteries; the scenery is fantastic. It is a much quieter, smaller place than Manali, definitely worth more attention than a brief overnight stop on the way to Ladakh. The main road to Leh is above the main part of the town, and there is a new bus station below the road. To reach the hotels nearby walk down from the bus station then follow the main street to the right (west) for around 200m. The Gyespa (www.gyespahotels.webs.com) is a nice simple hotel with a good restaurant (prices start at Rs300 for a double room). For a great *momo* (Tibetan dumpling) and *momo* soup check out a small restaurant on the main street, 100m from the Gyespa, on the right towards the bus station.

Donkeys grazing the meadows at the campsite in Pishu (Treks 5 and 6)

impossible here and the people, the Chang-pa nomads, depend solely on their stocks of sheep, goats and yaks. Sarchu is some 30km beyond the pass. It is the administrative border between Himachal Pradesh and Jammu and Kashmir state; there are restaurants and a police checkpoint.

Beyond Sarchu, the Yunam River joins the Tsarab, an important river of the Zanskar region that eventually becomes the Zanskar River. The road leaves the Tsarab Valley 25km beyond Sarchu and ascends to the Nakee La (4915m), 700m above the valley floor. It then descends to a valley and ascends again to the Lachulung La (5055m). From this pass there is a 20km+ descent to a police checkpoint in Pang. The trekking route from Kharu (see Trek 1) ends here and the Tsarab Chu trek (Trek 2) then follows the Toze Chu. There are tent restaurants and camps 1km beyond the checkpoint. Most buses stop here for a meal break.

Beyond Pang, the road climbs steeply to a wide plateau. After some 40km of crossing through the stark, deserted Morey Plains (the Plains) is the Taklang La (about 5300m). Beyond the pass, the descent leads to the first villages in the Gya Valley. At Lhatho, there is an alternative ending to the Markha Valley trek (see Trek 8). The road follows the Gya Valley to the Indus at Upshi village, about 20km beyond Lhatho. Leh (see below) is a further 55km (2hrs) along the Indus from Upshi, passing the spectacular Thikse Gompa.

Shikara (gondola) on Dal Lake in Srinagar

Getting to Leh via Srinagar

This route consists of a few stages: from Delhi to Jammu, from Jammu to Srinagar and from Srinagar to Leh (via Kargil). The first two stages are generally accessible all year round. The road between Srinagar and Leh normally opens in late April or early May and remains open until late November or mid-December (check the current status on www.kargil.nic.in). If you plan to visit Kashmir on the way to Ladakh earlier or later in the season, you could get to Srinagar as described below, then travel by air from Srinagar to Leh.

To get to Jammu, take a train from Delhi (Tawi or Jammu Tawi is the name of the station in Jammu). Book ahead (Sleeper Class about Rs260/berth) in Delhi or visit www.indian-railways.gov.in, www.indianrail.gov.in or www.makemytrip.com.

WARNING

The Kashmir region has suffered instability since 1986 as a result of disputes over the territory between India and Pakistan, as well as a separatist movement. This often takes the form of curfews, violent protests or even bomb attacks or armed fighting between militia groups and security forces.

If you are thinking about travelling via Srinagar and the Kashmir Valley, it is imperative to check your government's latest advice on the region before deciding whether to use this route. For those in the UK, see www.fco.gov.uk.

AMRITSAR

If you have time, be sure to visit Amritsar on the way to Srinagar. Go by train: Delhi to Amritsar, and then to Jammu. The highlight of Amritsar is the fabulous and atmospheric Sri Harmandir Sahib or Golden Temple – the most important Sikh shrine in India. The ornate temple stands in a large pool surrounded by equally exquisite, intricately decorated buildings. To really get the flavour of the place try sleeping and eating at the temple – it's all free! For information about the site, Sikhism, as well as sleeping in the temple and staying in Amritsar, visit www.goldentempleamritsar.org.

It is best to arrive in Jammu early in the morning (train No 2413) and continue by bus or shared taxi to Srinagar – the bus station is just next to the Jammu Tawi Railway Station (right from the station). The shared taxi stand is in front of the railway station. The price is around Rs200–500 in a bus/shared taxi and the journey takes about 8hrs. Spend at least a night in Srinagar (if you want to go to Leh the next day, book the bus first); preferably plan a few days in the city. Alternatively, fly from Delhi to Srinagar (for reservations try www.makemytrip.com).

SRINAGAR

Hidden behind the Pir Panjal Range of the Lesser Himalayas, the Kashmir Valley and its main city Srinagar enjoy a cooler climate than the plains of India. It's worth spending a few days around Srinagar, enjoying its fantastic location and pleasant people. Visit the historic but neglected old city for its amazing architecture and its mosques. Do not miss the vegetable market on Dal Lake and the fantastic Mughal Gardens.

Kashmir was a popular holiday destination under British rule. During that time the British did not have rights to buy land and build houses in Kashmir so they developed accommodation in boats, on the lakes of Srinagar. Today, hundreds of these boats are owned by local people and serve as hotels. Because the number of tourists coming to Kashmir is still limited, it is easy to find a place (no advance booking necessary) and the prices are quite low.

The majority of the houseboats in Srinagar are on Dal Lake, little more than 1km from the bus station; there are also boats nearer to the station on a canal next to a golf course. There are different classes and standards ▶

of houseboat accommodation, and you don't even have to look for it: houseboat owners wait for tourists at the bus station, airport and taxi stand. Ask for details of the boat and bargain. Important things to check are where the boat is situated, whether it has access from the land (if it does not, you will probably have to pay for a *shikara* or gondola to access the boat), and whether food is included in the price. A fair price for a room on a simple boat including food is Rs300–450 per person.

Avoid the touts (saying you have a reservation might help), leave the station and go to the right past the J&K Bank Headquarters. Turn right into the main street. Head for the canal (where the author found a friendly family who owned the *Cairo*, a boat 350m up the lane along the canal; they also had a more expensive boat on Dal Lake). For Dal Lake cross the canal by the road bridge and then follow the major road left for 350m to another bridge. Cross the bridge and then take a path to the right along the lakeshore. There are shops and hotels on the left and you will reach the houseboats after 400m.

The safest way to travel between Srinagar and Kargil is by bus. It's possible (but less advisable) to hire a taxi or to join other travellers in a shared taxi. Jammu and Kashmir State Road Transport Corporation

Floating vegetable market on Dal Lake, Srinagar

(www.jksrtc.nic.in) operates the route. Buses leave about 8am from the main bus terminal in Srinagar and arrive in Kargil the same evening. Book the ticket in advance at the bus station. Usually there is one ticket all the way from Srinagar to Leh (Rs700) on the same bus; the hotel in Kargil is not included. Buses stop en route for meals, but carry extra water, a torch and warm clothes in your hand luggage in case of delays. Have a string or rope with you to fasten your bag to the roof.

From Srinagar the route passes through the beautiful green landscapes of the Kashmiri Himalayas. Sonamarg (2750m) is the perfect place for an overnight break, surrounded by glaciated peaks and wooded slopes. There are dozens of simple restaurants or *dhabas*, shops and a few hotels. Spending time here helps with

acclimatisation. The famous Amarnath Cave, an important pilgrimage site for Hindus, is situated 25km up the valley from Sonamarg, and worth a visit if you stay in Sonamarg for a day or two.

Beyond Sonamarg the road starts its dramatic ascent of the Zoji La (3540m), a major road pass (closed in winter) of the Great Himalaya Range, marking the border of Ladakh. There is an amazing change in the landscape as you leave green, forested alpine scenery and enter a dry, treeless landscape, where green oases are limited to irrigated spots and valley floors.

From the pass the descent is gentle to Dras, the first settlement. It is reputedly the coldest, most snowbound spot in India and one of the world's coldest permanently inhabited places. Some 60km down the Dras River is the confluence with the Suru

Trucks approaching the Zoji La

River; and about 5km upstream along the Suru River is Kargil (2730m). This is the capital of Kargil District, one of the two districts that form Ladakh. Buses stop here overnight and leave the next day before dawn. There are plenty of hostels around the bus station, most of them quite dirty and relatively expensive.

The road to Leh leaves the Suru River beyond Kargil and crosses a ridge to the Wakha Valley. Mulbekh is some 35km along this valley – the first village en route where the majority of the people are Buddhist. There is a *gompa* (monastery) and a rock sculpture of the Buddha Maitreya (the future Buddha) that is thought to date from the 8th century.

Further on, the road climbs the Namika La (3822m), descends to the valley of Sangeluma and later ascends to the Photo (Fatu) La (4070m), the highest point on the way. A 15km descent brings you to Lamayuru (3500m), and another 15km further, after a dramatic descent, you reach the Indus Valley at about 3000m.

Khalatse marks the beginning of Central Ladakh. There is a checkpoint where foreign tourists need to register, and many restaurants, where most buses stop for lunch. Following the Indus most of the way, Leh is 4–5hrs' drive from Khalatse.

TRAVELLING AND SIGHTSEEING IN LADAKH

Leh

Leh is situated in a wide side valley of the Indus, north of the river. It is the historic capital of Ladakh and administrative centre of Leh District. This

Looking towards the Stok Range from Tukcha, Leh

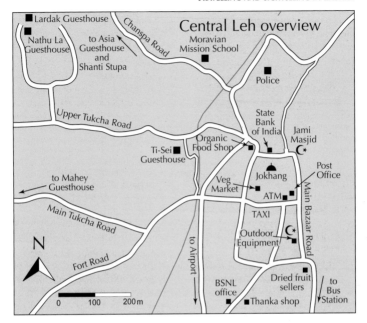

fast-growing town is now a tourist centre, but also houses a very important military base. There are cultural sights, craft markets for souvenir shopping and many pleasant guesthouses and hotels. Despite expansion, it is still a relatively quiet place, with some remnants of its village character still evident.

Arriving in Leh you will see the gleaming white new Shanti Stupa on a hill to the west. The ancient Leh Palace – reminiscent of the Potala, the palace of the Dalai Lama – and Namgyal Tsemo Gompa stand on the rugged hillside to the east. The town centre is at the foot of the palace, while the majority of guesthouses are on the

western side. Rugged mountains (part of the Ladakh Range) crossed by the Khardung La (approximately 5360m: incorrectly famous for being the highest drivable road in the world) dominate the northern horizon. South of town are the Indus River and the Stok Range. The highest peak is the much-climbed Stok Kangri (6150m), rising almost 3000m above the valley floor.

Accommodation

The number of hotels and guesthouses in Leh today is vast, and everyone has their favourite. The area most popular among travellers is Chanspa (also spelled Changspa).

It stretches along Chanspa Road, on the way to the Shanti Stupa. There are many guesthouses along Upper Tukcha Road and in the upper part of Leh, along Sankar Road. Generally you don't need to book, but if you come during peak season (mid-July to late August) or when a big event is taking place (the Dalai Lama's teaching, for example, or a major festival), book ahead (www.reachladakh. com is a good source for news on Ladakh, as well as dates of festivals and events).

The following list represents a few establishments that have been checked by the author.

- **Ti-Sei Guesthouse** This centrally located guesthouse with a garden is reminiscent of youth hostels across Asia. It is a good place to meet other travellers, but if you're looking for somewhere quiet, you could certainly do better. Rs300 for a double room.

- **Lardak Guesthouse** The author's favourite! It is a rural, traditional family house with a few rooms and a beautiful garden: the perfect place for a peaceful rest. It is accessible from Chanspa and Upper Tukcha Road. Tel. +91 9419 613714 or +91 9419 888568; Rs200–300 for a single room; doubles available too.

- **Nathu La Guesthouse** A modern house with a few rooms, located next to the Lardak. The standard is good for the price. Tel. +91 9419 342338; Rs300 for a double room.

- **Mahey Guesthouse** A nice peaceful place in tranquil surroundings on Main Tukcha Road. Tel. +91 1982 251263 or +91 9419 888705; Rs500–800 for a double room.

Lardak Guesthouse – one of Leh's traditional guesthouses

Shanti Stupa, Leh

- **Asia Guesthouse** More like a hotel; quite a big place with many rooms, it has a pleasant garden and a restaurant where excellent set dinners (different every day) are served for a reasonable price (the author's favourite place for dinner: about 7pm!): Rs70 per person for as much food as you want. They also arrange treks and tours. Tel. +91 1982 253403 or +91 9419 178689.

Many hotels and guesthouses in Leh – of varying standard – are listed on the official website of Leh District (www.leh.nic.in, under Tourism/Where to stay?).

Eating out

Leh has dozens, if not hundreds, of restaurants for tourists in season, offering both local and Western-style food. The majority are along Chanspa Road and the upper parts of Fort and Old Fort roads. For cheaper food, check the Tibetan restaurants mostly on the upper floors of buildings along Main Bazaar Road, opposite the post office. For a cheap, simple breakfast, try the small restaurants or *dhabas* near the Jama Masjid and along the upper part of the local bazaar.

Getting around

The airport is close to Spituk Gompa, southwest of central Leh, about 3.5km from the bus station and almost 5km from the centre. It is about 5.5km to Chanspa, so you'll probably take a taxi (don't be surprised to pay more than in Delhi – the fare from the airport to Chanspa is about Rs250–300). If you'd rather take a bus, you will easily catch these crowded vehicles on

81

the main road in front of the airport. To buy a flight ticket, check the offices in central Leh or buy online.

Bus stations for long-distance buses and minibuses are close to each other. The first is quite well arranged and has a booking/information office. It is better to buy tickets in advance and turn up well before the scheduled departure. Remember to bring string or a rope to fasten your bag to the roof.

The minibus stand is quite chaotic. There is no office or information board, but buses have a relatively fixed timetable. Nearer destinations, like Spituk or Choglamsar, have frequent connections throughout the day. Places like Alchi or Kharu only have one or two buses each day; others like Phanjila or Chiling have just one or two a week. The only way to find out what time they go is to ask conductors at the station or at a small canteen nearby. Booking is not possible; arrive early, about 30mins before departure, especially if you are taking an infrequent connection. Big bags are put on the roof. Prices for destinations in Central Ladakh range from about Rs12 for short distances to around Rs100 for the longest.

It is about 2km from the bus station to Chanspa – roughly 30mins' walk. Taxis are available at the bus station; the price to a guesthouse at Chanspa is about Rs200. For long-distance taxis check at the taxi stand in the city centre (see map).

Shopping

Leh is the perfect place to buy Tibetan handicrafts; there are a few Tibetan markets around town. Tibetan, Ladakhi and Kashmiri handicrafts are sold in dozens of shops, run mainly by Kashmiris. Kashmiri people are hard bargainers; you will need to be persistent to pay a low price. For local crafts, visit the local bazaar on the way to the bus station. For *thangkas* (religious paintings), check workshops – one is opposite the BSNL (telecommunications) office. Bargaining is customary in every shop or market.

To buy trekking equipment, go along Main Bazaar Road to find the area called Supermarket, a small market with a few shops specialising in sports gear, reached via a narrow lane off the main street. The Tibetan refugee markets sell items imported from China. For trek food check the local market at the southern end of Main Bazaar Road (dried fruits, *tsampa*, dry cheese) and organic food shops on Chanspa Road. Also try in the centre, near the State Bank of India. Kerosene can be bought in the upper part of the local bazaar, on the way to the bus station.

Leh has a few good bookshops. For books on Ladakh, the Himalayas and Buddhism, buy here – you will probably not find them in Delhi. Many novels can be found too. Most books are in English, but some are in French, German or other languages. Books are cheaper in India than in the West, and many Western publishers have branches in India. Furthermore, posting books is cheaper than other items; ask about 'book post' at the post office. For secondhand books visit the Bookworm on Old Fort Road.

Leh has at least two post offices, banks, at least two ATMs, a few foreign exchange offices and dozens of Internet cafés, so communicating with the outside world and access to your funds is easy here.

Festivals

There are a number of festivals each year in Leh and its surrounds, many of which take place in summer.

Nearly every *gompa* or monastery has a yearly religious festival (dates depend on the Tibetan Calendar). The Ladakh Festival organised by the State Department of Tourism takes place in September each year and is aimed at promoting the rich local culture. Losar, or the New Year celebration, is the biggest winter holiday for the local community. Ladakhi Losar is celebrated two months before the Tibetan Losar, in the 11th month of the Tibetan lunisolar calendar. For dates of events in a particular year check www.leh.nic.in (Tourism/Fairs and festivals) or www.reachladakh.com.

If you attend a festival – particularly a religious event – respect the local people. Wear adequate clothes: no shorts or cropped or sleeveless tops. Don't disturb the locals watching the performance if you want to take a photograph; do it discretely. Be aware that you are not the most important person watching the events, and leave the front rows for the locals; for the Ladakhis these are important spiritual experiences. For information on the festivals and their dates see the websites listed at the end of the previous paragraph.

A girl from Zanskar performing a traditional dance

Sightseeing in Leh

Leh is a remarkable site. Here the legends connect the paths of Buddha and Christ. Buddha went through Leh northwards. Issa (Jesus) communed here with the people on his way from Tibet. Secretly and cautiously, the legends are guarded. It is difficult to sound them because lamas, above all people, know how to keep silent. Only by means of a common language – and not merely that of tongue but also of inner understanding – can one approach their significant mysteries.

Altai Himalaya Nicholas Roerich

Walks to the modern Shanti Stupa and ancient Namgyal Tsemo Gompa, situated atop opposite hills, will not only give you a glimpse of Buddhism but also test your fitness. Evenings, when the setting sun lights Leh and the peaks of the Stok Range, are the best times to visit the Shanti Stupa. It was built in the mid-1980s by an order of Japanese Buddhism. Walk around the *stupa* a few times (clockwise!). Look for the statues symbolising the four most important stages of Buddha Sakyamuni's life: his birth, meditation, his teachings and his death.

There is an impressive panorama of Leh, the Indus Valley and the mountains from the *stupa*. A quiet temple nearby is worth a visit as well as the Changspa Stupa, an exquisite structure that blends beautifully into the landscape. North of town is the much-venerated Shankar Gompa.

Vistas from Namgyal Tsemo Gompa are excellent. Visit it early in the morning to see Leh in the light of dawn. There are two temples and the

Namgyal Tsemo Gompa, Leh

LEH PALACE

King Sengge Namgyal built Leh Palace in the 16th century. It took only three years to complete, but was burnt down by the Tibetans and Mongolians in 1685. A Balti Muslim, Chanden Ali Sengee, was responsible for the design.

A large wooden door with three guarding snow lions above dominates the entrance. Visitors enter at the fourth level, with its various welcoming halls. The ground area was used for stables. The second floor was used for storage, with the third occupied by the servants; the fifth floor housed the King's Audience Hall, the Tsokhang.

On the sixth floor were the king's and queen's private areas. The seventh floor houses the image of Dukkar, known as the lady with a white parasol, as well as a 1000-armed aspect of Tara. The Samyeling Lhakhang has some Gelug-pa images, as well as Tara, Sakyamuni, Palden Lhamo (the fierce female Tibetan deity) and Guru Rinpoche. The eighth floor comprises of seven rooms of unknown use, and the top level, the ninth, has a prayer room.

ruins of the Tashi Namgyal Fort, built in the 16th century by Tashi Namgyal. Parts of the top building, a white-walled crumbling structure with elaborate wooden balconies, is a former Dard fortress dating back to the fifth century.

Walk downhill from Namgyal Tsemo to reach the imposing nine-storey palace, which is open to visitors. Other sights in this area are the Chenresig Lhakhang (chapel) and the Chamba Lhakhang.

Further down, passing through the narrow streets of the Old Town, is the Jama Masjid, the main place of worship for the local Muslim community. Just in the centre, opposite the State Bank of India, there is the gate to Soma Gompa or Jokhang Monastery, a modern Buddhist temple built in 1957. It is worth visiting, especially in

the morning or evening, when many Ladakhis come to perform their *kora* or ritual walk around of the temple.

Places to visit southeast of Leh

Choglamsar is southeast of Leh, in the Indus Valley, just a few kilometres from the town. This used to be the main settlement of Tibetan refugees in Ladakh but was badly affected by flash floods and mudslides caused by a sudden cloudburst in August 2010. A few hundred people died, and many houses have been demolished. The town is 20mins' bus journey from Leh and has frequent connections. Choglamsar has a number of Tibetan shops, restaurants and a temple. The Mahabodhi International Meditation Centre (www.mahabodhi-ladakh.org) and the Central Institute of Buddhist Studies are both located here.

Stok is opposite Choglamsar, on the south bank of the Indus River. It is a beautiful, large village at the foot of Stok Kangri peak. The 19th-century Stok Palace houses descendants of Ladakh's kings (currently the family do not have any royal authority). For a pleasant walk, take the morning bus (two or three buses a day to Stok), go to the last stop and walk down to the palace. There is a museum open to tourists. It is a little over 5km from the palace to Choglamsar, where you can easily catch a return bus.

Located some 15km from Leh, upstream along the Indus, **Shey** is a former Ladakhi capital with superb panoramic views. The ruins of the old fortification have an obvious strategic location on a ridge where the Indus Valley is narrow. The renovated palace below the ruins is a newer construction but the temple adjacent to it houses a 17th-century gilded statue of Buddha Sakyamuni that is approximately 12m high. A number of daily buses can drop you in Shey; take a Thikse, Kharu or Hemis bus (and possibly any other bus) going further up the valley. Taxis are happy to take you for a ride too!

Thikse Gompa
This stunning, impressive *gompa* complex is located a few kilometres beyond Shey along the Indus. The monastery buildings cling to a sheer slope, one above the other. The view from the *gompa* is magnificent: Shey down the Indus, Stakna Gompa upstream and the monastery of Matho on the opposite side of the river.

Painted mani stones displaying Buddhist mantras

MORE ABOUT THIKSE GOMPA

Two emissaries of Tsong Khapa – Sherab Zangpo, and his disciple, Spon Palden Sherab – founded Thikse Gompa in the mid-15th century. Rinchen Zangpo probably built a chapel here in the 11th century, a building that no longer exists. Today what remains are the old Dukhang, the Gonkhang and the red Chamba Lhakhang of Maitreya on the east side. Other chapels include the Kudung Lhakhang and the Drolma Lhakhang.

The red Chamba Lhakhang is the most imposing sight at Thikse, with its 12m-high golden statue of future Buddha, Maitreya. It was built in 1979 with Maitreya in a sitting position, wearing a golden crown. Behind and on the sides are images of Tsong Khapa and Sakyamuni.

In the Kudung Lhakhang, the newest of Thikse's chapels, are two large silver and gold *stupas*. The sixth reincarnate, Nawang Namgyal, and the seventh, Chamba Sokmit, are on display here, as well as the current ninth incumbent lama. The Drolma Lhakhang contains images of the 21 Taras, Kachokma, Vajrapani, Dorje Sempa and Chenresig, as well as Tsong Khapa. The Lhamo Lhakhang, which is normally closed, presumably houses a statue of Palden Lhamo, the fierce female deity.

The Nyingma Lhakhang has an imposing image of Demchok, a deity closely associated with Mount Kailash. One of the most astonishing chapels is the Gonkhang, where the ferocious mind-curdling protectors of Buddhism, Yamantaka, Kitapala and a four-armed Mahakala, are gathered in a dark and solemn temple. The original chapel might date back to the time of Rinchen Zangpo. The present chamber is around 500 years old.

The current *lama* is Nawang Chamba Stenzin, who was born in 1943 at Chushot village nearby. Educated in Tibet at Drepung and Tashi Lhunpo, he developed the monastic schools at Diskit in the Nubra Valley. About 100 monks are currently studying at Thikse.

Calling monks to prayer in Thikse Gompa

For a spectacular view of the *gompa*, get off the bus about 1km beyond the monastery. Walk back through the fields with the monastery in full view. If you come early in the morning (7am), you may attend the *puja* or morning prayers. Bring a cup for the tea that is served during the offering. There is a restaurant at the monastery complex.

Stakna Gompa

A few kilometres from Thikse, on an isolated hill in the middle of the valley (on the left bank of the Indus), lies Stakna Gompa. Its name, meaning 'Tiger's Nose' relates to the shape of the hill – said to resemble a tiger jumping to the sky. The place is quiet and peaceful, with several temples. Stakna Tulku is the highest reincarnated *lama* of the monastery.

To get to Stakna, take one of the frequent buses going to Thikse. Get off at the last stop, just beyond Thikse. It is just a short walk over a bridge across the Indus to Stakna Gompa. If not for cultural reasons, visit it for breathtaking views of the valley.

Hemis Gompa

This is the largest, richest and most frequently visited of the Ladakhi *gompas*. Founded in the 17th century, it is located in a side valley a few kilometres southwest of Kharu village and the Indus. A big religious festival devoted to Guru Padma Sambhava takes place here every year; once every 12 years, in the Year of the Monkey, there is a special celebration with an exhibition of a large, precious *thangka* of the Guru. Hemis Gompa is the main centre of the Druk-pa Lineage of Tibetan Buddhism (www.drukpa.org) and the main monastery of Ladakh. The Gyalwang Drukpa is the head *lama* of the lineage; he is regarded as the spiritual leader of Ladakh.

Two buses a day link Leh and Hemis; they stop just in front of the monastery. Accommodation is

---

MORE ABOUT STAKNA GOMPA

Stakna Gompa first appears in chronicles of Ladakh that link it to the Gelug-pa reformer, Tsong Khapa. Shenrab Zangpo, who developed the monasteries of Karsha in Zanskar and Diskit in Nubra, is associated with Stakna's origins. The monastery probably dates from around 1580. It has two main chapels; the Dukhang hosts some lesser-known deities. The most interesting chapel houses the Shabdrung Nawang Namgyal, the Bhutanese senior deity who is venerated throughout Bhutan as the founder of the Druk-pa sect. Other icons on display are two Bhutanese lamas, Stakpe Palzang and Tashi Tsampel on the left; Guru Rinpoche is on the right. The Indian mystic saint, Naropa, sits in front.

Hemis Gompa

available both in the *gompa* and in the village below. A good garden restaurant belonging to the monastery is just beside it; food is also available in the village. Hemis is a finishing point of the Markha Valley trek (see Trek 8).

Chemrey and Traktok Monasteries
Chemrey is located 47km southeast of Leh. It is one of the most attractive monasteries, located on top of an impressive hill, 8km from the road junction at Kharu. There are limited

---

MORE ABOUT HEMIS GOMPA

The monastery was built around 1630 by Kushokq Shambhu Nath. After 1730, Gyalsang Rinpoche, the third incarnate Kushokq Stagsang Raspa, extended the *gompa*, building more shrines, chapels and *stupas* to house the fine scriptures and murals. The Druk-pa school was established here in the 13th century. Gotsampo, the great sage, meditated in a cave about 2km above the *gompa*; this cave is now a pilgrimage site that makes a pleasant hike in summer.

A curious story that still persists about the Hemis Gompa is its possible association with Jesus Christ. Many years ago, the explorer-philosopher Nicholas Notovitch reported that there were documents proving that Jesus Christ had passed this way around 2000 years ago (see *The Lost Years of Jesus* by Elizabeth Clare Prophet, Summit University Press 1988).

A tiny path cuts across the slopes above the Tsarab Chu (Trek 2)

MORE ABOUT CHEMREY AND TRAKTOK MONASTERIES

Chemrey Gompa, devoted to the Kagyu-pa sect, presents a stunning sight. Houses and buildings flow down the hill surrounded by a clutter of old and new *chortens*. Chemrey is associated with Hemis Gompa. Begun under Sengge Namgyal and his chief Lama Stagsang Raspa, it was probably enlarged around 1644–46 as a dedication to Sengge Namgyal after his death. The Guru Lhakhang houses a prolific number of deities dedicated to Guru Rinpoche and the many different aspects of the Tantric magician. The main festival here, when Cham dances are performed, usually falls in November.

Traktok Gompa (also written as Tak Thog) belongs to the Nyingma-pa sect. Two large *chortens* stand before the monastery complex. The main sanctuary, one of the meditation caves of Guru Rinpoche (Padma Sambhava), gives the monastery its name, 'natural rock roof cave'. It is guarded by yak horns; the cave shrine is rarely accessible to visitors. The other cave, known as Tu Phuk, contains images of the eight forms of Guru Rinpoche, as well as an 11-headed Chenresig (Avalokiteshvara). The Urgyen Photang Lhakhang also houses images of Guru Rinpoche. The Traktok Tse-Chu festival is celebrated from the 9th–11th days of the sixth month while the Traktok Wangchok festival is held from the 26th–29th days of the ninth month.

Spituk Gompa

MORE ABOUT SPITUK GOMPA

Spituk – which translates as 'model community' – is one of the oldest monasteries in Ladakh. The site dates back to the time of Rinchen Zangpo and Yeshe O from the Guge Kingdom of western Tibet. It was initially a Kadam-pa monastery, founded by King Gas Ra Bum on the site of the original 11th-century monastery. Later, during the 15th century, it became the seat of the dominant Gelug-pa sect, when two emissaries of Tsong Khapa came from Tibet to grant it full status. The monastery comprises a number of chapels; the main ones are the Chokhang, Tara Lhakhang, Tsogchen and Dukhang-Chikhang. The new golden *stupa* room on the south side is impressive, and the Gonkhang on the hilltop holds some frightening images.

buses to it in summer and only a basic guesthouse in nearby Kharu. On the way you pass into a 'plastic-bag-free zone,' a new initiative on the eco front.

Traktok Gompa is located about 50km southeast of Leh. The main structures of Traktok cling to a steep hillside on the south side of the valley. To reach it, you must continue up the valley past Chemrey from Kharu. Traktok is about 15km from Kharu. A visit here is best combined with an excursion from Leh to other monasteries in this part of the valley. Buses to Tangtse (and Pangong Lake) may pass by in summer. There is no accommodation in Traktok.

Places to visit southwest and west of Leh
Spituk Gompa

This *gompa* is located on a dramatic hill at the end of the airport runway just southwest of central Leh. Buses from Leh go to Spituk every 15mins. For a magnificent view of the Indus Valley from the monastery, late afternoon is the best time to visit.

Phyang Gompa

West of Leh in a side valley is the quaint settlement of Phyang. The large monastery sits on a hill dominating the village and its surroundings and is one of the oldest such buildings in Ladakh. Tashi Namgyal probably founded it in the 16th century. Some historians think he built it out of remorse for the blinding of his elder brother, Lhawang. It is one of two monasteries devoted to this sub-sect of the Kagyu-pa. About 60 monks are practising here at present.

Three buses a day go to Phyang Gompa from Leh (in the morning, at noon and about 4pm), returning to Leh about 15mins after their arrival. Visit the *gompa*, then walk down from the monastery hill through the picturesque village fields and across the desert to the main Leh–Srinagar road, where you can catch a bus. It is 5km from the monastery to the main road.

The main road from Leh to Srinagar leaves the Indus Valley for a while

MORE ABOUT PHYANG GOMPA

Phyang was probably once a Kadam-pa monastery before becoming associated with the Drigung-pa nearly 500 years ago. The Drigung sub-sect has its head monastery in Tibet, east of Lhasa. The various chapels include the Dorje Chang Lhakhang (also known as the Dukhang Sarwa), the Padma Gyalpo, the Tsokhang and the Gonkhang. Kashmiri artists of the 14th century were responsible for the intricate artwork. The Tsokhang is an amazing room, containing a multitude of imagery; even before entering, one is accosted by the four Lokapalas. The main altar is devoted to Skyoba Jigjen, with images of Atisa, Amitabha, Manjushri and Avalokiteshvara, with four arms and his *mala* – prayer beads. Elsewhere Vairocana takes centre stage, with two Skyoba Jigjen Buddhas on each side. Other icons are Sakyamuni, Maitreya and Vajrasattva.

beyond the turn-off to Phyang. It climbs up, crosses a deserted plateau and returns to the Indus, passing high above its impressive **confluence with the Zanskar**.

Basgo

The road descends to the fertile village of Nyemo. Basgo is the next village, located some 40km from Leh, and a capital of Lower Ladakh in the 15th and 16th centuries. The impressive *gompa* and fort (partially ruined, under renovation) is said to have held out for three years against invasion in the second half of the 17th century.

Basgo is easily accessible, as all buses to Likir, Saspola, Alchi, Khalatse

Phyang Gompa

and Kargil pass it. There is a restaurant and a guesthouse at the western end of the village.

Likir Gompa

This monastery is on a hill about 3.5km off the main Leh–Srinagar road, in a side valley. To get there, take the only direct bus (about 4pm) or get off any bus going to Saspola (or further) at the crossroads near the village. The walk along the road leading to the monastery is not particularly pleasant. The return direct bus leaves Likir early in the morning. There are a number of guesthouses near the *gompa* and in the village, near to the main road. An interesting educational

MORE ABOUT LIKIR GOMPA

In 1470, learned sage Lhawang Lotos came from Central Tibet and converted this former Kadam-pa monastery to the Gelug-pa sect. There are a number of temples at the monastery, but the first thing you will probably see is the enormous statue of Buddha Maitreya. The monastery is famous for its paintings, a collection of manuscripts and *thangkas*. It is also noted for its religious Cham festival, when the famed masked dancing monks perform. Likir Gompa is also the seat of successive reincarnations of Ngari Rinpoche (the present incarnation is Tenzin Choegyal, brother of the 14th Dalai Lama). About 100 monks live at the monastery.

Likir Gompa

initiative of establishing micro-libraries for children in villages across Ladakh has been recently started in Likir. For more information on the project check www.facebook.com/FriendsOfLikir, or visit the school just next to the monastery.

Opposite the monastery, on the other side of the Indus, the mountains rise dramatically. The top of the mountain range is just 6.5km from the Indus and over 2000m higher. The Stakspi La is clearly visible from Likir and marks the start of the Alchi to Alchi Trek (see Trek 7).

Saspola

This beautiful village, with its apricot orchards, has well-tended and peaceful caves, sometimes used for meditation. It is on the main Leh–Srinagar road, beyond the turn-off to Likir. To visit the caves, get off near the State Bank of India and walk through the fields towards the rock face, where the caves are clearly visible.

Alchi Gompa

Alchi is one of the most famous places in Ladakh, if not in the entire state. The main reason for its pre-eminence is its unique ancient paintings, which date back to the 11th century, the time when Buddhism was spreading from Kashmir. Once an important religious centre, Alchi Gompa was abandoned for unknown reasons in the 16th century and then became the responsibility of monks from Likir. The temples are well preserved and definitely worth a visit, although the place, being very popular among tourists, is rarely quiet or peaceful.

MORE ABOUT ALCHI GOMPA

Alchi is one of the oldest monasteries in the region, and the complex was originally surrounded by high walls. It was built under Rinchen Zangpo and his Kashmiri artists; its paintings show the distinct Kashmiri/Indian style. The chapels here include the Manjushri Lhakhang, Lotsa (Lotsawa) Lhakhang, Sum Tsek Lhakhang, Kangyur Lhakhang and the Lhakhang Soma, as well as some significant *chortens*. The Manjushri chapel is noted for four elaborate, colourful and stunning images. The Lotsawa Lhakhang is devoted to the translator (Lotsawa) Rinchen Zangpo. The large chapel and internal courtyard structure is the Vairocana Lhakhang. There is an image of the future Buddha Maitreya and the main deity popular across Ladakh, Vairocana. The Sum Tsek temple is an ancient-looking three-storey building with an elaborate, beautifully carved wooden façade; it is covered with exquisite murals and paintings. The Lhakhang Soma has exquisite Kashmiri-style paintings and should not be missed.

The Zanskar Mountains as seen en route from the Dungdungchen La towards Chiling

Alchi is situated about 65km from Leh, on the left bank of the Indus, opposite Saspola, a few kilometres from the main Leh–Srinagar road. There are two direct buses a day, at about 8am and 3pm. The return buses leave Alchi at the same time, taking 3–4hrs. There are guesthouses and restaurants in the village, but none is very cheap. Alchi is the start and finish point of Trek 7.

Rizong

Rizong is about 70km west of Leh, 5km north of the road to Lamayuru and Srinagar. Either take a bus to

MORE ABOUT RIZONG GOMPA

Rizong (also Ri Dzong) Gompa is well hidden, sitting high on a steep-sided hillside. There is a new arched entrance, a *chorten* and new monks' quarters below the main complex. Visitors can view two main chapels. In the Dukhang, the Buddha Maitreya is prominent in front of a *chorten*, eight small images of Buddha and an image of Guru Rinpoche. The other chapel is the Thegchen, the yellow-coloured building that tops the complex. It is probably the more interesting, with some imposing images: earthly Buddha Sakyamuni, Avalokiteshvara and a fearsome Vajrapani. The monastery dates from about 1840 and was built under the supervision of Lama Tsultrin Nyima and conforms to the reformist Yellow Hat Gelug-pa sect. There are around 40 monks at the monastery.

Lamayuru and get off, or charter a taxi from Leh for the day. There is no accommodation at the monastery and no village here. The monastery is reached by a small track (often cut off by snow in winter), and is a long walk from the main road. A sign states 2km, but that is only the distance to the Chullichan nunnery, picturesquely set in a small grove of trees. After the nunnery is an unmarked junction near some *stupas*. Take the left fork, which is also a jeep track, and follow this uphill. The road straight on goes eventually to Yangtang, but also forks and doubles back to Rizong further on, if you prefer a less steep path. The walk to Rizong from the main road will take about 1hr 20mins. To sleep nearby, you might try in Uletokpo, or continue to Lamayuru.

Lamayuru Gompa

This is one of the oldest, largest and most spectacularly situated *gompas* in Ladakh. It is located some 120km along the main road west of Leh. Situated on a hill, above a deep valley, it is surrounded by an incredible moon-like landscape of extraordinarily shaped rocks, sculpted by wind and water from the alluvial detritus of an ancient lake that once existed here.

Most of the houses of Lamayuru village cling to the hill below the *gompa*, leaving the valley floor free for agriculture. This is the starting (or finishing) point of one of the most popular trekking routes in Ladakh: from Darcha to Lamayuru (or the reverse) across Zanskar, through Padum (see Trek 3 and Trek 5). Lamayuru is also

MORE ABOUT LAMAYURU GOMPA

This was once called Yungdrung Gompa, with its origins linked to the Bon faith of early Tibet, making it one of the oldest monasteries in Ladakh. It also had the name Tharpa Ling, which means 'place of freedom'. Since the 16th century, Lamayuru has been one of two major Drigung Kagyu-pa *gompas* in Ladakh, Phyang being the other. Large *stupas* and *chortens* are clustered around the main structure, with the Dukhang, Chenresig Lhakhang and the Gonkhang being the main chapels. In an older section is the Sengge Lhakhang that dates back to the 11th century, to the time of Rinchen Zangpo. The Chenresig Lhakhang is devoted to Avalokiteshvara, who is depicted here in his 11-headed 1000-armed version. The main Dukhang is a newer chapel and is the meditation cave of Indian Buddhist sages, Naropa and Marpa – the principle founder of the Kagyu-pa. The chamber of the protecting guardians, the Gonkhang, is located above the Dukhang. It houses some of the more common deities, Skyoba Jigten, Dorje Chang, Milarepa, Marpa, Guru Rinpoche, plus their protectors – a four-armed Mahakala and Vaisravana.

on the less popular but more demanding trek from Zanskar over the Kanji La (see Trek 6). It is also possible to finish the trek from Alchi (see Trek 7) here.

To get to Lamayuru from Leh, take a bus to Kargil, but make sure it passes through Lamayuru; there is an alternative road. There are a number of lodgings in Lamayuru. If you need one, you may start by checking the author's favourite: Tharpaling. This is a beautiful house by the main road, 200m from a small square where buses usually stop; prices depend on the room, but are generally budget.

Padum – the heart of Zanskar

Zanskar is the southwestern part of Ladakh, an area of big river valleys. The Stod (Doda) is one, flowing from the Pensi La southeast along the Great Himalayas. The Kargyak Chu flows roughly in the opposite direction, from its source in the Great Himalayas near the Shinkul La. It meets the Tsarab – a big river running from the Baralacha La – and continues northwest as the Lungnak (Tsarab, Lingti or Tsarab Lingti) Chu. Stod and Lungnak join in a huge valley – at the foot of the Great Himalayas – to form the Zanskar River, which flows initially northeast in a wide valley. This upper part of the Zanskar Valley, with its tributary valleys, forms the Zanskar sub-region. Padum, situated roughly at the confluence of Stod and Lungnak, is the major settlement.

Zanskar is a remote country, guarded by high passes and still quite isolated from the outside world by the solid barrier of mountains; it is cut off for most of the year, with the only winter route leading along the frozen Zanskar River. It used to be a separate kingdom; it has its own dialect (of the

Looking from the Stagrimo Gompa towards Padum, situated at the confluence of the Lungnak (right) and Stod rivers in the wide Zanskar Valley

Ladakhi language) and some differences in culture, local customs and even ethics. This beautiful and peaceful region is well worth a visit, even if you don't plan to trek.

Getting to Padum

Currently, there is just one road linking Padum with the outside world. It follows the Stod River up to the Pensi La and then descends along the beautiful, long valley of Suru to Kargil on the main Srinagar–Leh road. This Padum–Kargil route is open for only a few months of the summer; its current status can be checked at www.kargil.nic.in.

Two additional roads are under construction (one to link Padum and Chiling along the Zanskar Valley, the other to Padum from Darcha via the Shinkul La). The construction of the latter has speeded up in recent years: on the Darcha side the road had extended as far as the Shinkul pass in 2014, and on the Padum side it was possible to reach Enmu village by car in late season that year. Although it will certainly still take some time to complete these roads, Padum and Zanskar – no doubt – will change significantly once they are open. There is no civil airport in Padum.

There are two options for getting to Padum in summer:
• By road
• By any of the trekking routes that finish here (see Trek 2 and Trek 3).

Buses between Padum and Kargil do not have a fixed timetable and run rather erratically, every few days. Some cover the distance in one long day, some in two. Occasional mini-buses and shared taxis make the journey from Padum to Leh in two days, with an overnight stop in Kargil or Lamayuru. It is over 230km on a very rough road between Padum and Kargil and it takes at least 12hrs to cover the distance. It is advisable to divide the journey into two stages with an overnight stop in Rangdum. For transport to Padum, ask at the bus station or taxi stand in Leh or Kargil. Padum does not have a bus station, but buses leave from the eastern part of town or the main crossroads; the latter also serves as a taxi stand. Ask the taxi drivers, in your guesthouse or at a restaurant (the Lhasa Restaurant owner has proved to be helpful in the past).

There are two main roads in Padum. One runs northwest–southeast, parallel to the Great Himalaya Range; the other heads northeast towards Pibiting Gompa, situated on a hill in the middle of the valley 2km from Padum. The main part of the town, and most of the guesthouses, are near the crossing of these two roads and along the road to the south, towards the mosque and the old part of the settlement.

Accommodation

Padum has a few guesthouses and a campsite. Group trekkers will probably camp or stay in one of the bigger guesthouses, such as Hotel Kailash or Ibex, located near the main junction.

A few smaller, family-run guesthouses have been checked by the author. Expect shared bathrooms, warm water limited to a few hours a day, a nice quiet atmosphere, and charges of around Rs300 for a room for one person. If you need to charge a battery (your camera, perhaps) make sure your guesthouse is connected to the solar network.

As you walk south from the main crossroads the first accommodation option is a room in a big, green house owned by a Muslim family. There is no sign; it is 50m from the junction, to the left of the main road, behind a building.

Further towards the mosque, on the left side of the main road, some 300m from the crossroads, is the Himalaya Guesthouse. It has a few reasonably big rooms with shared bathrooms for Rs300. The Mount Blanc Hotel, a further 170m on the same side of the road, is similar in price and conditions. Further along the road, on the right, about 150m beyond the mosque, is the Khar Ging Guesthouse.

Facilities

Padum has a number of restaurants serving local, Indian and European food. The author's favourite is the Lhasa Restaurant by the main road (try *momo* – Tibetan dumpling, or *ruchos* – a momo soup).

Padum is one of the few places where buying food supplies for a trek is possible. You will not find freeze-dried food, but rice, noodles, instant soups, tinned tuna, milk powder and so on are available. Fresh fruit is brought to Padum from Kashmir and is easily available in a few shops next to the crossroads.

As many trekking groups pass through Padum in the season, with some finishing in the town, it is usually possible to find horses for a trek here. Ask at the campsite. To arrange in advance, check www.trekzanskar. org – it may be helpful. Don't expect to buy or hire any trekking or photographic equipment here.

Although there was an Internet café in Padum in 2009, usually there was no connection. The BNSL mobile phone service generally works (BNSL J&K SIM cards only), but often the connection breaks or is halted for a few hours. Landline phones are available, but do not expect to be able to call whenever you want. There is a post office, but it takes significantly longer for letters to get to an address from here than from Leh.

Electricity (cable) is available in some houses at night, but make sure that your guesthouse is connected and be aware that there may be power cuts (load shedding). There is no ATM and the only bank does not offer any foreign currency exchange service!

Getting around Zanskar

There are bus or shared jeep connections from Padum to some places in Zanskar. There is a bus to Zangla and a bus to Karsha; both leave Padum six

Eighth-century rock carvings of meditating figures, Padum

times a week around 4pm and return the next morning. Ask the locals for details.

Places to visit in Zanskar

There are a few interesting sites in and around Padum. Some are within a short walking distance; others can be reached either by a few hours' walk or by bus or taxi. You might also visit some on trekking routes that do not involve carrying camping equipment, where you can sleep and eat in family houses en route.

Buddhist rock carvings, said to date from the eighth century, can be seen on a boulder by the Lungnak River, about 200m down from the southern bridge in the southeast part of Padum. There are a few well-preserved meditating figures. To get there, follow the main road towards the old part of the village, past the mosque. At the crossroads in front of the Khar

Ging Guesthouse go left towards the river. As the road turns sharp right continue straight ahead, along the fields with the river below right. After 400m a small hill with a few prayer flags is reached. The carvings are on its southwest side, on rock faces above the river.

Stagrimo Gompa

This pleasant *gompa* is in the southern part of the settlement, on a hill at the foot of a high slope. It is visible from the town and you will get there easily by wandering through the fields – a nice walk with great views from the *gompa*.

Pibiting

The temple is on a hill in the middle of the Zanskar plains some 2km northeast of the main crossroads in Padum. It is a particularly picturesque site, especially in the late afternoon.

Karsha Gompa

This large *gompa*, located on a sheer slope above the plains north of the town, is certainly the most impressive site around Padum. Although more than 7km away as the crow flies, it is clearly visible from the town. Head towards it through the fields (see the start of Trek 5 or Trek 6). The first half of the walk is pleasant, the next quite tiresome. Carry water with you. Alternatively, take a bus; it leaves Padum daily in the afternoon and returns the next day. You could also try taking a shared taxi. Karsha has a campsite and a few guesthouses.

Stongde Gompa

Probably founded in the 11th century, this *gompa* is worth a visit even if you are not a lover of Buddhism. It is situated on a hill, high above the valley floor and Stongde village on the east of the Zanskar River, about 12km north-east of Padum. There are incredible views of the village, the Zanskar Valley and the Great Himalaya Range from the monastery.

Stongde is at the end of the Round Sultanlango trek (see Trek 4). If you want to visit it from Padum, take an afternoon bus to Zangla and get off in Stongde. The bus returns in the morning; it is possible to sleep at the monastery. Zangla village, further down the Zanskar River, has ruins of a castle and a nunnery.

Bardan and Mune Monasteries

These two are within a day's walking distance from Padum up the Lungnak Chu, on the way to Phukthal (see Trek 4). Both are on the trail from Pang (Trek 2) and Darcha (Trek 3). Mune has a hotel next to the *gompa*. Both monasteries are accessible by jeep.

The view from Phukthal Gompa

Phukthal Gompa

There is no doubt that Phukthal, located on a cliff in the narrow valley of the Tsarab Chu, is the most spectacular place in the region. Part of it is in a huge cave, high above the river. Although its age is not certain, its history is said to date back to the 11th century. Trekking routes 2 and 4 pass the monastery; a short side-trip off the 'Darcha Padum Trek' (Trek 3) also leads to it. Phukthal can be accessed within three days' hike from Padum (six days for a return trip). It is an easy route and no supplies or camping equipment are necessary, as you can sleep and eat in the villages on the way.

If you don't have time for hiking, you could reach Phukthal in a day going by car to Enmu on the new road (or even further, to Cha, if the road is ready when you're there) and continuing on one of the trekking routes described in the 'Round Sultanlango' chapter (see Trek 4, Stage 3 for details).

Rangdum Gompa

This *gompa* between Padum and Kargil, near the main road, is worth visiting if you are approaching or leaving Zanskar this way. Again, it is located on a hill, above the wide plains of the upper Suru Valley. The village below the *gompa* is an alternative start point of the trek via the Kanji La and an alternative finishing point for the trek along the Oma Chu and over the Pikdong La (for both, see Trek 6). At over 7000m high, the twin-peaked Nun Kun massif dominates the landscape around Rangdum.

ON THE TREK

Finding the route

All the routes described in this book follow trails that have been used by people and their animals for hundreds of years. Therefore the paths are generally clear and usable by pack animals. If you are on a path that is indistinct or seems to be too difficult, you have most probably lost your way and should return the way you came. In many places there is more than one path – often the result of domestic animals taking different tracks – and the main trekking route is not easily identified. Read the route description carefully to make sure you pick the right path!

In some places, paths traverse sheer slopes, and are often narrow and precipitous. Sections of the path are rough and broken up, or have fallen away. Take special care; read the route description and be alert. Note the small signs with which locals often mark the route: a row of small stones laid horizontally across the path means that the route does not continue that way, and you should search for another. A small pile of stones (cairn) normally marks the correct way – look for one of these when you have doubts about the right way to go.

MOUNTAIN SAFETY

All mountain walking can be hazardous, but with prior awareness and concentration on trek risks can be minimised. The following advice is relevant for all trekkers, whether independent or in a group: it is important to be responsible for yourself even when in the company of others.

In Ladakh the biggest danger in the mountains comes from the high altitude, severe cold and bitter winds. Be sure to keep well wrapped up first thing in the morning and make sure you are carrying enough warm clothing for the whole day. Group trekkers will not be carrying all their baggage and it will not be accessible during the day, so be prepared. In deep canyons the sun sets very early in the afternoon and temperatures plummet.

Take particular care on the rough and rocky trails; bear in mind that the next hospital is hundreds of miles away. Remember that you may not be thinking as clearly as normal at these altitudes; don't take unnecessary chances, such as leaping carelessly across rivers or boulders. Breathing through a scarf at higher altitudes helps to retain some of the fluid that would otherwise be lost as moisture in the exhaled breath. It also gives some protection from dust and icy winds.

There is a limited danger in Ladakh from guard dogs in villages and from bears in isolated wilderness areas.

Please don't be put off by the above advice; just take care and enjoy the trek! Forewarned is forearmed.

When walking along paths that traverse sheer slopes, or on the floor of a narrow valley, be aware that wild animals on the slopes above could dislodge stones. Keep a sharp eye on your surroundings.

Crossing rivers

Mountain streams usually flow fast and strong, the water is cold and riverbeds stony and slippery. Usually it is impossible (and dangerous) for a single person to cross a mountain river if the water is higher than mid-thigh level. Water levels over knee height

are very difficult to cross. Observe the river and try to find the best place to cross. Generally, the wider the section of the river is, the shallower it is. Many rivers split into multiple channels in places – it's usually easier to cross there than over a single fast-flowing channel.

Note that on a meandering stretch of river the shallowest place to cross will be found on the straighter sections. On the bends the force of the water is intensified and so the current cuts into the bank and riverbed more fiercely. The shallowest

Smiling children from Photoksar village (Trek 5)

route from one bank to the other will be found by walking along the riverbed between the meanders, along the straight section, where the main current moves more gently from one side of the riverbed to the other. The shallowest crossing is usually not the shortest one.

Before you enter the river, take off your boots to keep them dry and warm for putting on again after the crossing. Make sure your trekking sandals are on firmly. Undo the hip-belt and chest strap of your rucksack, so that you can get out of it quickly in case of a fall. Cross steadily, step by step. Test the depth in front of you with a trekking pole before you step forward. Stand firmly, legs apart. Support yourself with your poles. If you are with a friend or in a group, cross in a row; link your arms together.

As most of the rivers in Ladakh flow from glaciers, the level of the water may change during the day. If you find a river too deep to cross, it might become possible the next day, early in the morning.

Protecting against cold at camp

Generally the higher you go the colder it gets. However, altitude is not the only factor affecting the temperature of different places in a mountain area; wind and moisture are important too. Therefore, a camp at the lowest possible place will not necessarily be the warmest.

The wind blows, although usually not strongly, quite regularly in the mountains, particularly along the valleys. In the early hours of the day, when the sun warms the mountain peaks, the wind blows up the valley from lower elevations towards the higher ground. In the evening and throughout the night, the peaks lose warmth quickly through radiation and cold, heavier air flows downwards along the valleys, towards lower elevations and local depressions. To avoid the stream of cold air passing downwards at night, don't make camp in the lowest part of the valley floor. A place on a terrace, behind a rock, or at least among shrubs is usually better.

You will feel warmer camping on dry ground than on damp ground. It is sometimes worth ignoring a nice green, grassy place in favour of a dry, dusty one. If you choose to sleep near a river or lake, or next to a patch of snow, do not make camp too close to it; you will be warmer 10m away.

The coldest time of day is usually just before dawn. At dawn places lit by the sun will warm up quickly, but those in the shade remain cold. Remember that when you make camp, especially on higher elevations and late in the season. Try to find a spot with an open aspect towards the east. The sooner the sun shines on a campsite in the morning, the sooner you will get warm. Needless to say, it is much easier to get up when you are warm!

A space blanket is a light foil covering that reflects thermal radiation. If you have one, put it under your sleeping mat. It is also a good idea to put spare clothes underneath the mat. Isolate yourself from the cold air by placing clothes, bags or anything you have between you and the tent wall. Close the sleeping bag properly; sleep in a hat and dry socks. On cold nights, try putting your rucksack underneath your legs, or put your legs into it.

In order to prevent your camera or torch batteries being drained on cold nights, either sleep with the items in your bag, or take the batteries out, slip them inside a glove and put that inside your sleeping bag overnight.

Managing waste

Always remember the rule that a camp should be left in the same condition as it was found. The same rule applies to the trails. However, the amount of litter left by tourists and their staff at camps along the trails and in the rivers of Ladakh indicates that this rule has evidently been forgotten by many.

Carrying your rubbish out of the mountains is the best thing to do. Most of the waste produced on a trek consists of plastic materials that are light and easy to carry out. Tins should be carried out by anybody trekking with pack animals. If trekking on your own, crush the tin and bury it deep in the ground, away from the camp and from any streams. Any batteries or electric and electronic waste must be carried out.

If you trek with pack animals, you should take responsibility to convince your staff to carry out all rubbish. On an organised trip, arrange the waste management before the trek.

Unfortunately there are obvious signs that some trekkers are not smart or civilised enough to care about leaving no trace of their personal waste. Don't be one of them! Never defecate along the valley floor or in a dried-up riverbed. Find a higher place, away from any water, away from the camp and the trail. Dig a small hole; cover the faeces with some soil and a few stones when you have finished. Burn the toilet paper if you use it – it doesn't take much effort. Tampons and sanitary towels are harder to burn. Make an effort to burn them properly (you will need some wood) or carry them out.

In organised campsites and in the villages, use the composting toilets. Remember that no tampons, sanitary towels or condoms should be thrown down the hole. Throw some earth down the hole when you have finished. The faeces dry out and then are used as a fertiliser for agriculture.

Ladakh is mostly a pristine environment, but it is also extremely fragile. With ever-growing numbers of visitors, imagine how the region could deteriorate in years to come if we do not respect nature. The future of Ladakh depends on all of us. Act responsibly and care for the unique environment of the region!

Read the *Mindful Traveller in Ladakh* brochure issued by one of the organisations working for the protection of Ladakhi culture; visit www.localfutures.org and choose 'Ladakh project'.

THE LAST WORD

I hope that this book will inspire, guide and nurture an interest in Ladakh and its unique culture that will stay with you forever, as it has in me. However you trek in Ladakh, it will be one of the most exceptional places you have ever visited. In a world that is rapidly changing, a visit to Ladakh will kindle a renewed optimism; the call of wild places remains, but the number of such seemingly unaffected destinations is shrinking fast. As is often lamented, it is our duty – as privileged visitors – to let Ladakh change us; it is not for us to change Ladakh.

Although I have done my very best to give you sufficient and accurate information for successful and safe trekking, I cannot guarantee there are no mistakes; and obviously in an area such as Ladakh local conditions can change. I would be very grateful if you would share your comments on this guidebook with me, and please contact me through Cicerone via info@cicerone.co.uk if you find any of the inevitable changes that will occur on the ground, so that they can be included in any reprint or new edition.

1 KHARNAK

The Zalung Karpo La, approached along this stony riverbed, is one of a few approximately 5000m-high passes on this trek, and one of many with spectacular views (Stage 5)

INTRODUCTION

Start	Kharu in the Indus Valley (3345m); alternatively Hemis or Shang Shumdo
Finish	Pang, on the Manali–Leh road (4514m); alternatively Sarchu (Manali–Leh road), Padum or Stongde (Zanskar Valley)
Distance	148km
Time	73hrs (10 days)
Altitude range	3345m (Kharu) to 5287m (Gongmaru La)

COMBINATIONS AND ALTERNATIVES

It is possible to skip Stage 1 by taking a bus from Leh to Shang Sumdo (a daily bus leaves Leh in the early afternoon). However, do not take this option unless you are well acclimatised; the camp at the end of Stage 2 (your first camp if you miss Stage 1)

lies 1000m higher than Shang Sumdo and you would overnight at an altitude of 4600m. If you are not well acclimatised your trek may well end there when you find you have to descend immediately due to altitude sickness!

If you want to visit Hemis Gompa at the beginning of the trek, stay the

Impressive rock walls in the upper Kharnak Valley (Stage 6)

109

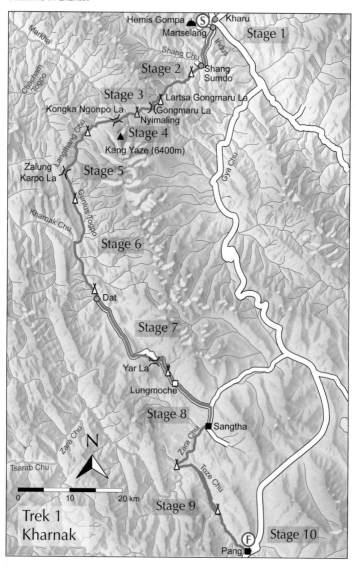

Trek 1
Kharnak

A magnificent view of the mountains surrounding the Kharnak Valley (Stage 6)

night in Hemis and start walking in the morning. There are two buses a day from Leh to Hemis; accommodation and food are available both at the monastery and in the village.

From Hemis you can either walk down to the Indus Valley and join the main route in Martselang village (see below), or go to Shang over a pass (about 4550m) to the southwest of Hemis (the author has not tested this route: ask for details from locals in Hemis). For the Martselang route, go down the valley from Hemis until you reach the Indus Valley. Do not descend any more, but find a clear path to the right that goes along the main valley high above the river. You will reach a road that goes up a side valley at a big *chorten* in Martselang village (about 1hr walk from Hemis); follow this road along the Shang Chu according to the main route description.

You can also combine the route with the Markha Valley trek (Trek 8). When in the Markha Valley, walk as far as the confluence with the Langthang Chu Valley beyond Hangkar and then go along the Langthang River. Join the Kharnak trek route and continue to the Zalung Karpo La. The Markha Valley trek can also be followed as far as Nyimaling, where the two routes cross. Note that combining the two routes makes a very long and demanding trek.

It is also possible to continue the trek as far as Padum by not turning from the Zara Valley into the Toze Valley, but by following the directions given in Trek 2. This would be a beautiful but extremely long, remote and demanding trek. It takes at least five days to walk from the confluence of the Toze and Zara rivers to the first inhabited place! As snow remains

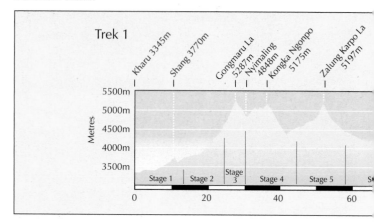

longer on the Morang La than on the other passes, this option is only accessible in late summer and autumn.

GENERAL INFORMATION

Good acclimatisation before the trek is vital. You will reach an altitude of 4600m on the second day and will not descend below 4000m until the end of the trek! The Gongmaru La, a very high pass, is crossed on the third day, and 5000m-high passes are crossed on Stages 4 and 5. There are many difficult river crossings on the way, and it is vitally important to have good trekking sandals and poles for these.

DIFFICULTY, SUPPLIES AND ACCOMMODATION

This is a long and remote trek. The possibilities of leaving the route or getting any help or support anywhere

beyond Nyimaling are limited. In 2009, on the way between Nyimaling and Pang (seven days), the author saw nobody except two people in Dat. Although there are two villages in the Kharnak Valley and two in the Zara Valley these are usually deserted, as people leave in the summer to go to high pastures with their animals. No supplies or accommodation are available on the major part of the trail. You may find accommodation in family houses at the beginning of the route in Shang Sumdo and Chokdo, and there are tent-shops with basic supplies up to Nyimaling.

WHEN TO GO?

In the second half of June (when the author walked this route) there was some snow on the Zalung Karpo La, but not enough to make the route inaccessible. June is probably the

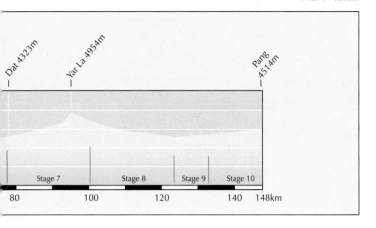

Dat 4323m

Yar La 4954m

Pang 4514m

| Stage 7 | Stage 8 | Stage 9 | Stage 10 |

80   100   120   140   148km

earliest time of the year when this trek is possible. However, in late June and July, the water in the Kharnak, Zara and Toze rivers may be so high that crossing them is very difficult or even impossible. River levels start to lower in August and do not rise again till the following spring, so late summer (August) and autumn (September and the first half of October) are good times for trekking. If planning to depart in mid-September or later, be aware that the water in the rivers, particularly that of the Toze Chu, will be extremely cold. At this time remember that the Manali–Leh road might already be closed for winter, or the traffic occasionally halted due to weather conditions when you need

to get away from the end of the trek near Pang.

ACCESS

There is a minibus from Leh to Kharu at about 8am (ask the locals for up-to-date information on buses). Get off at the bridge on the Indus; that should be the last stop. If taking the bus to Hemis, ask to be dropped approximately 1km beyond the bridge on the Indus, at the turn-off to Martselang. Pang, at the end of the trek, is on the Manali–Leh road. Food is available there, as well as accommodation in tent-dormitories (open as long as the road is open). Buses in both directions pass Pang before noon each day.

STAGE 1
Kharu to camp beyond Shang Sumdo

Start	Kharu (3345m)
Finish	Camp beyond Shang Sumdo (3742m)
Distance	14km
Time	5hrs (including optional visit to Shang Gompa)
Altitude range	3345m (Kharu) to 3770m (Shang)

This is an easier stage compared to many on this trek as there is a road to Shang Sumdo. There are no major ascents on the way. It is usually hot between Kharu and Shang Sumdo.

Alternatives
There are two other possible starting points for Trek 1:
- It is possible to take a direct bus from Leh to Shang Sumdo, but only use it if you are well acclimatised. Skipping Stage 1 makes the ascent of the Gongmaru La too quick and increases the risk of altitude sickness if you are not properly acclimatised.
- The trek can also be started in Hemis, accessed by bus (see Places to visit southeast of Leh). From the *gompa* set off along the stream, downwards, passing the village and fields. On reaching the road, about 1.4km from the *gompa*, follow it for approximately 150m to find a clear path on the right, high above the Indus River. Follow this for 1.7km to a big *chorten* in Martselang village and the road to Shang.

Water supplies
Carry sufficient water for 1½hrs when starting the trek. There are no side-streams along the Shang Chu, so refilling your water bottles from the river is the only choice. A convenient place is at the bridge over the Shang Chu. Shang Sumdo village, where you can refill your bottles again, is 1½hrs further on. Leaving Shang Sumdo, you need supplies sufficient for ½hr.

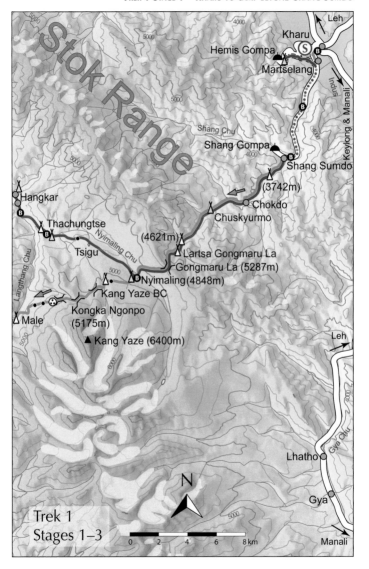

There are villages on the early stages of this route, but the surroundings become wilder and more remote further into the trek – the upper Kharnak Valley (Stage 6)

This is where the path from Hemis joins the road.

Take a side-trip to Shang to visit the monastery, then return to Shang Sumdo.

Route

Kharu is a village in the Indus Valley, on the Manali–Leh road, about 40km from Leh. The bus should drop you next to the bridge on the Indus, below the main part of the settlement. As you look from the bridge towards the SW, with the river behind you, the valley leading to Hemis is in front of you. The valley leading to Shang and on to the Gongmaru La is next on the left. From the bridge follow the looping road on the true left (west) bank of the Indus River until it forks (you will cross a big irrigation channel on the way). Take the left turn (the right leads to Hemis) and cross a small stream in a fairly wide valley. Follow the road as it passes **Martselang** village and comes to a big *chorten* (stupa) where the Shang Valley begins. ◄

Leave the Indus Valley and follow the Shang Chu SW on its true left bank (on your right facing upstream). About 1½hrs from Kharu you will reach a road bridge. Cross it and follow the road on the true right bank as far as the next bridge in **Shang Sumdo**, where the valley forks (another 1½hrs). The route to the Gongmaru La leads towards the SW, along the true left bank of the river (Kitshan). The road leading along the valley ahead goes to Shang village. ◄

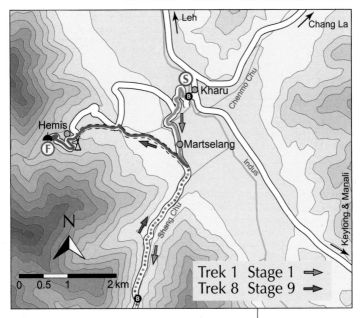

There is a campsite in **Shang Sumdo**, a tent-shop and a few houses offering homestay accommodation. It is often possible to arrange to pick up horses here if you feel you need them, as many organised groups finish their treks here and some horsemen wait for a new job.

In Shang Sumdo, start on a new road SW (towards Chokdo village), traversing the violet-coloured rocks on the true-left slope of the valley above the village. You will arrive near to the valley floor in about 30mins. There is a place for a few tents on the terraces among bushes. Camp here and use water from the river. Alternatively, continue to Chokdo village where homestay accommodation is available.

STAGE 2
Camp beyond Shang Sumdo to waterfall camp

Start	Camp beyond Shang Sumdo (3742m)
Finish	Waterfall camp (4621m)
Distance	11km
Time	8hrs
Altitude range	3742m (camp beyond Shang Sumdo) to 4621m (waterfall camp)

This is quite a long, hard stage with sheer exposed slopes in places making it both precipitous and thrilling! You climb 900m and camp high. If you are not well acclimatised or you start to feel any symptoms of altitude sickness split this stage up: perhaps sleep at Chuskyurmo on the first night and at Lartsa Gongmaru La the next. Note that Stage 3 is even harder (crossing Gongmaru La), and that you will not descend below 4300m for several more days.

Alternatives
As mentioned above, divide the stage to aid acclimatisation and for an easier ascent.

Water supplies
As you will be walking along the river all day you don't have to carry much water on this stage.

Route
Continue along the valley, on the left bank, upstream. The road, which was under construction in 2013, probably extends now as far as the first houses of Chokdo village, which are reached just over 1hr from the camp. If it is indeed there, follow it, or continue along the path on the true-left bank of the valley, upstream. It climbs gradually, traversing the slope, and is exposed in some places. Blue sheep often clamber on the rocks above, so beware of falling stones. You will return to the valley floor some 30mins from the camp; climb again and then reach the first fields and houses of **Chokdo**

village, which are reached just over 1hr from the camp. There is no campsite here, but it's possible to find lodgings further on in the village.

Himalayan blue sheep (bharal)

There is a minor valley on your left at the start of the village. The main valley turns sharply to your right, towards the W. Follow its true left bank (on the right, facing upstream). Still in the village, you will see the valleys fork ahead. Go down to the river and continue upstream, crossing the water a few times (easy). The path may not be very clear here, especially at the beginning of the season. As you get to the clear fork mentioned above (45mins to 1hr from the first house), turn into the valley on your left, heading SW. First, go along the river near the water and then take the clear path on its true left bank (on your right, facing upstream). You will pass a big campsite above you on the right and a tent-shop next to it, just on the path. This is **Chuskyurmo**.

Continue a gradual ascent along the river, first on its true left and then on its right bank. The valley narrows; pass a rocky gorge and a small stream on your right. Continue along the main valley as it turns to the left. Cross over to the true left bank. Leave the valley floor, climb steeply and go along a clear traverse, high above the river for about 45mins.

You will reach a spot where there are paths on both sides of the valley. **Do not continue on the true left bank!**

This path is dangerous! Descend to the river, cross it, climb to the other side and continue walking high above the river along its true right slope (on your left, facing upstream). The path is clear, although sometimes narrow and precipitous, and descends to the valley floor further on. The valley is narrow here and the path (not very clear) leads along the stony riverbed.

After around 600m look for a path climbing the slope on your left (the right slope of the valley). Follow it. You will descend to the valley floor again and then reach a clear fork. You need to leave the valley on your right and continue straight along the valley heading straight on, towards the SW. Just at the fork climb a steep, clear path on the right slope of the valley (on your left) – another precipitous one. The Gongmaru La can be seen occasionally along the way, and the valley turns left (SSW).

You will soon come to a waterfall. There is a small place for one tent just above it, next to the path (where the author slept); alternatively continue for another 30mins to the **Gongmaru La Base Camp (Lartsa)**, where there is space for many tents. You might meet some groups here in the peak season.

STAGE 3
Waterfall camp to Nyimaling via the Gongmaru La

Start	Waterfall camp (4621m)
Finish	Nyimaling (4848m)
Distance	6.5km
Time	5½hrs
Altitude range	4621m (waterfall camp) to 5287m (Gongmaru La)

The steep climb to the pass will certainly make you tired, but there are great views from the top. The descent is short and much easier. The setting of the camp at Nyimaling is beautiful.

Alternatives
- If you suffer any symptoms of altitude sickness before the pass, return and spend an extra night at the base camp.
- If you get symptoms after crossing the pass, do not stay in Nyimaling, but follow a clear, high path down the left bank of the main valley to Thachungtse camp (4249m) or, better still, go on to Hangkar village (3990m). If you feel fine the next day, go to the confluence of the Langthang and Nyimaling rivers and then follow along the Langthang until you pick up the trail en route to the Zalung Karpo La.

Countless peaks of the Zanskar Mountains, the Ladakh Range and the Karakoram, as seen from the Gongmaru La, looking north

Water supplies
Gongmaru La Base Camp (Lartsa) is the last place to get water before the pass and the following descent to Nyimaling. Take enough water for 5hrs.

Route
From the camp, continue by the main valley (on its right bank) for 15mins and then leave it, turning into a valley on your right, towards the SW. In another 15mins you

will reach **Gongmaru La Base Camp (Lartsa)** (4744m). It's also a good place for a camp; there is no shop.

The pass is over 500m higher, SSW of Lartsa. The pathway, however, does not lead directly up. The valley forks; take the trail on your right, heading W. There is a clear path across meadows, climbing a steep slope; look out for marmots.

About 500m from Base Camp the path leaves the valley, turns left (S) and then follows the slope, cutting it with long, clear zigzags. It's a laborious ascent; the final climb is very steep and tiring and you will be relieved to reach the pass (5287m), 4hrs from camp.

There are great views from the **Gongmaru La**. Towards the northeast is the Indus Valley, and beyond it, the Ladakh Range. The beautiful meadows of Nyimaling lie to the southwest, just below you, and Kang Yaze peak (6400m) is on the other side of the valley, 1000m higher than the pass. Right of Kang Yaze, on its ridge, a pass can be seen, clearly lower than the Gongmaru La. It's on the way to Langthang Chu and Zalung Karpo La; you will cross on Stage 4.

It takes 1hr to descend to **Nyimaling**. Go steeply down at first and then over a plateau, a little to the right, but generally heading towards the obvious valley straight down in front of you.

NYIMALING

Nyimaling is in the upper part of the Markha Valley. The valley is wide here and the abundance of plants makes it a perfect pasture. Some people from the surrounding villages move here for the summer each year with their yaks, sheep and goats. There is a tent-shop with basic supplies and a toilet. You will have to pay a camping fee. As most of the groups doing the Markha Valley trek stop here, the place may be crowded and the water polluted. Therefore it's better to take water from the small stream flowing from the direction of Kang Yaze (if it's not dry) than from the main river.

STAGE 4
Nyimaling to Langthang Valley via
the Kongka Ngonpo

Start	Nyimaling (4848m)
Finish	Langthang Valley (4552m)
Distance	13.5km
Time	8½hrs
Altitude range	4379m (path junction in Langthang Valley) to 5175m (Kongka Ngonpo)

This is a long and hard day of ups and downs, mainly at around 5000m in wild and remote country. You will probably not meet many people during the next few days.

Alternatives

If you don't feel up to crossing a few passes in one day, and prefer an easier (but longer) option – about 17km to the point where the main route is rejoined, possible in one long day – walk down by the main route along Nyimaling Chu (high above the valley floor) to its confluence with Langthang Chu, beyond Thachungtse camp

The beautiful valley of the Langthang Chu as seen on the way from the Kongka Ngonpo at the end of Stage 4

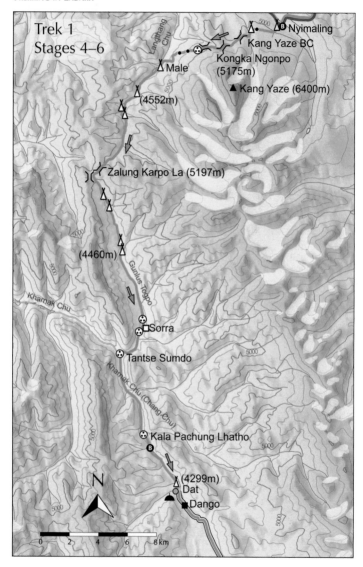

Trek 1
Stages 4–6

Langthang Chu

△ Nyimaling
△● Kang Yaze BC
Kongka Ngonpo
(5175m)

△ Male

▲ Kang Yaze (6400m)

(4552m)

Zalung Karpo La (5197m)

(4460m)

Kharnak Chu

Gunlus Togpo

Sorra

Tantse Sumdo

Kharnak Chu (Chang Chu)

Kala Pachung Lhatho

(4299m)
Dat
Dango

N

0 2 4 6 8 km

and before Hangkar village (Langthang is the first big river on the left). Then, turn left up the Langthang Chu until you meet the route that crosses the passes at the place described below.

Water supplies
Take water for the first 2hrs from the camp and then, from Kang Yaze Base Camp, take supplies sufficient for the rest of the day.

Route
From **Nyimaling** climb the steep left slope of the valley. Head S, towards Kang Yaze (which you will leave on your left later in the day). There is no clear path. The easiest way leads along a small steep valley (it might be dry in summer). As you pass the steepest part of the slope, head W till you get to the ridge (1½hrs from the camp) – you don't have to reach its highest point, as you will be descending soon anyway. Although it is usually windy here, the ridge is a good place for a rest. ▸

Towards the SW, on the other side of the valley, you can see the next pass to be crossed. There is no other option than to descend to the river and then climb again to the pass. There is a good place for a camp, on the trail, down in the valley (the **Base Camp** – at 5042m – for climbing Kang Yaze peak).

Crossing the stream at the base camp is easy. Take water for the next 5–6hrs, as you will probably not find any further on. Climb to the pass – it can be clearly seen to the SW. There is no clear path, so try to find your own, zigzagging up the slope to reduce the gradient. Look out for marmots.

From the top of the pass (5104m) the next one can be seen to the SW, almost 2km away and about 70m higher. To get there, walk down and left towards a clear path traversing the stony slope on your left. Follow this path; it vanishes in stones and tufts next to a small stream that probably exists only in the spring period. Climb steeply to the pass – the **Kongka Ngonpo** (5175m), 4hrs from Nyimaling.

There are marvellous views of the Stok Range, with its famous culmination Stok Kangri (6150m), the Markha Valley and Kang Yaze peaks.

From the pass, go steeply down on quite a good path left of the valley, which cuts a number of gullies on the steep slope. The path gets narrow and the slope sheer further on; keep going, but watch out for falling stones from above. The trail will get much easier as you come to rough grass, where you may also see marmots and blue sheep. Descend a little then go W to another pass (1hr from the Kongka Ngonpo).

From the pass continue W to a very simple shepherds' shelter (a small wall of stones) on a ridge. Descend for a while. The path becomes unclear, but the terrain is easy. Ascend slightly to a ridge below another shelter (about 130m lower and 20mins from the previous ridge, 5½hrs from Nyimaling).

Leave the valley leading from the Kongka Ngonpo and follow the main valley of the Langthang Chu from here on, to the SW. The path descends gradually to the river, cutting small valleys on the slope and climbing the ridges that separate them. You will reach the valley floor (4379m) 7½hrs after leaving Nyimaling. ◄ There is a summer shepherds' settlement and a perfect site for a camp a bit further on at **Male** (4424m). From Male

You will join the path from the Markha Valley (from Hangkar) here.

Wintry scenery on an early spring morning in the Langthang Valley

continue on the true right bank of the river (on your left). The path is clear here.

It is possible to camp an hour further on, by a major eastern tributary (where the author slept). There are also good sites between these places, and a few further on towards the pass. You can sleep in any of them, but bear in mind the following:

- The closer to the pass you sleep, the easier the ascent on the next day.
- Because the camp will be at a high elevation it will probably be cold – so the more open the aspect towards the east, the earlier the sun will warm up your tent.
- Don't camp too close to a steep slope – there are many blue sheep here that might dislodge stones.

STAGE 5
Langthang Valley to Gunlus Valley

Start	Langthang Valley (4552m)
Finish	Gunlus Valley (4460m)
Distance	14km
Time	9hrs
Altitude range	4460m (Gunlus Valley) to 5197m (Zalung Karpo La)

Both the ascent to the pass and the descent are long and laborious. Awesome views from the top!

Alternatives
- It is possible to join the path to Zangla in Zanskar via the Charchar La (not described in this book).
- Another option is to walk back to the Markha Valley via the Rabrang La.

For both options, from Zalung Karpo La go to the right (northwest) instead of descending ahead (south).

The Zanskar Mountains as seen from the way to the Zalung Karpo La

Water supplies
Fill up with enough water for the trek to the pass and for part of the descent before the stream en route dries up. There is water about 1hr beyond the pass.

Route
Continue up the Langthang Valley, which turns right (SW) just beyond the camp. The path crosses to the true left bank (on your right, facing upstream); follow it. Half an hour from the camp there is a valley on your right and a good place for a camp. The main valley turns slightly left, towards the SSW, here. Further on there are big valleys on both sides. Continue along the main, central one, crossing the stream to the true right bank. There is a perfect place for a camp that can accommodate many tents (4638m).

Climb a 10m-high rock step. The valley narrows and turns towards the S here. Follow the rocky valley floor, crossing the stream a few times. You will pass a beautiful ravine on your right. 10mins further, 30mins beyond the rock step, you will reach a fork in the valley. There is a small grassy spot here, a good place to camp for one or two tents (4747m).

Follow the valley on your right, SW. The water supplies soon dry up, so fill up your water bottles whenever you can. There is another fork 30mins further on (4869m). Take the valley on your right towards the WSW. It is further to the pass from here than it appears to be. After another 15mins of walking pass a valley on the right and turn left (SW). The spot on top of the steep, dry valley in front of you is not Zalung Karpo La, alas: it is still 2hrs of walking to the pass.

Ascend steeply. Where the slope lessens, turn slightly left and then slightly right, following the main valley until you reach the **Zalung Karpo La** (5197m, 5hrs 30mins from the camp). If there is snow on the path, climb the slope on your right and follow the ridge to the pass.

The **Zalung Karpo La** is a very obvious pass, with prayer flags and a *lhato* (cairn) on the top. The view is one of the best in Ladakh, including the peaks of Kang Yaze towards the northeast, the Gyamshu massif to the southeast and the rugged Zanskar

The Zalung Karpo La, with prayer flags and great views of the Gunlus Valley and snowy peaks of the Gyamshu massif

Range to the south. There is a beautiful, wild valley towards the south, ahead of you. This is the Gunlus (Sorra) Valley, which you will follow beyond the curve that can be seen far below.

Descend by a clear path to reach another pass, just below the Zalung Karpo. ◄ If you're heading to Kharnak, do not cross the second pass, but continue down by a clear path towards the southeast.

If you cross it you could go to Zangla (in the Zanskar Valley) via the Charchar La or back to the Markha Valley via the Rabrang La.

From the pass keep ahead to soon reach the valley floor and continue along the left bank of the river. There are places to make camp. An hour from the Zalung Karpo La you will pass a simple shepherds' shelter, which is a good place for a camp (4784m). The valley narrows beyond here and the path traverses its left slope high above the river. **Beware: the slope is sheer and the path precipitous in some places.**

At the end of the traverse there is a nice place to camp (4697m). It is still above the river, on a high terrace, so if you stay there, you will need to descend and reascend to get water. The next place for a camp is 50mins further on.

From the high terrace, the path descends to the valley floor. Follow it and then continue along the river; a tiring walk on a stony path. The first place for a camp (4467m) is right in the middle of the valley, where it can get cold and windy at night. The author slept 500m further on by a big valley on the left, in a beautiful grassy place. It takes more than 2hrs to cover the distance from the Zalung Karpo La to this site.

STAGE 6
Gunlus Valley to near Dat village, Kharnak Valley

Start	Gunlus Valley (4460m)
Finish	Near Dat village, Kharnak Valley (4299m)
Distance	19.5km
Time	9hrs
Altitude range	approximately 4200m (confluence of upper Kharnak and Gunlus rivers) to 4460m (Gunlus Valley)

Although this is a long walk in both time and distance, it is a relatively easy stage. There are no passes or any major ascents so enjoy the walk along beautiful, wild valleys.

Alternatives

Instead of turning left up the Kharnak Valley from the confluence of the Gunlus Togpo and the upper Kharnak Chu (Chang Chu), continue down the river as far as Tilad Sumdo. This is a very demanding route, requiring about

Independent camp in the Kharnak Valley, near Dat village

200 river crossings (cutting across most of the meanders). It takes more than a day to get from the confluence to Tilad. It is not possible to take this route in late June and July, when the water is high. From Tilad Sumdo, turn left towards the Charchar La to Zangla in the Zanskar Valley. It is a beautiful, wild trail (the author did this route in 2004 but it is not covered in this guidebook).

Water supplies
You will be walking along the river, so you don't need to carry water.

Route
Walking down the valley becomes easier below the camp as the path leaves the stony riverbed and leads along grassy terraces, crossing the stream periodically. There are plenty of good, scenic places to camp.

Following the true right bank, 1½hrs after leaving the camp, you will reach some house ruins and old fields (4227m). Soon ford the river to the left bank, heading to the abandoned villages of **Sorra** and Khar, situated at the confluence of three big valleys. At the village, the main river flows through a deep ravine that is only about 1m wide. There is an interesting bridge over the ravine; you don't need to cross it.

The valley widens and soon turns sharp right. Continue on the left bank, passing a sheer, high slope. The valley narrows and forms a ravine again. Although there are paths on both sides of the stream, the one on the right is easier. There are willow bushes on the valley floor that you will walk through for some time.

About 30mins from Sorra you will come to a big valley on your left, flowing from the S: the upper Kharnak Chu, also called Chang Chu. You need to follow this valley upstream. Find a clear path ascending a ridge on your left, which divides the two valleys. Climb it, pass a shepherds' shelter (**Tantse Sumdo**), then descend to the valley floor and ford the river to its true left bank (on your right, facing upstream). It's not a difficult crossing, but you will need to take off your boots.

Continue through the willow bushes upstream to arrive at the confluence of three rivers, some 40mins after leaving Tantse Sumdo. There are massive rock towers in the middle of the valley and a cave high above on your left. Walk towards the SE, between the towers, up the central valley that forms a canyon here. It looks like a paradise for rock climbers!

Just 20mins further the valley floor becomes wide, grassy and almost flat. The willows disappear and the stream meanders tranquilly. The path leads on the true left bank – perfect places for a camp. One hour from the rock towers, there are tributaries on both sides. Here is the shepherds' settlement of **Kala Puchung Lhatho** (not permanently inhabited; 4213m). The valley turns SSE here. You will come to a solid bridge in another 20mins, but don't cross it. ▶ After a further 20mins' walk, the valley opens to a view of impressive 5600m peaks.

A bit further on, climb to a high terrace – an alluvial fan formed by the river flowing from a big valley on your right. Follow a clear path past a few massive *mani* walls. It is about 15mins to **Dat** from here. Unless you want to sleep in the village (4323m), cross the first terrace to the tributary stream and go to the left towards the Chang River. Find a place to camp just below the terraces.

Nearby is a cremation ground, and there are a number of mani walls and prayer flags.

Approaching Dat

133

STAGE 7
Camp near Dat, Karnak Valley, to camp near Lungmoche

Start	Near Dat village, Kharnak Valley (4299m)
Finish	Camp near Lungmoche (4743m)
Distance	23km
Time	9½hrs
Altitude range	4299m (Kharnak Valley) to 4954m (Yar La)

This is a long walk through wild, remote and dry country. You follow an unpaved road that starts in Dat, but will probably not see any vehicles or people. There is a steep final climb to the pass, but generally the trail is easy to follow.

Alternatives
There are no alternatives for this stage.

Rupshu – Eastern Ladakh – as seen from the Yar La

Water supplies
This stage enters a very dry region; even the big rivers may occasionally dry up. There is no water en route

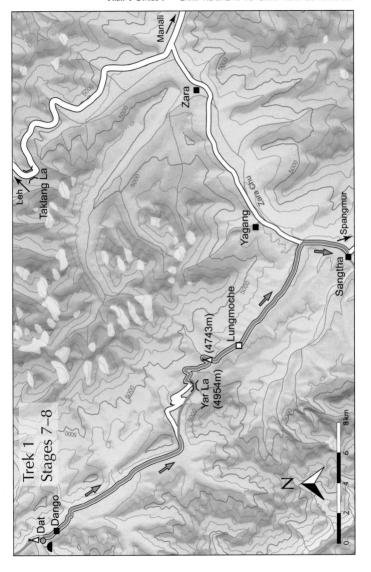

Trek 1
Stages 7–8

between Dat and the foot of the Yar La, or in most of the places along the valley on the other side of the pass. Whenever you do find water, take some reserves to cover the next few hours!

Route

Return to the path that you left the previous evening. Follow it until you reach **Dat** village (4323m) in the next side valley on your right. There are no fields in the village. Another settlement, **Dango**, is just 15mins' walk further along the main valley, left of and just below the road. There are no fields here either; both villages depend solely on breeding animals, and both might be empty in summer as people leave with their stock for the high pastures. There is a small monastery in Dat. ◄

Unless you want to visit Dango (which is by the river, off the main route), take enough water from Dat to cover the next 5hrs.

From Dat, follow the dirt road along the main valley towards the SE. You walk on a terrace, 10m above the valley floor for the first hour and will then arrive at the wide dried-up riverbed of a valley coming from your right. Cross it; when you get to the other bank, cross the main valley's dried-up riverbed too. Continue up the main, wide valley on its right bank. It is hot but windy here; kiangs (Tibetan wild ass) are often seen in this area.

There is a mountain range at the end of the valley. The way to the Yar La turns into the last big valley on your left. It is more than 9km from the main valley crossing to that turn and it takes 3hrs to cover the distance. About 1km beyond the turn, leave the road and head towards a clear path ascending to the pass along a valley's axis on your right (ESE).

You will arrive at a small stream 40mins later. The pass is SE of here, 300m above; the path leads directly to it. You should be able to see the road on your left clearly as it climbs gradually, zigzagging uphill. Take water for a few hours. If the riverbed is dried up, there should be another stream just before the final ascent to the pass. You will ascend along a stony wall that marks a border to a *stupa* at the top. This is quite a tough climb.

The **Yar La** is 4954m high (8hrs from Dat). The road pass to the left is a little lower. From the pass, walk down to the road which traverses the left slope of the valley. Follow it, occasionally cutting its curves. The road enters big tributary valleys on the left on its way down the main valley. There is a river and a good place to camp in the second one, within 1½hrs of the Yar La. Camp here, although the place is shaded from the morning sun. Don't go any further, as the main valley becomes dry beyond here and there is no water in the abandoned settlement of **Lungmoche**.

The Yar La is crossed en route to Lungmoche

BEING PREPARED – A WATER CRISIS!

I was on this route in mid-June. As I found it cold a few times at night, I started to be careful about the places where I camped. The earlier your tent is lit by the sun, the faster you get warm in the morning. When I arrived at camp by the tributary stream on my way from the Yar La, I expected it would be cold there in the morning. My guidebook suggested a camp in Lungmoche village, so I went on.

When I got there, it turned out that the settlement had been abandoned and that there was no water there. The riverbed in the main valley was dried up too! Although I had already been walking for 10hrs that day, I decided to go further, towards the Zara River. According to the map, that river would be quite large; and according to the map, Yagang village was on the way and would be an important settlement. As it was on the road, I imagined shops and small restaurants there.

It became dark, but I kept on walking without any light. I didn't want to lose time by stopping and taking the torch out of my bag, as I was hoping to arrive in Yagang at any moment.

Soon I felt quite thirsty. In one place I felt soft ground under my feet. I thought it was wet and expected to find water, but when I knelt, it turned out to be just a dry, soft dust. I got my torch out, looked at the map and looked around. I was on the right trail, on the dirt road. The riverbed was where it should be, although dried up. There were no signs of the village.

Half an hour later I stopped to pitch my tent. No village, no people, no water. I had no more than a glass of water in my bottle. I drank half of it and went to bed after 12hrs of walking, without any food.

In the morning it turned out that I was still on the way from the Yar La to the Zara Chu in the dried-up valley. There was still no sign of Yagang village. There was no movement on the road. Having no water, I could not prepare food. I just drank the remaining half glass, packed my stuff and continued down the valley. Needless to say, I felt very thirsty.

I reached the Zara Chu Valley after 2hrs. Its riverbed was dried up too! And there was no village! I felt thirsty and increasingly anxious. I looked at the map and decided to walk up the valley; there was no other option. Yagang should be up there and the valley led to the main Manali–Leh road, where I was hoping to find water. There was a water pump on the way, and the ground in the riverbed was wet. I pumped a dozen times, but the water still did not come.

I started to walk along the riverbed, hoping to find water soon. The village could be seen about 2km ahead. It seemed to be empty and the small valley there looked dry. As I approached it, I felt more and more nervous. I realised that I could not manage to walk as far as the main road! I felt really bad and was starting to panic, as there was no sign of water or any people in Yagang.

Surprisingly, while on a small hill, I saw a tiny stream in the valley below Yagang! I ran to it, knelt down, still with the bag on my back and drank, drank, drank! The danger was over.

STAGE 8
Camp near Lungmoche to Zara Valley camp

Start	Camp near Lungmoche (4743m)
Finish	Camp before confluence of Zara and Toze rivers, Zara Valley (4310m)
Distance	23km
Time	6½hrs
Altitude range	4310m (Zara Valley) to 4743m (camp near Lungmoche)

A relaxing day walking down the valley. Desert dominates the landscape, although there are green meadows along the river further down the valley.

Alternatives

- On reaching the Zara Valley, instead of going downstream towards the Morang La and Pang turn left (northeast) and follow the dirt road to the main Manali–Leh road, just below its ascent to the Taklang La. Unless it is very early or very late season, you will almost certainly find transport to Leh or Manali.
- The Manali–Leh road can also be found by following the road from Sangtha to Spangmur and continuing from there over the Spangmur La. It makes sense if you want to avoid fording the Toze River dozens of times.

Note that these alternatives have not been checked by the author.

Water supplies

There is no water in the main valley that comes from the Yar La below the camp, and at times no water in the Zara Chu either. During research, the latter was dry one day, but flowing the next day. Perhaps the author was unlucky in searching for water at the wrong time; but whatever the reason, take as much water as you can whenever you find it. In the Zara Valley, there is a water pump in Sangtha settlement about 1hr from the confluence.

Route

From the camp, continue walking by the dirt road, on the left side of the valley. The riverbed is usually dry. You will pass the abandoned settlement of **Lungmoche** (4620m) and eventually reach the main Zara Valley (2½–3hrs).

The Zara Chu flows from your left (NNE) towards the right (S). Turn right down this valley, on its left bank, on a dirt road. It's possible to find a place to camp around here. The settlement of **Sangtha** (4416m) is reached 1hr after turning into the Zara Valley. ◄ This is another village (often empty in the summer), that depends solely on the breeding of yaks, sheep and goats. There are no fields but take a look at the very simple houses and impressive *mani* walls.

In Sangtha, the road turns left, towards the SE, into a quite narrow valley. ◄ Leave the road and ford the Zara River. One might expect a boring day along the wide, dry valley, but surprisingly the Zara Valley narrows beyond Sangtha and the landscape changes. Continue down the valley on the right bank. You will have to cross the Zara Chu again, 5mins later, back to the left side. The path is not very clear but leads along the river channel for some time, then rises above the floor.

While on quite a high terrace, 45mins from Sangtha, you pass a valley on your right and a few small *mani*

See map: Trek 1 Stages 8–10

The road goes to Spangmur village on the way to the Spangmur La.

Chortens and mani walls near Sangtha

walls. Soon descend to the valley floor that forms an 'S' shape here, cutting through resistant rocks. There is a good place to camp at 4372m (1hr from Sangtha, 5hrs from the previous stage's camp).

Follow the river on its left bank. In 30mins arrive at a grassy place with a dry valley on your left – a perfect spot to make camp (4345m). There is a summer shepherds' settlement at the foot of a sheer rock, on the opposite side of the river. Have a look at the picturesque *chortens* there.

Continue on the left bank, with plenty of good places to camp as far as the confluence with the **Toze Chu**. In 30mins you will reach a place where the river narrows and bends sharp right to round a spur of flat rock. It takes 40mins to cover the remaining distance to the Toze Valley. Camp anywhere on the way.

STAGE 9
Zara Valley camp to Toze Valley camp

Start	Camp before confluence of Zara and Toze rivers, Zara Valley (4310m)
Finish	Toze Valley camp (4360m)
Distance	10km
Time	5hrs
Altitude range	4268m (confluence of Toze and Zara rivers) to 4360m (Toze Valley)
Note	If you decide to camp on the valley floor, find a place a few metres above the water.

The time required to cover Stages 9 and 10 depends on the number and difficulty of river crossings, which may change according to the water level. In late season it is possible to cover both stages in one long day.

The Toze Chu (as well as the Zara Chu below the confluence with the Toze) is a braided river, flowing through a number of channels. Unstable bars and small islands separate the channels (a channel full of water one day may be abandoned on another, and a dry island might be flooded after a few hours); the water level changes too. The river is different season-by-season, day-by-day, and even hour-by-hour.

Generally, the more channels there are the easier it is to cross. Sometimes a channel is impossible to cross one day, but can be forded the next morning. Use your poles and take care. Unless you have a rope or cross in a group, don't ford if the water is above thigh-level. Read the 'Crossing rivers' section in the Introduction.

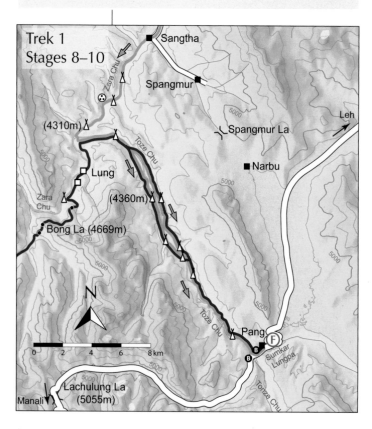

Yaks in the Toze Valley, bred for their power and used for ploughing and transportation; the females (dimo/drimo) and yak/cow crosses (dzomo) are famed for their nutritious milk

Alternatives

You can pass the confluence with the Toze and continue down the Zara Chu for about 2hrs, then you could leave the valley and cross two passes to the Tsarab Chu Valley. While there you could either continue to Zanskar, or join the Manali–Leh road near Sarchu. For both options see Trek 2. These routes, however, may be inaccessible in June, when there can be snow on the Morang La.

Water supplies

There are no side-streams, so water from the Zara and Toze rivers is the only choice. These are big rivers. The Toze Chu carries glacial flour (rock flour) or very small grains of sand, and is grey in summer. Additionally, as it passes Pang it picks up a lot of rubbish. It is not seriously contaminated, but if you have a filter or water purification tablets, use them. The glacial flour may irritate your stomach. If you don't have a filter, leave water in a bottle overnight to let it settle and clear.

Route

The **Toze Chu** is a large, left-bank tributary of the Zara Chu. Ford the Toze Chu and go upstream along its true left bank (ENE). It should be unnecessary to cross the river for about 1hr, till you get to a clear right turn of the valley. Cross to the true right bank (on your left, facing upstream) just before this.

The valley narrows and small terraces appear. Try to follow the right bank as far as possible. There are small places to camp here and there. In 40mins you will come to a place where the valley widens and the river's channels meander from one side to the other.

Pass quite a large valley on your right in another 40mins, and the next one 20mins later. It forms quite a big alluvial fan in the main valley, on its true left bank. Although it is not a perfect place for a camp, the author slept there. Better places on both sides of the river are found about 1hr further on.

STAGE 10
Toze Valley camp to Pang

Start	Toze Valley camp (4360m)
Finish	Pang (4514m)
Distance	15km
Time	7hrs
Altitude range	4360m (Toze Valley) to 4514m (Pang)

Continue along the river upstream, on either of its banks, until you reach the Manali–Leh road. Try to avoid unnecessary river crossings.

Alternatives
There are no alternatives for this stage.

Water supplies
The same conditions as for Stage 9 apply.

Route
If you are on the true right bank of the river, you should be able to continue along it for a few hours. There is an indistinct pathway following green terraces by the river or on high terraces, around 10m above the valley floor. While on the high terrace, **watch out for its sheer ending** – find a gradual descent instead!

The Toze Chu, a braided river

If you are on the river's left bank, continue above the valley floor for about 40mins, then descend to the river-bed and cross a tributary stream in a side valley on your right (4393m). You come to a grassy terrace and a simple shepherds' shelter in 30mins. It is a good, although quite littered, place for a camp. You'll reach another meadow on the left bank in a further 30mins. The valley narrows sharply here for a short while; cross the river and continue on its true right bank.

After 1hr of walking the valley narrows substantially, and the trail to Pang becomes more difficult. The high terraces often end in sheer drops, so be careful to search for easier descents. The river flow is deeper here, making crossing difficult (but unavoidable). Continue along the river on either side until you reach the road in Pang. It will be a shock to encounter the noisy road and polluting trucks after being in the wild.

Two rivers meet here: the Sumkar Lungpa flowing from your left, and the Tonze on your right. At the road there is a police checkpoint. The road bridge to Keylong and Manali is on your right. **Pang**, which consists of a few simple restaurants, tent-dormitories and a military camp, is left of the checkpoint, by the road, in the direction of Leh.

The majority of buses and minibuses going in both directions stop in Pang for a meal break. The public bus to Keylong (an overnight stopping place on the way to Manali) should arrive about 10am; the bus to Leh arrives at about 2pm. Ask the locals for details.

TREK OPTIONS FROM PANG

If you plan another trek, starting south of Pang, it is better to go to Keylong than to Leh. It's a good place for a short rest, where you can also buy supplies for further trips. If you stay overnight in Pang, try to choose a quiet tent-hotel, and be considerate of your fellow guests. It's also possible to camp by the river just below Pang.

The trekking route towards Tso Moriri Lake starts in Pang (not described in this book), but the lack of good shops in Pang limits the possibility of buying supplies for another trek here. Additionally, trekking on this route requires a special permit, which cannot be arranged in Pang.

2 TSARAB CHU

The confluence of the Tsarab and Zara rivers (Stage 6); big rivers, many passes and remoteness characterise this trek

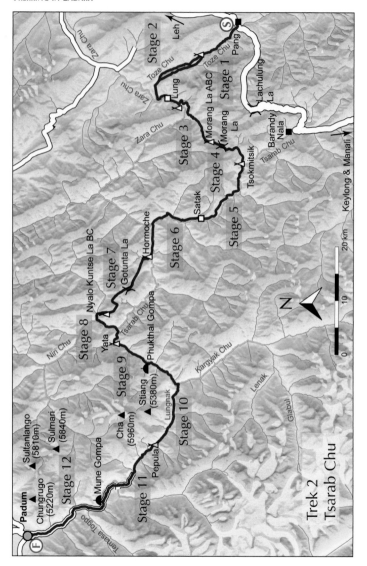

Trek 2
Tsarab Chu

INTRODUCTION

Start	Pang on the Manali–Leh road (4514m); alternatively Zara (on the Manali–Leh road, just south of Taklang La), Kharu, Hemis, Shang, Sarchu, Spituk or Chiling
Finish	Padum, Zanskar (3600m); alternatively Sarchu (on the Manali–Leh road), Padum or Stongde (Zanskar Valley)
Distance	174km
Time	75½hrs (12 days)
Altitude range	3600m (Padum) to 5355m (Morang La)

COMBINATIONS AND ALTERNATIVES

Instead of starting in Pang, it is possible to start along the Kharnak trek (Trek 1) and then pick up the Tsarab Chu trek; just continue along the Zara Chu instead of turning into the Toze Valley. However, this would make a very long and remote route.

The trek can be made even longer by starting in Spituk or Chiling and walking along the Markha River (see the Markha Valley trek) to join the Kharnak trek at Nyimaling, and then continuing on the Tsarab Chu trek.

The trek can also be started near Zara, south of Taklang La on the Manali–Leh road (see the map for Trek 1 Stages 7–8). From there, take a dirt road along the Zara Chu as far as Sangtha, then continue as described in Trek 1 to the confluence of the

The Zanskar Mountains as seen from the Bong La (Stage 3)

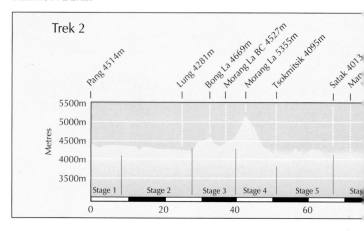

Trek 2

Pang 4514m

Lung 4281m
Bong La 4669m
Morang La BC 4527m
Morang La 5355m
Tsokmitsik 4095m

Satak 4013
Man

Metres		
5500m		
5000m		
4500m		
4000m		
3500m		

Stage 1 Stage 2 Stage 3 Stage 4 Stage 5 Stag

0   20   40   60

Zara and Toze rivers, where you meet Trek 2.

Another possibility is to start at Narbu, north of Pang, and join Trek 1 in Sangtha near the Spangmur La (see the map for Trek 1 Stages 8–10).

Note that these last two options have not been checked by the author.

You can also start on the Manali–Leh road, about 25km north of Sarchu, in Barandy Nala (Gian on some maps), where the main road leaves the Tsarab Chu Valley and climbs towards the Lachulung La (so avoiding many river crossings and the steep climb to the Morang La). Go to the lowest bend of the road and follow a clear footpath traversing the right slope of the Tsarab Valley. Tsokmitsik, where you meet the route from Morang La, is by the second major tributary valley on your right, about 11km from Barandy

Nala, and it takes 3–4hrs to get there. This last route (in reverse) can also be used if you wish to shorten the trek considerably and finish in Gian.

An interesting finish to this trek is by taking the trail via the Stongde La to Stongde in the Zanskar Valley. While in the Niri Valley, near Thantak, it is possible to head upstream, following the Round Sultanlango trek (Trek 4).

You could also leave Zanskar, avoiding Padum. While in Purni beyond Phukthal, turn left to go up the Kargyak Valley. You need to cross Shinkul La and will eventually reach Darcha (the route is described in this guidebook in reverse: see Trek 3).

GENERAL INFORMATION

Regardless of all its difficulties (see below) this is one of the best routes – if not *the* best – that the author did in Ladakh. It is wild and beautiful,

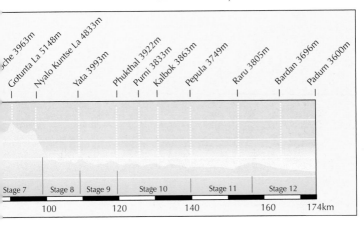

che 3963m Gotunta La 5148m Nyalo Kuntse La 4833m Yata 3993m Phukthal 3922m Purni 3833m Kalbok 3863m Pepula 3749m Raru 3805m Bardan 3696m Padum 3600m

| Stage 7 | Stage 8 | Stage 9 | Stage 10 | Stage 11 | Stage 12 |

100   120   140   160   174km

especially in September, when the Tsarab Chu turns an incredible blue.

DIFFICULTY, SUPPLIES AND ACCOMMODATION

This is a long, remote and difficult trek with many river crossings and passes. The path is often narrow and precipitous. Days are long at high elevations, rarely dropping below 4000m for the first eight days. You must be well acclimatised and experienced to undertake this trek; there are no inhabited settlements, supplies or accommodation as far

The wild valley between the Bong La and the Morang La Base Camp (Stage 3)

Long traverse high above the Tsarab (Stage 5)

as Phukthal Gompa (Stage 9). After Phukthal you can rely on homestays in the villages.

WHEN TO GO?

This is a trek for late summer and autumn. In June, snow on the Morang La makes the pass very difficult or even impenetrable; in July, the rivers are high, making crossings very hard or impossible. The author did the trek in September, the recommended time. In October, it would probably be very cold, making the river crossings even more arduous.

ACCESS

Buses from Leh to Keylong (or Manali) arrive at Pang in the morning, usually not later than 10am. Buses from Keylong (an overnight stop en route from Manali) reach Pang about 2pm (leaving Keylong at 5am.) There is generally a daily service between mid-June and mid-September. The minibus service starts earlier in the season and operates longer. It is not unusual for the road to be closed occasionally in September for a few days, and it generally closes for winter in mid-October.

STAGE 1
Pang to Toze Valley camp

Start	Pang (4514m)
Finish	Toze Valley camp (4431m)
Distance	9km
Time	3hrs
Altitude range	4431m (Toze Valley) to 4514m (Pang)
Note	If you are camping on the valley floor, try to find a place a few metres above the water level.

The Toze Chu (and the Zara Chu on Stage 2) is a braided river. Small unstable islands separate the channels; water levels vary constantly and islands can be flooded within hours. It's easier to cross where there are more channels. Take care and use poles on the many crossings encountered during this stage. Unless you are in a group and have a rope, don't ford if the water is higher than your thighs. Read the 'Crossing rivers' section in the Introduction.

Alternatives
From Pang there is no other option for this trek than going down the Toze Chu. However, there are other possible starting points (see Combinations and alternatives).

Water supplies
There are no side-streams, so water from the Toze Chu is the only choice. The river carries glacial flour and, as it passes habitation at Pang, could become contaminated. Filter or purify the water here. The glacial water might irritate your stomach, so if you don't have a filter leave it to settle overnight to clear. For the first day, take water from Pang (there is a water pump near the restaurants).

Route
If you travel by bus to **Pang**, make sure it stops there for a meal break. From Leh, the road follows a big, wide, dry, almost flat valley and then descends to Pang. From Keylong, the road crosses the Lachulung La, follows a

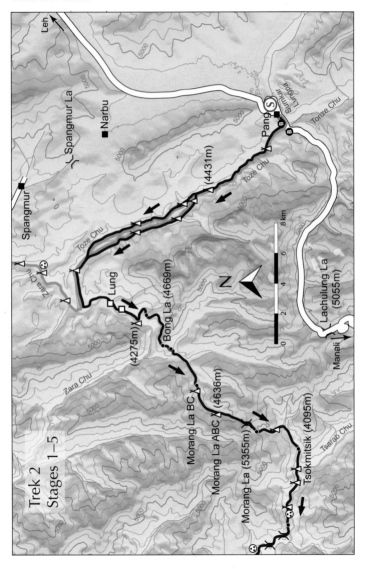

Trek 2
Stages 1–5

The braided river of Toze Chu flows in a number of channels separated by stony islands; the river changes constantly

stream, then crosses the bridge on Tonze river and arrives at the police checkpoint in Pang. The restaurants are 1km further. The Toze Chu, the river you need to follow, is to the left of you, flowing towards the NW. You can alight at the police checkpoint, but it's more convenient to get off near the restaurants, where you can have lunch and fill your water bottles from the pump. ▶

From the restaurants, walk down along the road towards Keylong (SW). Cross the bridge over the Sumkar Lungpa. Soon, before reaching the next bridge, you will arrive at a police checkpoint. You will need to register here. Just right of the road, towards the NW, the Sumkar Lungpa and Tonze rivers meet, forming the Toze Chu. Leave the road, cross the left tributary to its left bank and walk downriver (NW). There is no clear path; the river meanders from one valley slope to the other and you will probably need to ford it at each turn.

A green terrace, reached 40mins after leaving the checkpoint, is a good place to camp. However, unless it is very late, continue downriver. After 1½hrs from Pang, you will come to a sharp right turn, with a big terrace on the right bank (4445m) and a rocky wall on the left. It

Note The exact location of the police checkpoint may change.

155

should be possible to walk on the right bank, along terraces above the valley floor, for some distance. The valley widens further on. Three hours from Pang, you come to a grassy terrace by the river, on the right. Camp here (where the author slept) or continue 10mins further to a high, quite flat, dry terrace above the path (the grassy spot is nicer, but the dusty one above is warmer). There are other good places to camp a little further on.

STAGE 2
Toze Valley camp to camp beyond Lung

Start	Toze Valley camp (4431m)
Finish	Camp beyond Lung (4275m)
Distance	19km
Time	7½hrs
Altitude range	Lung (4275m) to 4431m (Toze Valley)

Stage 2 continues down the Toze Chu to its confluence with the Zara Chu. The time required and the number of river crossings depends largely on the river level – you may not be able to follow the description below exactly. In this case, just walk down the river. From the confluence of the Toze and Zara rivers, walk downstream along the Zara Chu.

Alternatives
There are no alternatives for this stage.

Water supplies
See Stage 1 for information on the Toze Valley. There is a small stream in Lung in the Zara Valley, and there should be a small stream at the camp at the end of this stage.

Route
From the grassy camp noted at the end of Stage 1 climb a narrow pathway to a dry terrace above the valley floor

and then follow the path along the terrace. You will pass a good camp just left of the path 30mins further on and will then descend to a grassy terrace – another good place to camp. Walk along this terrace for 20mins; climb to another dry terrace about 15m above the valley floor to find another camp area.

The tiny traverse 300m above the valley floor followed on Stage 3, as seen from Stage 2

Drop to the valley floor 10mins further along to find another green terrace. Continue along the valley floor for 20–30mins to a fairly clear path which traverses the right slope. Continue much the same for another 20mins. About 40mins further, beyond a larger valley on the right, the main valley narrows gradually and turns left. You will probably need to cross to the left bank of the river and then back again before you reach the narrowest section of the valley and its sharp left turn. There is a place to camp on a green terrace just before the curve.

The large valley of the Zara Chu comes into view ahead, almost 3km away; it takes about 45mins to get to the confluence. Cross the Toze Chu and walk along the left bank to where the rivers join, at a right angle (14km and 5½hrs from the previous camp, and another 5km (about 2hrs) to the end of this stage).

Once in the Zara Valley, turn left and continue downstream on the left bank. The valley meanders here as it cuts through the mountain range, turning left and then, 15mins from the confluence, right (SSW). As you look down the river, you will see a sharp right turn about 4km further on. Note the path on the slope, high above the valley floor; it is the route for Stage 3.

Nearer to hand are the ruins of an abandoned settlement, **Lung**. There are some buildings on alluvial terraces, in the middle of the valley and on its left bank. Head towards the latter. You will probably have to cross some river channels, but do not cross to the right bank; try to keep to the left side. **Be careful; the river is really powerful here.** There is a small stream in Lung on the left bank of the Zara Chu (4281m).

Walk down the main valley, keeping to its left bank. There are no more river crossings. In 15mins you come to some more ruins. Continue along green terraces, passing a thin, braided path climbing a 30m-high ridge on your left. Some trekkers start the climb towards the high traverse here, but it's easier to take a slightly different route as described below. It's also possible to camp here.

Continue down the main valley until you get to a narrow, medium-sized valley on your left, 10mins later, still before the main valley makes a major right turn. There should be a small stream here. Enter the valley and make camp. If the riverbed has not dried up, you may walk upstream along it for 15mins to a grassy camp.

STAGE 3
*Camp beyond Lung to Morang La
Advance Base Camp*

Start	Camp beyond Lung (4275m)
Finish	Morang La Advance Base Camp (4636m)
Distance	12km
Time	6½hrs
Altitude range	4275m (Lung) to 4669m (Bong La)
Note	The beginning of this stage is incorrectly marked on some maps. Check the route details below and follow them carefully

The main part of this stage is an impressive traverse of the Zara Valley slopes, 300m above the river. The traverse is not so scary as it looks from a distance. There is a pass and then the confluence of big dry valleys. You follow one of them to a stream; then pass the Morang La Base Camp and follow the river to Morang La Advance Base Camp.

Alternatives
There is an alternative start for the ascent to the high traverse passed in the main valley 10mins before reaching camp (see Stage 2 for details). However, this option requires an unnecessary climb to a series of ridges, since the two paths join about 15mins beyond the camp.

Water supplies
Stock up when you leave the valley about 15mins beyond the camp. There is no water until Morang La Base Camp, 5hrs away. You will follow a stream beyond the Base Camp.

Route
From the camp go ESE first, then E, upvalley, leaving the Zara Chu behind. There is a narrow pathway along the true left bank of the stream. In 10mins, at a dry grassy terrace, a gradual ascent of the slope on your right begins.

The Zara Chu and the mountains of Rushpu as seen from the traverse 300m above the river

Soon you arrive at another greener, grassy terrace; it is also a good place to camp. There is a path on the other side of the valley, above. ◄

This is the alternative route from the Zara Valley which descends to the stream and crosses it to rejoin the main route on the grassy terrace.

Follow the path leading uphill from the terrace to your right (S at first); the way becomes clearer further up. Head to the left of the rocks above right. Mind the rock debris at the end of the ridge straight above you; it should eventually be on your left.

Beyond the rocks, keep ascending towards a pass-like flattening between two hills. From there, continue gradually up to the right, where the traverse starts (at about 4565m). It takes about 1½hrs to get here from the camp and you should be able to see the path ahead. If the path is not clear, you are in the wrong place!

It takes about 1½hrs to do the traverse, finishing at the Bong La. Try to avoid stopping on the way and look out for falling stones from the slopes above which may sometimes be dislodged by animals. There are outstanding views of the Zara Valley on the traverse. While on the **Bong La** (more like a ridge than a pass), traverse to the next ridge (SSW). ◄ The Morang La is more than 7km away to the southwest, but cannot be seen from here.

From here you will see a large valley just below and an impressive mountain range further to the south. Great views!

160

Descend steeply to the floor of the valley that comes in from the left. Cross it and go towards the SSW, to the next valley. Follow it upstream until it forks. Take the branch to your right, heading SW. Pass a rock column and then continue along the usually dry riverbed, bearing to the true left side of the valley (on your right as you follow the route). It is more than 1km to the next fork. Turn right towards the WNW and follow that valley. It narrows 300m further on and turns sharply left. Water should show up somewhere around here. You come next to a very narrow ravine. The path leaves the valley floor, crosses a small ridge on your left and descends to the floor again.

There is a beautiful place to camp for a few tents (5hrs from the last camp). This is **Morang La Base Camp** (bigger and nicer than the Advance Base Camp) and it is possible to climb the Morang La from here. However, if you want do that it is better to continue on to the **Advance Base Camp**, which is 1½hrs further and 100m higher. Follow the stony riverbed, crossing the stream easily many times. The path is indistinct. The valley heads W first and then turns towards the SSW. The Morang La can occasionally be seen – a clear pass at the top of a very steep slope.

Morang La Base Camp, a lovely (if limited) spot to camp

Pass a tributary valley on your right, then go through a steep section of the valley. Soon you come to a few small flat camping places by a valley on your left. The Morang La (which cannot be seen from here) is straight ahead (SSW). A distinct pathway begins here, ascending the valley's true left slope (on your right as you approach). Make camp around here.

STAGE 4
Morang La Advance Base Camp to Tsokmitsik

Start	Morang La Advance Base Camp (4636m)
Finish	Tsokmitsik (4095m)
Distance	11.5km
Time	7hrs
Altitude range	4095m (Tsokmitsik) to 5355m (Morang La)

This is a tough stage, because the Morang La is a very high pass and the ascent is steep. It takes 3hrs to get to the top, followed by more than 1250m of descent (4hrs) to Tsokmitsik in the Tsarab Chu Valley. Unless covered with snow, the pathway is clear.

Alternatives
There are no alternatives for this stage.

Water supplies
You need to take water from the camp for the next 5–6hrs.

Route
Leave the valley floor and follow the clear path cutting across the true left slope of the valley (on your right as you approach). You will cross the riverbed (it might be dry) twice further on and come to a steeper section of path. Ascend to a fork in the valley (a little over 1hr from

the camp). The Morang La is straight ahead towards the S, at the top of the steep slope. ▶

From the fork, follow the valley towards the S, straight towards the pass. Keep near the valley's true left side (on your right as you walk uphill). You will pass a small valley on your right, a bigger valley on the left and then two more on your right. The gradient increases as you progress, and the final traverse is harder than it appears from a distance. As on most of the passes, there are Buddhist prayer flags and a cairn on top of the **Morang La** (5355m). You will probably have great views from the pass (it was snowing heavily when the author passed this way).

Descend steeply, heading towards a ridge on your right, 300m below. From the ridge descend to the valley on your right, then steeply down along its dried-up riverbed. There is a confluence with a big valley coming from the left (1hr from the pass, elevation: 4800m). A few level earth platforms at the foot of a rock wall make a good place to camp if there is water in either of the valleys (in September both are dry).

Do not take another pass west-southwest of the fork (which may appear a good option if the Morang La is under snow); it does not lead towards the Tsarab Valley, and it is not possible to access the main trail from it.

The beautiful Tsarab Chu in autumn

Continuing down the valley you come to another place to camp in 30mins. If there is no water here you may find it just 10m below, but a large tributary on the left is reached in another 20mins; the valley turns right (SW) here. There is a good place to camp on a green terrace. It takes 1½hrs to cover the remaining distance to the camp in the Tsarab Valley.

Climb slightly to a moraine on the right and then continue down the pleasant valley above the river, descending to the valley floor 15mins further on. Follow the river and then take a traverse of the right slope for 20mins. Further on you will cross the stream, take a short traverse of the left slope and return to the valley floor. Continue on by a stony riverbed, crossing the stream many times (easy). The valley forms a narrow ravine in some places. Heading WSW, you arrive in the Tsarab Valley. Tsarab Chu is a big river and flows in from the left (SSE); the small stream that you have been following from the Morang La joins it at right angles. **Tsokmitsik**, at the confluence, has some good camping places.

STAGE 5
Tsokmitsik to Satak

Start	Tsokmitsik (4095m)
Finish	Satak (4013m)
Distance	15.5km
Time	7½hrs
Altitude range	4013m (Satak) to 4402m (first pass of the day)

Don't expect an easy day! Although the route follows the right side of the Tsarab Valley downstream this is an undulating stage, with a number of passes and ridges and no villages on the way. The path is generally clear, although narrow and precipitous in places. The landscape is beautiful, with excellent views. Late in the season the colour of the Tsarab Chu is amazing.

Alternatives

If you want to end the trek here, walk up the Tsarab Chu along its right bank. The path is clear and follows a high traverse most of the time. After about 11km you will reach the main Manali–Leh road at the place known as Barandy Nala (Gian on some maps). It takes 3–4hrs to get there. Buses in both directions should pass around noon. If you continue by road for 26km south you will reach Sarchu, where basic accommodation and supplies are found.

Water supplies

Although you follow the Tsarab Chu all day, the path stays high, away from the river. The side valleys are generally dry unless it is early season. There may be water in a stream 4hrs after the camp in July and early August, but none further on. Take water supplies for the entire day from the camp.

Route

Walk downstream along the right side of the Tsarab Valley. Stay near the river for the first 10mins – you don't need to take the path traversing the slope – to reach a dry terrace a few metres above the river (a good place to camp).

Settlements in this part of the Tsarab Valley have long been abandoned, leaving it wild and remote

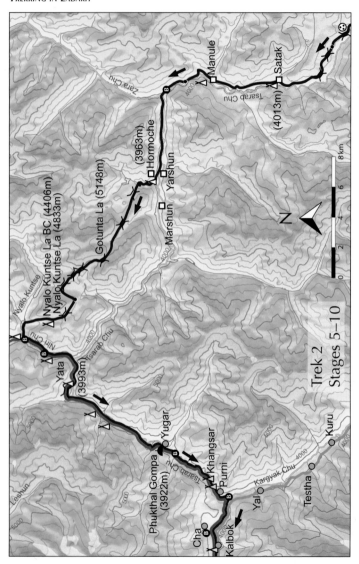

Further on, go down to a low terrace. Tsarab flows through a rock-gate just beyond it; note an incredible bridge above. Climb to a ridge that's in front of you. Beyond it, 1hr from Tsokmitsik, the path forks; take the left option down towards a huge, stony, well-like structure.

> This is a **wild animal trap**: examples are found all over Ladakh. Raw meat is used as bait, and animals – bears, foxes, wolves and snow leopards – trapped and killed by local villagers to protect their livestock. (In recent years wildlife protection organisations and campaigns have educated the locals about the wider importance of wild predators, and traps are used less frequently, if at all.)

There is a good place to camp 10mins further on, just below the path and ruins of a settlement. A gradual, clearly defined ascent towards a ridge high above the river begins here. While on that ridge, continue upwards along the ascending traverse crossing successive minor ridges to the first pass (4402m), 2½hrs from the camp. From the pass walk to the right, slightly down, to a dry side valley (4252m) and then steeply up on its opposite slope to another pass (4326m). Go right and downwards again to a green side valley (4173m) with shepherds' shelters. The river will probably still be flowing in July and August, making it a good camping place. It takes 4hrs to get here from Tsokmitsik and another 3½hrs to get to the next place with water (Satak).

Ascend to another pass (4268m, 30min) and then follow a long traverse high above the valley floor. The views are marvellous! You come to a ridge and then the next pass (4368m) – the fourth. It takes 1½hrs to get here from the last green, grassy valley. Next head slightly downwards to a pasture in the basin. Further on go slightly left and a little down to the floor of a side valley. Trek on upwards again to the next pass (4327m). Thankfully it's the last one today! It takes another 1½hrs to cover the remaining distance to the camp in Satak.

The people left the village (due to a shortage of water for irrigation) in 2006 for Sarchu, near the Manali–Leh road.

Descend gradually to a dry terrace, some 20–30m above the river, almost 2km from the last pass and 250m below it. Then ascend briefly and follow a precipitous traverse with a tiny waterfall on the way. You reach another dry terrace above the river. *Chortens* (*stupas*) can be seen from here and then the abandoned buildings of **Satak**. Camp here on the former fields and terraces. ◄

STAGE 6
Satak to Hormoche

Start	Satak (4013m)
Finish	Hormoche (3963m)
Distance	15.5km
Time	6½hrs
Altitude range	3925m (confluence of Zara and Tsarab rivers) to 4076m (first high traverse beyond camp)

Another day in the Tsarab Valley, with no major ascents or long descents. You don't need to carry much water and it is a relatively short stage. However, the way does traverse precipitous slopes, is really narrow in places and negotiates the wide Zara Chu.

Alternatives
There are no reasonable alternatives. Although there is a bridge just before the confluence with the Zara Chu and a good path on the other side of the Tsarab leading to the abandoned villages of Yarshun and Marshun on the left bank, crossing it means a difficult recrossing (no bridge) a few kilometres further on. Crossing the Tsarab Chu is very difficult even in September.

Water supplies
There are side-streams on the way, so you will have a chance to refill your bottles every few hours. From the

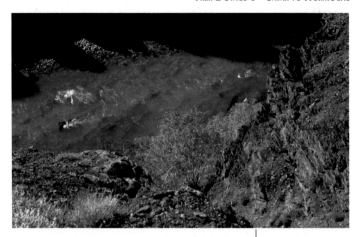

camp you need to take water for the first 45mins of walking; for supplies further on refer to the details below.

Route

From **Satak** ascend to the dry terrace high above the river just beyond the village and walk along a relatively easy traverse. You pass a small waterfall (the next place with water is 45mins further) and then descend to another dry terrace. The next traverse will take you to another terrace, 1km further on. Crossing it, you will reach a pretty large valley with a stream flowing from your right. Descend and cross the stream to find an abandoned house on the opposite side. This is **Manule**, roughly 1½hrs from Satak and a good place to camp.

Take water from Manule for 2½hrs. Follow the path traversing the slope until you come to a small, narrow side valley. The Tsarab Chu turns sharp left here. Descend gradually and then make a low traverse of the steep slope. Trekking on, you ascend steeply to a ridge at a right turn of the valley (about 1hr from Manule). Continue high above the river for a few hundred metres. Further on, go downwards and then ascend gently to an impressive stone and wood bridge over the Tsarab Chu.

Big mountain rivers such as the Tsarab are usually grey in colour in late spring and summer due to glacial flour; in autumn the current decreases and the river clears, becoming a beautiful blue

The footbridge on the Tsarab Chu near the abandoned village of Yarshun

If the river is too high to cross, there is no option other than going all the way back to the Manali–Leh road.

Do not cross the bridge: continue on the right bank of the Tsarab, traversing the slope. You reach a big tributary river coming from the north (right). This is the Zara Chu, the same river you followed a few days earlier, before crossing the Morang La. It is not easily forded, even late in the season, and probably impossible in July or early August. **Take extreme care here!** ◄

From the confluence, follow the path traversing the slope high above the Tsarab Valley floor. **Yarshun** is an abandoned settlement on the other side of the river. When opposite the first buildings, descend and walk along the river for a while. Further on, ascend to the uninhabited buildings on the right bank of the Tsarab and continue for 15mins to a large but narrow valley on your right. This is **Hormoche**; camp here. **Marshun**, another abandoned village on the left bank a little further downriver, can be seen from here.

STAGE 7
Hormoche to Nyalo Kuntse La Base Camp

Start	Hormoche (3963m)
Finish	Nyalo Kuntse La Base Camp (4406m)
Distance	16.5km
Time	9½hrs
Altitude range	3963m (Hormoche) to 5148m (Gotunta La)

This is no doubt the hardest stage of the trek. It is long, there are six passes (two major ones) and almost 1200m altitude difference between the camp in Hormoche and the highest point. You stay above 4800m for more than 10km and need to ascend about 1500m. Additionally, there is no water on the way so you will have to carry supplies. Luckily the views are marvellous – a good reward for your efforts.

Alternatives
If there was clean water at the base of the Gotunta Pass, it would be a good idea to split Stage 7 in two, but since water is only available early in the season, it is not usually possible to camp anywhere on this stage. There is a path from Hormoche downstream along the Tsarab River, but the valley gets narrow and steeper beyond the camp. The path is indistinct, narrow in places, precipitous and dangerous. Only go there with a good local guide!

Water supplies
In the main season, there is no drinkable water on this stage. The tiny lake 4½hrs beyond Hormoche at the base of the Gotunta La is not clean. Apparently there is sometimes a stream flowing into the lake early in the season, but it is dry in late summer. Take water for the whole day (9–10hrs) from the stream just beyond Hormoche.

Route

Leave the Tsarab Valley and go N, into the narrow side valley just above the camp in **Hormoche**. Walk upstream for 20mins. Take some water, leave the valley and start ascending the steep clear path ahead (on the true right side of the stream). Climb a series of zigzags to reach the top of a gully that forms a gently ascending valley, heading generally NW. Follow the valley along the slope on the right until you get to the first pass (4382m), about 1½hrs from Hormoche.

From the pass go slightly to the right and then slightly left (generally NW), very gently up, through a dry valley, to the foot of a steep slope on your left about 500m from the pass. Climb steeply for 30mins and then more gradually on a long traverse leading towards a clear pass left of an impressive wall ahead. It's a steep climb at the end. The pass is 4738m high, roughly 3½hrs from the camp. Do not descend from the pass, but go upwards to a ridge on your right (W). ◀

Look out for the small picturesque lake in the valley behind you.

Continue NW, by a long traverse. The Gotunta La can be clearly seen on the opposite side of the valley. There is a small lake in the valley on your way. If there is a stream above it, you may camp here to divide the stage. It takes 4½hrs to cover the distance from Hormoche, but there is more than 5hrs to go. Both of the two main passes of the stage are still to be crossed! Ascend the opposite slope of the valley, heading WNW. Climb steeply at first, then proceed to the left (W), gradually traversing to a dry valley. The trail is again steep up the dry valley. At the fork go right, NW, to a clear pass. This is the **Gotunta La** (5148m), some 6hrs from Hormoche.

Have a look at the way ahead from the pass (the traverse below right, then another one, on the opposite slope, 3.5km in distance, towards the NW).

Descend to the path cutting the slope on your right. You come to a ridge and two following passes further on. Do not descend to the valley from the second one, but go NW, left, part way around a hill, traversing the slope. Soon you come to another ridge. Follow it down to a saddle-like pass and then up, along the opposite

ridge, towards the WNW. Turn left a little further on, then follow a long traverse (seen from the Gotunta La). The path turns slightly right after 1km and comes to a ridge pass. Cross it, turn right again (NW) and walk along another 1km-long traverse to the last pass. This is the **Nyalo Kuntse La** (4833m).

Prayer flags and an astonishing number of Zanskar Mountain peaks as seen from the Gotunta La

Descend steeply on the opposite side of the pass (NNW). The only place to camp is on a few small platforms, some 400m below, about 45mins from the Nyalo Kuntse La. There is a very tiny spring.

STAGE 8
Nyalo Kuntse La Base Camp to Yata

Start	Nyalo Kuntse La Base Camp (4406m)
Finish	Yata (3993m)
Distance	10.5km
Time	4½hrs
Altitude range	3896m (bridge over the Niri Chu) to 4406m (Nyalo Kuntse La Base Camp)

Almost the whole of Stage 8 is in descent, but it's not an entirely easy day. The path is narrow and precipitous in many places, so the walking demands your concentration. The highlight of the day is the valley itself, particularly below its confluence with the Tsarab Chu.

Alternatives

- The trail meets Trek 4 during this stage. On meeting the Niri Chu Valley turn right and go up river (north), to Thantak, instead of going left to Phukthal. It is possible to finish this trek in three days, but is a hard option.
- A side-trip is also possible. When in the Nyalo Kuntse Valley (below the camp) turn right, upstream, for about 2hrs to a lake. It is said to be a beautiful and wild place.

Water supplies

Take water from camp for 1hr, and for another 1hr before leaving the Nyalo Kuntse Valley. The next place to refill is at the bridge on the Niri Chu – take supplies for 2–3hrs.

Route

Descend to the Nyalo Kuntse Valley that comes in from your right (E). The valley could be dry in mid-September, but you will certainly find water a bit further down. 20mins on, just before reaching the confluence with the Niri Chu, you come to a bridge. ◀ If you need to camp here, an excellent choice is N up the valley, less than 1km from the bridge.

The bridge leads to Thantak village and the Stongde La (see Trek 4); it is also the way to Shade village and Zangla in the Zanskar Valley (not covered in this book).

To continue on Trek 2 towards Phukthal, do not cross the bridge. Just beyond it the confluence is reached with the deep gorge of the Niri Chu coming in from the right. Don't go down to the valley floor here unless you want to camp by the riverbank. Walk up to a clear and broad path traversing the left slope high above the river. Head SW, downstream. About 40mins from the confluence you will pass above a bridge. You need to cross it, but to get to it continue for 100m then take a clear path, marked with small piles of stones, which descends to the bridge.

Cross the bridge and continue along the valley, downstream on a traversing path above the river on the right bank. Although the path on the left bank continues too, it is narrow and dangerous further on. You will be traversing this exposed slope (on the right bank) as far as Phukthal. **The path is narrow in many places and may be dangerous, so be careful!** If the path is damaged, search for an alternative.

> Note that this trail is quite popular, as this is the **best and easiest route** to Thantak and Shade villages; even if parts of the path are damaged, there should be a clear and safe alternative. Do not use the path if it seems to be abandoned, and look out for signs put out by locals: a horizontal row of small stones indicates that the path does not continue. Small piles of stones (cairns) mark the correct way. **Note** Do not take this route just after or during serious rain or snowfall.

Around 15mins after crossing the bridge, you come to a dry, high terrace. It's a good place to camp, but if you stay here, you need to carry water from the river (there is a path). Continue on the high traverse. Just before the confluence with the Tsarab Chu, in a big valley coming from the left (SSE) about 45mins beyond the bridge crossing, you will pass above an old rope bridge. ▶

This marks the end of the alternative and dangerous route along the Tsarab Chu trail from Hormoche.

Follow the path on the right slope. After the confluence, the valley forms an impressive canyon. The Tsarab Chu turns sharply a few times as it cuts through resistant rock. About 30mins from the confluence you will have to skirt around a damaged section of the trail: descend steeply and then climb back to the high traverse. Before a major sharp left turn of the valley (SSW), almost 1hr from the confluence, just past a high dry terrace, there is a small cave a few metres above the path. Shortly you will start climbing along a very steep valley. While ascending, pass a row of willow bushes on the left. Although there is a path leading straight ahead as well, go upwards. (The section ahead used to be very precipitous and dangerous but was renovated in 2013 and should be fine to follow. If you do so, be careful.) On the ascent you will reach a small spring and a few small flat areas. This is **Yata**, and you can camp here.

STAGE 9
Yata to Phukthal

Start	Yata (3993m)
Finish	Phukthal (3922m)
Distance	10.5km
Time	4½hrs
Altitude range	3822m (side valley en route) to 4103m (pass above Yata)

This stage sees the continuation of the traverse of the Tsarab Valley's right bank. The path was renovated in 2013 and is better now, but it needs high concentration all the same. The same warnings as for Stage 8 apply.

Alternatives
Instead of climbing to the small pass at the beginning of the stage, return to the traverse below you and follow it

Phukthal Gompa clings to the rock face high above the valley

down the valley. This path used to be very dangerous but was renovated in 2013 and should be fine. Be careful.

Instead of staying overnight at one of the guesthouses at Phukthal Gompa, you could continue down the Tsarab Chu to Purni and stay at one of the campsites there.

Water supplies

There are a few streams on the first half of the stage. After that, take sufficient water for 2hrs from a deep valley between two green terraces (see below for details).

Route

Climb to the small pass that is towards the NW, 100m above camp (20mins). From the pass descend gradually (WSW), to a side valley just above its confluence with the Tsarab. Take water for 1hr. From the side valley, begin a traverse high above the Tsarab. The path is clear, although narrow and precipitous at the beginning. It's better not to delay here; watch the slopes for falling stones.

There is a small green terrace high above the valley floor about 1½hrs after leaving Yata (if there is water, this is a good camping spot for one or two tents). Cross a tiny stream 10mins later and reach a deep side valley in another 20mins. Take water for 2hrs. (Another good place for a camp is at a high, green terrace, a few minutes further along). Further on, about 2hrs from Yata, the path leads downwards. Descend and walk just above the river for a short time, then ascend to the high terrace. After 15mins there is another descent where the path forks. The right fork leads up to a pass. Although the two trails meet further on, go left, downwards, as it is not necessary to ascend here.

Traverse above the river for a few minutes and then ascend to the different higher traverse. Pass a rock face on your right and follow a slight right turn of the valley. From here a narrow part of the valley, 1km further on, and a ravine on the right can be seen. Climb steeply on a clear path, then follow a traverse about 100m above the river to the deep valley of a tributary stream. Across the ravine continue high above the Tsarab on a clear

It is possible to watch the monks at Phukthal Gompa performing religious rituals

It is possible to watch the monks at Phukthal Gompa performing religious rituals

path. It will take about 30mins to cover the remaining distance to **Phukthal**. There is a *chorten* (*stupa*) on a ridge as the valley turns. The monastery clings to a sheer slope on the other side of the ridge, just to the right. **Yugar** village is on the opposite side of the valley. The views are stunning!

PHUKTHAL GOMPA

It is definitely worth staying at the amazing monastery – the monks are hospitable and friendly. You will be welcome to attend most of the assemblies, prayers and meals (pay for your food when leaving). Staying at Phukthal gives you a glimpse of the real monastic life of the region. However, if you are a single woman trekker it is best not to stay there (for cultural reasons).

There is a 'hotel' – a dormitory room – at the *gompa*, and a new guesthouse situated just below it on the way to Purni. The guesthouse is the less interesting option, but the monks really prefer to accommodate tourists there. It may be better to take a long rest at the *gompa* and continue to one of the camps in Purni.

STAGE 10
Phukthal to Pepula

Start	Phukthal (3922m)
Finish	Pepula (3749m)
Distance	20km
Time	7½hrs
Altitude range	3749m (Pepula) to 3922m (Phukthal)

In Purni, you join a very popular route – Darcha to Padum – and follow it as far as Padum (see Trek 3). Most trekkers take a side-trip from that trail to Phukthal. The walk follows a very clear path, often busy with trekking groups. There are settlements along the way with at least a simple shop, and it is possible to find accommodation in most of them.

Construction works on the Darcha–Padum road have been progressing quickly, so you will follow the road at least in some sections below Purni. In 2014 the road head on the Padum side was in the village of Enmu on the right bank of Lungnak (a bit east of Changpa Tsetan). On the Darcha side, it was already at the Shinkul pass.

Alternatives
The main trail from Purni to Padum follows the left bank of the Tsarab River. Another, less popular, one follows the right bank; that path is not as clear and is dangerously precipitous in some places, but it is perfectly fine for advanced trekkers (although there are a few sections where the path is very narrow and might be challenging for some trekkers) and it's no more difficult than the route from Morang La. It takes about 2hrs to get to Cha, and the views are superb! When in Phukthal ask about the current condition of this route and whether local people are using it (ask for the way to Cha).

To take this option do not cross the bridge below Phukthal, but follow the right bank high above the river. At Cha village there are two options:
• Cross the bridge to the left bank and join the popular trail.

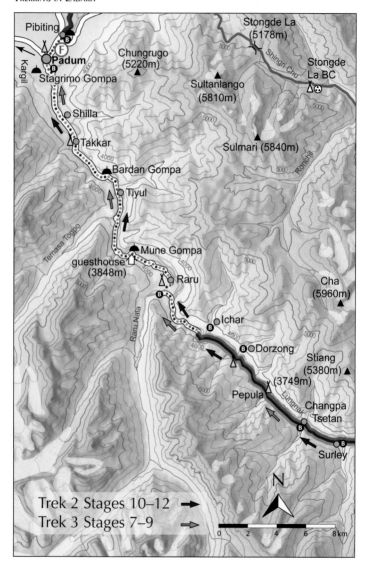

- Continue on the right bank to Enmu. It used to be a beautiful and infrequently used traverse, but the road extends on this side of the river so it's hard to say what it'll be like in the future. (In September 2014 the head of the road was in Enmu.) Ask the locals about the condition of the route when you are there. If the path still exists, it follows a high traverse between Cha and Enmu. It's up and down in places so it's not an easy one. It passes a small nunnery (Ani-Gompa) or a nun's monastery, Dolmaling, which clings impressively to a sheer slope. The path is good; the route is scenic with fantastic vistas. It takes about 2hrs to cover the way. It was possible to arrange transportation to Padum in Enmu or in any place below it in 2014. You can also continue the trek from Enmu on either side of Lungnak.
- There is a beautiful two-day alternative that was tested by the author in 2013 and 2014. It's a wild option with fantastic views, and it lets you avoid busy routes and a part of the extending road. From Phuthal, go down the valley on the right bank no more than 5mins beyond the new guesthouse. Do not cross the bridge but reach a side valley on your right just beyond it. The path is clear at the beginning

Phukthal Gompa, viewed from the bridge over the Tsarab Chu

– it enters the side-valley, climbing steeply to a step, then descends and continues at the floor. From here on the path may disappear in places, but just follow upstream at the valley floor. The valley is probably called Zherin. You will pass some shelters and a pasture (and maybe also some yaks) by a big valley on your right, which is called Yugar Doksa. Continue by the main valley slightly to the left until you reach a big side-valley on your left with places for a camp. This is Zaya, about 6–7hrs from Phukthal. Sleep here. On the next day continue by the main valley until you reach another side-valley on your left, behind rocks, at the right-turn of the main valley. Turn into this one to reach a pass with fantastic views of the Great Himalaya Range. Descend at the valley floor first, then take a clear path traversing the left slope and eventually crossing the ridge on your left. After the ridge, descend by a clear path to the village of Enmu in the Lungnak (Tsarab/Tsarab Lingti) valley and on the Darcha–Padum road. It takes about 6hrs to cover the way between Zaya and Enmu.

From Purni you could go up the Kargyak Chu in the direction of the Shinkul La, leaving Zanskar. The route finishes in Darcha on the Manali–Leh road. See Trek 3 (reverse the route description) for more details.

Water supplies

On Stages 10 and 11 water is generally not available between the settlements, so carry supplies sufficient for 2hrs. The path undulates and it is usually hot in summer. From Phukthal take sufficient water supplies for 2hrs.

Route

From the monastery descend towards the S. Mind the cultural custom and keep left of the impressive *mani* walls and *chortens* (*stupas*). At the bridge, where the valley turns right, cross to the left bank and follow the clear path downstream. It forks in some places – take the one that seems to be more frequently used. It takes less than 2hrs to cover the distance to Purni; the first house, **Khangsar**, is passed around 15mins before the main part of the village is reached. There is a campsite here and meals are served at the house. It's a very nice place and usually quieter than the main campsite in **Purni**, where most of the big groups stop. There are two restaurant-shops and a big campsite in the main part of the village. If you are in need of supplies, it is the best place for shopping. When leaving, take water for 1½hrs.

The Kargyak Chu coming from your left (SE) meets the Tsarab Chu in Purni. ▸ The river is called the Lungnak ('dark gorge') from the confluence down to Padum, but is also frequently marked on maps as the Tsarab Lingti, Lingti or Tsarab.

A path on the true left bank up the Kargyak Valley leads to Darcha via the Shinkul La.

> The **road connection between Darcha and Padum** along the Kargyak and Tsarab valleys is under construction. Sadly for trekkers, the works have speeded up in the recent years. In late 2014 on the Darcha side the road under construction already crossed the Shinkul pass, and will probably reach Kargyak village in 2015. On the Padum side the road head was in Enmu in September 2014, opposite Changpa Tsetan. There is also a link road to Surley, which you'll see further on in this stage. To avoid walking on the road, check the alternatives for Stages 11 and 12.

Cross the bridge over the Kargyak and walk to the right, downstream. There is another path above you – both paths meet 30mins further on. You come to a bridge on the Lungnak 20mins beyond the junction and a house a little further on. Cha village is on the opposite side of the river. ▸ Continuing on the left bank, the trail reaches **Kalbok** village (3863m) in 20mins. It is situated on a terrace high above the valley floor. There is one house, a shop, a campsite and field; only one family lives here. It's a beautiful place; you can either camp or stay at the house.

The alternative route from Phukthal joins here.

Cross the bridge (3786m) in a side valley roughly 30mins after Kalbok. Take water sufficient for 1hr.

Above is the village of **Surley** (3908m), on high terraces and accessed by a steep path, just beyond the bridge. Accommodation (homestay) is available in the village.

Continue straight ahead, along the main valley. High above the valley floor, you reach a *chorten* and a junction with a new road (under construction in September 2014) leading to Surley (left) and a planned bridge on Tsarab Lingti (right). Continue straight on a traversing path. (If you reached Enmu following one of the alternatives described above, you can join the main route here crossing the bridge from Enmu.) After 15mins, pass above a settlement called **Changpa Tsetan** about 1hr from the last bridge. The path turns left and descends steeply to another side valley. ◄

There is an interesting mill up the stream, on the right – the small building with a water channel.

Take water sufficient for 1½hrs to Pepula, cross the bridge and climb steeply the opposite slope of the side valley. Continue along the Lungnak with some tiring ups and downs. **Pepula** (only a campsite with a small shop-restaurant) is at the next tributary stream beside the Lungnak. The monks from Phukthal run this place.

STAGE 11
Pepula to Mune

Start	Pepula (3749m)
Finish	Mune (3848m)
Distance	17km
Time	6hrs
Altitude range	3730m (bridge over the Raru Nala) to 3848m (Mune)

A tiring day along the left bank of the Lungnak, with a succession of ascents and descents before joining the road in Ichar. From here on the main trail follows the road (see alternatives below). Arranging transportation to Leh might be possible in Ichar, Raru or anywhere on the way.

Mune Gompa is one of many monasteries of the Gelug-pa order

Alternatives

- According to local people, there is a trail from Ichar to the Ronchil Valley. It joins the Round Sultanlango trek (Trek 4) just before the ascent to the Stongde La. It is probably a nice trek that few Westerners do. Ask for details in Ichar.

- It is possible to walk on the harder, right side of the Lungnak between Ichar and Raru, as this option would save you the road walk. The route is perfectly fine, and has beautiful views, but it requires some steep ascents and is precipitous in places. The author tested it in 2013 and 2014. It is a fantastic, scenic alternative to the usual walk between Ichar and Raru, which follows the road. From Ichar you need to climb steeply to the main part of the village, then go into the side valley, cross it and climb again. This is on a very well used path as villagers take this route to get to their fields high above Lungnak (Tsarab Lingti). Pass the fields and continue on the high traverse. Finally descend to the bridge on Lungnak just after its confluence with Raru Nala, then climb the slope and reach Raru. It takes approximately 3hrs to cover the way between the Ichar bridge and Raru on this route.

Water supplies

There are small streams between Pepula and the Dorzong bridge, but it is better to take water from Pepula sufficient for 1½hrs. At the Dorzong bridge pick up supplies for 2½hrs, and at Raru for 1hr. Bear in mind that it is usually dry and hot along this route in summer.

Route

From **Pepula**, continue down the Lungnak. The path ascends at first and then continues above the valley floor. The clear, safe track has short descents and ascents with nice views. When opposite a village 1½hrs from Pepula, descend and cross a bridge over a side-stream. Another 200m further on, there is a bridge over the Lungnak, with a simple restaurant and a campsite. On the other side is **Dorzong**. In 2009 road construction works were in progress on the right bank.

Refill your water bottles and follow the left bank to reach another bridge in 40mins opposite **Ichar** village with trees growing around the settlement: a pleasant surprise! Cross the bridge, turn left and reach the road. Follow it down the valley, which bends here a few times. Further on the road turns left into the side-valley of the Raru Nala – a big tributary fed by meltwater from a few glaciers of the Great Himalaya Range.

Follow the road to the bridge over the Raru Nala. Cross it and then leave the road. Take a path to the right, downriver on the left bank and ascend to the ridge on your left. This path is a shortcut to **Raru** village, seen from the ridge; the large buildings house a school. Near the village you will join the road again. There is a shop and a simple restaurant, and a few houses offer accommodation. Occasionally, shared jeeps go to Padum from here.

The 4km from Raru to Mune takes 1hr, following the road from Raru or taking a shortcut on a path. The latter ascends to the ridge NW of the road. There is a lake and a campsite on the way. Head NW from the lake, keeping the Lungnak on your right, until you meet the road again. Follow the road to the **Mune Gompa**, on the right of the road with a hotel on the left, which belongs to the monastery. Prices are similar to those in Padum at the end of Trek 2: about Rs250 for a double room.

Monks of Mune Gompa

STAGE 12
Mune to Padum

Start	Mune (3848m)
Finish	Padum (3600m)
Distance	18km
Time	5½hrs
Altitude range	3600m (Padum) to 3848m (Mune)

A boring stage following the mainly asphalt road to Padum. The town offers the basic luxuries of modernity, but still remains a relatively quiet place.

Alternatives
- It's a good idea to skip this stage by taking a jeep from Raru but you might also ask in Mune, or further down in Bardan. Hitch-hiking anywhere along the way may be possible.

- To avoid following the road on the major part of this stage, cross the bridge on Tsarab Lingti (Lungnak) to the scenic Pibcha village. From there follow the traverse on the right bank of the river to Shilla, where you join a road leading to Padum. You may either stay there for the night, try to arrange transportation to Padum or continue the walk on the road. It takes about 2hrs to cover the way between Pibcha and Shilla.

Water supplies

From Mune take water for about 1½hrs. In Bardan refill bottles for 1hr, and at the camp in Takkar for the remaining 2hrs.

Route

Follow the road along the valley. You will cross a few side-streams on the way, the last one about 1hr beyond Mune. After 1½hrs you come to a house. This is **Tiyul** (Tiengul) settlement and there is picturesque Pibcha village on the opposite side of the river, connected by a

Set on a crag, the 17th-century Bardan Gompa, and chortens below

bridge. **Bardan Gompa** is less than 30mins' walk further, on a hill. The monastery is worth visiting.

The distance between Bardan and Padum is about 10km (2½–3hrs). The asphalt road starts on the way. You arrive at **Takkar** (one house and a campsite) about 1hr after leaving Bardan. **Padum** is 6km further on.

Padum is located in a wide valley, at the confluence of the Lungnak and Stod (Doda) rivers, at the foot of the Great Himalaya Range. The two rivers flow from opposite directions and join to form the Zanskar River. There are several guesthouses in the town, a few restaurants and two campsites. (For more information about Padum see Padum – the heart of Zanskar in the Introduction.)

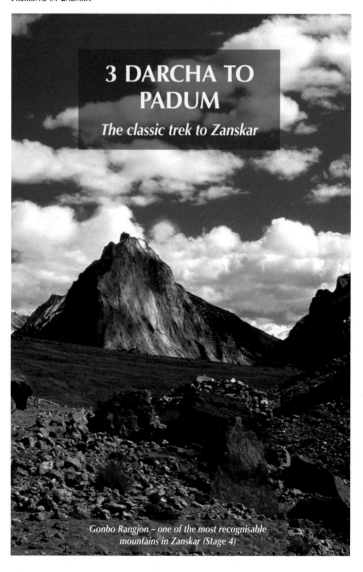

3 DARCHA TO PADUM

The classic trek to Zanskar

Gonbo Rangjon – one of the most recognisable mountains in Zanskar (Stage 4)

INTRODUCTION

Start	Darcha on the Manali–Leh road (3378m); alternatively Pal Lhamo, Zanskar Sumdo
Finish	Padum, Zanskar (3600m); alternatively Stongde (Zanskar Valley)
Distance	135km
Time	60hrs (9 days)
Altitude range	3378m (Darcha) to 5054m (Shinkul La)

COMBINATIONS AND ALTERNATIVES

From Purni (Stage 6), go up the Tsarab Chu to Phukthal and then continue up the valley along the Round Sultanlango trek (see Trek 4: a demanding route that is not accessible in July and early August). Pal Lhamo is between Darcha and Zanskar Sumdo and can be reached by bus or jeep, so you could skip the initial part of Stage 1. For proper acclimatisation, however, it is best to start to trek in Darcha. You can continue trekking from Padum to Central Ladakh either by Trek 5 (Padum to Lamayuru: the classic trek from Zanskar) or Trek 6 (Padum to Lamayuru via the Kanji La).

The Great Himalayas as seen from the Shinkul La (Stage 3) in early summer

GENERAL INFORMATION

This is a relatively easy route, passing at least a summer settlement and usually a few villages every day. Basic food and home accommodation (homestay) is available in almost every village on the way. The path is easy to follow, as this is a popular and quite busy trail. In the high season you will meet a few groups of trekkers each day and, regardless of the season, a few locals. Stages are shorter than those on the other treks and most of them can be divided however you wish. It is a beautiful trek, but go soon before ongoing road construction changes it forever.

Sadly for trekkers, a road bridge on Jankar Nala was built in Zanskar Sumdo in 2013 and the road under construction extended beyond Ramyak. It is said that the road construction reached the Shinkul La in late 2014, and it may reach Kargyak village in 2015. The tunnel under Shinkul pass has also been planned.

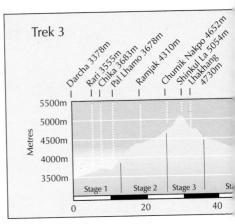

Trek 3

DIFFICULTY, SUPPLIES AND ACCOMMODATION

The Shinkul La is the major difficulty of the trek – it is a serious pass across the main ridge of the Great Himalayas, over 5000m high – and you have to climb it from a starting altitude of about 3380m at Darcha.

Unless you are well acclimatised do not skip Stage 1 by taking a jeep. Regarding acclimatisation, it is a good idea to divide the first stage into two shorter days, or spend a night in Darcha before starting out.

Most of the small shops and campsites are only open in the high season (mid-July to the end of August). At other times you need to carry more food. If you need ponies or horses, it should not be difficult to arrange them in Darcha in the high season. Many horsemen finish their work there and hope for extra employment on their way back home to Zanskar.

Using homestay will give you a great opportunity to interact with local people and observe their way of life, and this is a cheaper option compared with an organised trek; normally homestay accommodation for one person costs the same as pitching a tent at a campsite. Generally

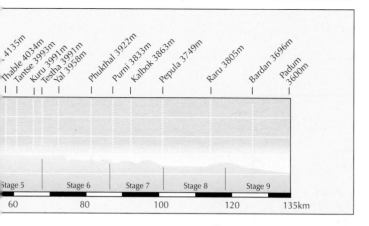

4135m
Thable 4034m
Tantse 3993m
Kuru 3991m
Testha 3991m
Yal 3958m
Phukthal 3922m
Purni 3833m
Kalbok 3863m
Pepula 3749m
Raru 3805m
Bardan 3696m
Padum 3600m

| Stage 5 | | Stage 6 | | Stage 7 | | Stage 8 | | Stage 9 | |
| 60 | | 80 | | 100 | | 120 | | 135km | |

the home-cooked food is much better than that at the tent-restaurants on the way, and reasonably priced too. In 2009 it cost Rs250–400 for food and accommodation per person per night in a family house. For a great experience that is also good fun, spend a day or so in a village, working with a family in the fields!

WHEN TO GO?

Usually, it is possible to trek the route between early June and late October. However, the Shinkul La receives heavy snowfall in winter, and is often snowbound until mid-July. This does not mean that it is impossible to cross it before then, or that you need any special equipment, but it does make

The fields of Zanskar near Padum in autumn, with Pibiting Gompa in the centre and Karsha Gompa far left, clinging to the valley side (Stage 9)

193

Padum

Chungrugo (5220m)

Sultanlango (5810m)

Shingri Chu

Niri Chu

Stage 9

Sulmari (5840m)

Temasa Togpo

Mune Gompa

Cha (5960m)

Leshun

Stage 8

Raru Nala

Tsarab Chu

Stiang (5380m)

Pepula

Lungnak

Phukthal Gompa

Purni

Stage 7

Kargyak Chu

Stage 6

Testha

Stage 5

Lenak

Giabul

Kargyak

Stage 4

Kargyak Chu

Gonbo Rangion

Lhakhang Sumdo

Shinkul La

Stage 3

N

Stage 2

Chumik Nakpo

Sangpo

Zanskar Sumdo

Leh

0   10   20 km

Stage 1

Trek 3
Darcha to Padum:
the classic trek to Zanskar

Pal Lhamo

Chika

Rari

Jankar Nala

Bhaga

Keylong & Manali

Darcha

Great Himalayas

the path hard and you might need to allow more time for that stage.

Rainfall is more likely on this than on any other trek. While trekking in September or October, be prepared for snowfall. Because conditions are far more humid south of the Great Himalaya Range than in Zanskar and Central Ladakh, you will feel the cold more intensively here. Therefore, when trekking in the late season, try to avoid camping at high altitudes. Weather-wise August is probably the best, but is also the busiest time for this trek. Early September is recommended, as there are fewer tourists and you can experience the beauty of the Zanskar autumn.

ACCESS

Darcha is situated on the Manali–Leh road, south of the main pass of the Himalayas. Therefore it is usually accessible for longer in the year than Leh. Early in the season, when buses do not go as far as Leh, they do go to Keylong, and Darcha can be easily accessed from there. Keylong is a good place to prepare for the trek; to acclimatise properly stay there for at least two nights. There are two buses taking under 2hrs from Keylong to Darcha, at 6.30am and in the early afternoon.

There are several restaurants, simple accommodation, a campsite and a police checkpoint in Darcha where you have to register. From Padum there are a few different options when leaving Zanskar (by foot or road). There are buses or jeeps to Kargil, and then on to Leh or Srinagar. Buses do not go every day and it may take you more than one day to arrange a jeep – allow some extra time for the journey out of Zanskar.

In Kargyak, as in most places in Ladakh, the buildings are on the valley edge, leaving the valley floor free for agriculture (Stage 4)

STAGE 1
Darcha to Zanskar Sumdo

Start	Darcha (3378m)
Finish	Zanskar Sumdo (3932m)
Distance	13.5km
Time	7½hrs
Altitude range	3378m (Darcha) to 3932m (Zanskar Sumdo)

Following the deep, wide, gradually ascending valley of the Jankar River, the route is on the road that will link Darcha and Padum. There is only one steep ascent, just beyond Darcha. The overall altitude gain of 550m is not great but is still a significant challenge so early in the trek, especially on a day spent mostly above 3500m.

Alternatives
As the road already extends beyond Pal Lhamo, you can skip this stage by taking a jeep or even a bus (for a part of the journey) – check in Keylong or Darcha. However, don't take this option if this is your first trek of the season at high altitude. According to some maps there are two paths from Darcha to Zanskar Sumdo. Indeed, a path can be seen across the Jankar Nala (on its true right bank) from the road between Darcha and Rari (which is on the true left bank of the river). However, the author has not checked this, and as far as can be seen from the road it does not look like a safe route. Don't take this option unless you have reliable information that it does exist and is usable.

Water supplies
You need to take water supplies from Darcha sufficient for 1½hrs. Further on, it is possible to refill bottles at least once an hour.

Route
Cross the road bridge in **Darcha** to the left (north) bank of the Jankar Nala. Follow the road until you have passed

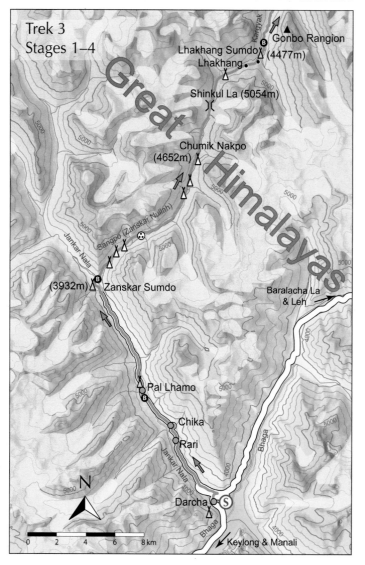

Trek 3
Stages 1–4

Great Himalayas

Gonbo Rangion
(4477m)

Lhakhang Sumdo
Lhakhang

Shinkul La (5054m)

Chumik Nakpo
(4652m)

Sangpo (Zanskar Nullah)

Jankar Nala

(3932m) Zanskar Sumdo

Baralacha La
& Leh

Pal Lhamo

Chika

Rari

Jankal Nala

Bhaga

N

Darcha

Keylong & Manali

0 2 4 6 8 km

Bhaga

Groups of chortens are seen in many places in Zanskar; always pass to the left of these (Stage 5)

all the *dhabas* (restaurants), then turn left on to a clear path that starts about 300m beyond the bridge. The path climbs the steep slope and joins an upper loop of the same road. Don't leave the road for another path above it, but simply follow it upwards as far as a sharp right curve. At a junction the road to the right leads towards Leh; take the road straight ahead, which follows the valley towards Zanskar Sumdo (NW).

The village of **Rari** is reached about 1½hrs after leaving Darcha, and the settlement of **Chika** some 45mins later. Further on, 3hrs from Darcha, there is a road bridge over the main river that flows here in an impressive, narrow, deep gorge. Cross to the true right bank. You come to a campsite and the **Pal Lhamo** settlement 30mins later. There is a tent-restaurant, which offers basic food, situated at an altitude of 3680m. **Stay there for the night if you feel slight symptoms of altitude sickness, such as a headache. If the symptoms are serious (bad headache, sickness), you must descend back to Darcha.** If you feel fine, continue up the valley along the road.

You will reach a side-stream roughly 2hrs 40mins' walk beyond Pal Lhamo. Cross it. The Sangpo, a large tributary, can be seen in a deep ravine to the right; the onward trail towards the Shinkul La leads along it. Soon a bridge over the Jankar is reached, and a campsite at **Zanskar Sumdo**.

STAGE 2
Zanskar Sumdo to Chumik Nakpo

Start	Zanskar Sumdo (3932m)
Finish	Chumik Nakpo (4652m)
Distance	12km
Time	7–8hrs
Altitude range	3932m (Zanskar Sumdo) to 4652m (Chumik Nakpo)

After a steep initial ascent, the trail climbs gradually along the true right bank of the Sangpo River. There are no major river crossings and the path is clear. There is a road under construction all the way to the pass; you will follow it in places and sometimes you'll walk on a pathway that is parallel to the road.

Alternatives
It is a good idea to spend another night at Zanskar Sumdo to aid acclimatisation. Leave your tent and heavy equipment at the camp and take a walk up the main valley; at the fork you can take either of the valleys, before reversing your route and returning to camp.

Water supplies
Take water for the initial ascent to the ridge on the opposite side of the Jankar Valley (1½hrs). You will be walking along the river later on where there are frequent side-streams, so you don't need to carry much water.

Route
Cross the Jankar Nala by the bridge and then climb a steep slope on the opposite side of the valley on a clear path.

Sangpo Valley and the peaks of the Great Himalaya Range

From the ridge (4089m) head NNE, traversing the Sangpo Valley's true right slope (on your left, facing upstream). It is precipitous in some places. You reach the valley floor about 1½hrs after leaving Zanskar Sumdo; this is a good place to camp. Another camping possibility is 30mins further on, and there is a third after another 20mins.

Beyond an alluvial fan on your left and a small side-stream crossing, just before a relatively big side-valley on your right, there are simple stone shelters and a possible camp (3–3½hrs from Zanskar Sumdo). The valley starts a gradual left turn further on. It's over 7km (4hrs) from here to Chumik Nakpo (Shinkul La Base Camp). Note the following relatively big side-valleys on your right (true left tributaries of the Sangpo River) beyond these shelters, and the side-valley that's almost opposite them. **Chumik Nakpo** (or Upper Chumik Nakpo – the last place to camp) is almost opposite the third one, just beyond a small stream flowing in from the left (a true right tributary). There are good places to camp every 30mins en route. Chumik Nakpo (or Upper Chumik Nakpo, as there's another place an hour earlier and 100m lower, with a tent-shop usually, which is also sometimes called Chumik Nakpo as well as Lower Chumik Nakpo) is the last convenient place to camp before the pass with enough places for a few small tents. It is the best place to start the final ascent. Be prepared for a cold night.

STAGE 3
Chumik Nakpo to Lhakhang Sumdo

Start	Chumik Nakpo (4652m)
Finish	Lhakhang Sumdo (4477m)
Distance	10km
Time	6½hrs
Altitude range	4477m (Lhakhang Sumdo) to 5054m (Shinkul La)

The Shinkul La is not a difficult pass and the ascent is not steep. However, weather and snow conditions may make the crossing much more testing. When the author was on the pass in October, it was raining; in early July more than a metre of snow covered it, making the climb hard. If this is the case, leave camp early in the morning when the snow is frozen and hard, and to allow more time to get to and cross the pass; it took the author 3hrs to get to the pass early in July.

Alternatives
There are no alternatives for this stage.

Water supplies
You do not need to carry much water; bottles can be refilled almost anywhere on the route.

Route
Follow the stream on its true right (W) bank (on your left, facing upstream) along masses of loose stones. One hour from camp you will pass a big valley on your left. Follow the main stream towards the NNE. At a glacial cirque on your right (E), there is a steep scree slope and a small stream opposite the glacier on your left (NW). Although the pass is not at the top of this slope, this is the main part of the ascent. Climb to the top of the scree slope; the path levels off. The **Shinkul La** is towards the N, just 1km further and 30m higher, on the opposite

*If crossing the Great
Himalayas via the
Shinkul La in early
summer leave camp
early before the snow
gets soft*

side of the small lake ahead. The path is to the right of
the lake. The pass (5054m) is well marked with cairns
and prayer flags.

Descend by a clear path along the main valley,
towards the NNE. In 1hr arrive at a big valley coming from
the left (4730m). This is **Lhakhang**, a good site for camping. Follow the main valley towards the ENE, traversing
the right slope. You come to a ridge (4713m) 45mins from
Lhakhang. Descend gradually to another ridge (4634m)
ahead and then steeply to the main Kargyak Valley just
below to reach **Lhakhang Sumdo**. There is a campsite and
a small shop-restaurant offering basic food (sometimes
the campsite is located a bit further down the main valley). Don't be surprised if you have to pay here for the
camping in Chumik Nakpo in addition to the normal fee
for camping at Lhakhang Sumdo.

STAGE 4
Lhakhang Sumdo to Kargyak

Start	Lhakhang Sumdo (4477m)
Finish	Kargyak (4135m)
Distance	15.5km
Time	5–6hrs
Altitude range	4135m (Kargyak) to 4477m (Lhakhang Sumdo)

Today's trek is a gradual descent on a clear trail along a wide and beautiful valley.

Alternatives
There are no alternatives for this stage.

Water supplies
The river is followed all day, so you don't need to carry much water.

Route
Cross the river of the main valley to its right bank (by a bridge). Follow the path downstream. The peak on your right with an impressive wall is Gonbo Rangjon; just beyond this mountain, 1½hrs from the camp, cross the river flowing in from the right. It is easy to ford.

Follow the path on the right bank of the river. (You will pass good places to camp every 15mins.) **Kargyak** is the first village in the valley. It is a picturesque place and the people living here are charming and hospitable; a few families offer food and homestay. Lobsang, the school caretaker, does really good food. If you prefer to sleep in your tent, the campsite (with a shop in high season) is 15mins before the village, below the path. Some groups stay here and continue the next day along the left bank of the river.

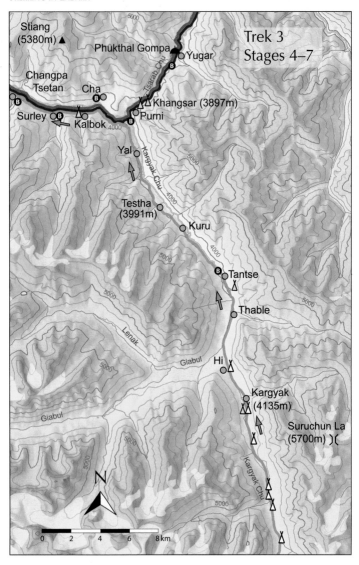

Stiang
(5380m) ▲

Phukthal Gompa

Yugar

Changpa
Tsetan

Cha

Khangsar (3897m)

Surley

Kalbok

Purni

Trek 3
Stages 4–7

Tsarab Chu

Yal

Kargyak Chu

Testha
(3991m)

Kuru

Tantse

Thable

Lenak

Giabul

Hi

Giabul

Kargyak
(4135m)

Suruchun La
(5700m)

Kargyak Chu

N

0   2   4   6   8km

EDUCATION IN KARGYAK

A school has been built in Kargyak recently, funded by a Czech organisation, to provide education locally for 80 children from the surrounding villages; most Zanskari children have to go to boarding school, and are away from home for 10 months or more every year. The building is a great example of how modern architecture can be designed to complement local culture. It is also environmentally friendly, heated by solar energy and so kept at a pleasant temperature all year long. The school is situated above the village, next to a small temple, and is worth a visit. If you want to stay there longer (volunteering is possible), ask at the school or contact Surya Civic Association (www.suryaschool.org).

STAGE 5
Kargyak to Testha

Start	Kargyak (4135m)
Finish	Testha (3991m)
Distance	16km
Time	5hrs
Altitude range	3991m (Testha) to 4135m (Kargyak)

This stage continues down the valley on a good path through villages with no major ascents.

Alternatives
- In a side valley east of Kargyak, above the village, is a trail to Sarchu (on the Manali–Leh road). It is probably a demanding route, as it crosses a very high pass, the Suruchun La, about 5700m. The author has not done this, so ask local people if you plan to leave Zanskar this way.
- If you want to spend more time in the area, try a two–three-day trek into the Giabul Valley. The river joins

the Kargyak Chu from the left (west), 1hr beyond the village. Although no path is marked on any maps, there must be one, as the locals take their animals there for grazing. The valley leads to the glaciers coming from the main ridge of the Great Himalayas. Ask the villagers of Kargyak about this route since it has not been tested by the author.

Water supplies
Early on water is available at least every 30mins. From Thable you need supplies to Tentse (1hr); at the bridge just beyond the latter take water for another hour. There is a stream halfway between Kuru and Testha.

Route
Follow the path down the valley. There is a good place for a camp 30mins beyond the village, just by the river, opposite **Hi**. Continue along the right bank, passing the confluence with a tributary coming from the left, the Giabul Chu (30mins). In another hour the village of **Thable**, situated on an alluvial fan, is reached.

The next village of **Tantse** is 1hr further on. There is a campsite and shop, and homestay is available. Beyond the village walk gradually down to the river, crossing it by the bridge (3985m). It takes a bit more than 1hr to **Kuru**

Typical Ladakhi houses have flat roofs, used for drying and storing hay, as well as different types of fuel for fires in winter

village (3991m) and then 30mins more to **Testha**. The path is precipitous in some places; watch out for falling stones. In Testha ask for a homestay (Tashi's house is one possibility) or ask the villagers to show you a good place to camp.

STAGE 6
Testha to Purni (and Phukthal Gompa)

Start	Testha (3991m)
Finish	Purni (3897m)
Distance	8.5km (+8km for Phukthal)
Time	3½hrs (+3½hrs for Phukthal)
Altitude range	3801m (bridge over the Kargyak River in Purni) to 3991m (Testha)

Although Phukthal is not on the main route to Padum, a visit to the spectacular *gompa* should not be missed. Leave your rucksack in Purni, and take a round trip to see it. From this stage until the end of the trek at Padum there are no places for wild camps; sleeping at paid campsites or in family houses are the only options.

Alternatives
If you don't want to visit the monastery, do not descend to the bridge about 30mins beyond Yal, but continue straight ahead, high above the valley floor, on the left bank of the Kargyak. Kalbok, a quiet, tiny settlement 1hr further, is a good place to spend the night. If you continue on, a good option is to visit Surley village above the main trail (see Stage 7 for details). Spending a night at Phukthal Gompa is a great experience.

Water supplies
The way down from Testha, as far as Padum, is mainly high above the valley and side-streams are rare. Usually water is only available in villages; see the details below.

Footpath above the Kargyak River

Route

There are two paths along the river about 1km beyond **Testha**. Both traverse the slope. Choose the lower one, descend to the valley floor and cross a side-stream. Beyond a side valley, continue on the left bank of the Kargyak River, ascending gradually to reach **Yal** village (3958m) in 1hr. It is much smaller than Testha and finding accommodation here may be difficult.

Straight ahead is towards Padum.

The valley forks after 30mins. ◄ For Purni and Phukthal turn right and cross the bridge over the Kargyak (3801m). Just beyond here the river meets the much bigger Tsarab Chu. From the bridge continue by a good path towards the N. It takes no more than 15mins to reach the main part of **Purni** village (3833m). There are two restaurant-shops and a big campsite, and it's usually busy. If you are running out of supplies, it's the best place for shopping. A quieter and nicer camp can be found at **Khangsar** (3897m) about 15mins further along, on the way towards Phukthal.

Pitch your tent (or ask the owner to store your bag), take your documents, money, camera and a cup and continue up the Tsarab Valley on the left bank for a little over 1hr. Cross a bridge (3838m) over the Tsarab, and soon come to some long *mani* walls and *chortens* (*stupas*). Clinging to a sheer slope, **Phukthal Gompa** (3922m) is an amazing place.

You will be welcome to attend most of the **ceremonies and monks' gatherings**. You can have meals with them (pay before you leave); Tibetan tea or sweet milk tea is usually served, but you need to take your own cup.

It takes 2hrs from Purni to Phukthal and a bit less for the return to your camp. It is also possible to stay at Phukthal (see Trek 2 Stage 9).

STAGE 7
Purni to Pepula

Start	Purni (3897m)
Finish	Pepula (3749m)
Distance	15km
Time	5½hrs
Altitude range	3749m (Pepula) to 3897m (Purni)

The waters of the Kargyak and Tsarab merge in Purni, then flow as the Lungnak ('dark gorge') from the confluence in a narrow valley almost as far as Padum. The trail, although very clear, is precipitous in many places, with numerous small ascents and descents.

Construction works on the Darcha–Padum road have progressed rapidly, so you will follow the road for at least some sections below Purni. In 2014 the road head on the Padum side was in the village of Enmu on the right bank of Tsarab (a bit east of Changpa Tsetan).

Alternatives
• There is also a route that follows the Tsarab Chu upstream to Stongde in the Zanskar Valley (see Trek 4). Note that this route is not accessible in June, July and early August because of high river levels; it is a demanding route.

- The old trail between Cha (the next village along the Lungnak Chu) and Dorzong on the right bank is said to be unsafe, particularly since road construction is in progress. Only take this option if locals confirm it is usable.
- Cars from Padum were going to Enmu (opposite Changspa Tsetan) in September 2014. You may try to arrange transportation and finish the trek there.

Water supplies

From Purni, take supplies for 2hrs. From Kalbok, you need water for just 30mins and then for 1½hrs from the side valley below Surley. Next, from the side valley beyond Changpa Tsetan take supplies for 1½hrs to cover the rest of the way to Pepula.

Route

*See map:
Trek 2 Stage 10.*

The alternative route on the right bank starts here.

Traverse of the Lungnak Valley below Purni

◄ Return to the bridge on the Kargyak Chu just below the main part of **Purni** (3833m). Cross it, turn right and walk downstream above the river. The path coming from Testha runs higher up and is joined in about 30mins. A further 20mins on, there is a bridge over the Tsarab and the village of **Cha** is on the opposite side. ◄ Continue on the left bank, passing a solitary house. Some 20mins later you will reach **Kalbok**, situated on a terrace above the valley floor. There is one house, a shop, a campsite and fields. Only one family lives in this beautiful place; you can either camp or stay at the house.

Next hike on and cross a bridge in a side valley about 30mins beyond Kalbok. Continue straight ahead along the main valley, below the terraces of **Surley** just beyond the bridge; a steep path climbs towards the village, where homestay is available. Continue straight ahead along the main valley. While high above the valley, you will reach a *chorten* and a junction with a new road (under construction in September 2014) leading to Surley (left) and a planned bridge on Tsarab Lingti (right). Continue straight on a traversing path. After 15mins you pass above the settlement of **Changpa Tsetan** (1hr from the last bridge).

Now the path turns left and descends steeply to another side valley. Take water for 1½hrs (to Pepula). ▸ Cross the bridge and climb steeply up the opposite valley's slope. Continue along the Lungnak. **Pepula** is at the next tributary stream. It is not a village, just a campsite and a small shop-restaurant.

Check out the local mill (a small building about 100m upstream along the right bank).

STAGE 8
Pepula to Mune

Start	Pepula (3749m)
Finish	Mune (3848m)
Distance	17km
Time	6hrs
Altitude range	3730m (bridge over the Raru Nala) to 3848m (Mune)

See Trek 2 Stage 11 for map and route description.

STAGE 9
Mune to Padum

Start	Mune (3848m)
Finish	Padum (3600m)
Distance	18km
Time	5½hrs
Altitude range	3600m (Padum) to 3848m (Mune)

See Trek 2 Stage 12 for map and route description.

4 ROUND SULTANLANGO

Trek 4 combines remote places, wild valleys and high passes with cultural highlights such as the impressively situated Phukthal Gompa (Stage 3)

INTRODUCTION

Start	Padum in the Zanskar Valley (3600m); alternatively Raru, Enmu, Shilla
Finish	Stongde, Zanskar (3800m); alternatively Padum
Distance	112km
Time	45½hrs (6 days)
Altitude range	3595m (Padum) to 5178m (Stongde La)

COMBINATIONS AND ALTERNATIVES

This route can be extended from the end point, Stongde, to Lamayuru or other places in Central Ladakh by joining Trek 5 (Padum to Lamayuru: the classic trek from Zanskar) or Trek 6 (Padum to Lamayuru via the Kanji La) in Pishu. When in Stongde, take a bus or walk to Zangla and then cross the bridge over the Zanskar River to Pishu. From Pishu continue as described in Treks 5 or 6. You could also join Trek 4 in Purni on the way

Bardan Gompa (Stage 1)

213

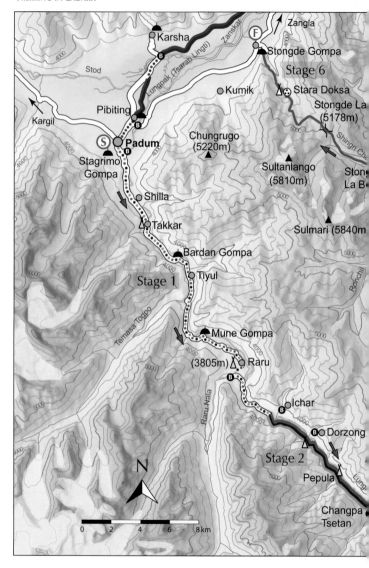

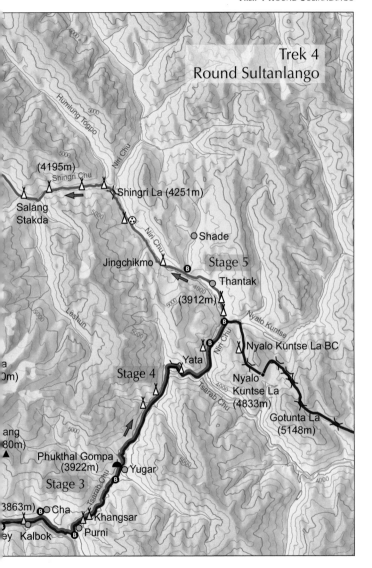

Trek 4
Round Sultanlango

Humlung Togpo

Niri Chu

(4195m)
Shingri Chu
Shingri La (4251m)
Salang
Stakda

○ Shade

Jingchikmo
Stage 5
○ Thantak
(3912m)

Leshun

Nyalo Kuntse

Nyalo Kuntse La BC

Yata
Niri Chu

Stage 4
Nyalo
Kuntse La
(4833m)

Tsarab Chu

Gotunta La
(5148m)

a
0m)

ang
80m)
▲

Phukthal Gompa
(3922m)
Yugar

Stage 3

Tsarab Chu

3863m) ○ Cha
ey Kalbok
Khangsar
Purni

from Darcha (see Trek 3). If you do so, Purni would be a good place to replenish your food supplies. Don't expect to buy everything you want, but you will certainly be able to secure your basic needs.

The Stongde La, crossed on this route, can also link to the Tsarab Chu trek (see Trek 2), but that would create a strenuous and exhausting expedition. If you choose this option it is strongly recommend that you allow extra time to visit the famous Phukthal Gompa. You can try to restock food supplies there or in Purni, have two nights' rest and then continue to Stongde.

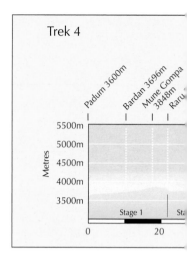

Trek 4

GENERAL INFORMATION

Chungrugo peak (over 5200m) stands 1600m higher than Padum, to the east of the town. Sultanlango peak, just 5km further east, is 600m higher. From

these peaks, a mountain ridge extends south-southeast to Cha peak, almost 6000m high. This range is surrounded by valleys: the Lungnak to the south-west and south, and the Tsarab to the

The mosque in Padum serves the Muslim community in the town, which settled here in the 19th century (Stage 1)

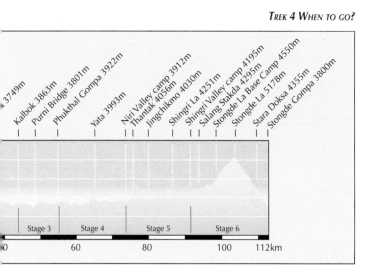

southeast. The Niri is to the east, the Shingri to the north and the Zanskar to the northeast. The Round Sultanlango trek follows these valleys, crossing from the Shingri to the Zanskar Valley by the Stongde La.

DIFFICULTY, SUPPLIES AND ACCOMMODATION

The trek consists of two parts. The route to Phukthal is rather easy on a busy path, and the section beside the road may be boring, at least between Padum and Raru (the road connecting Padum with Darcha is under construction). You will pass villages frequently and may find accommodation. The second part starts with a narrow, precipitous path traversing a sheer slope. There are dozens of serious river crossings, the Stongde La is both high

and steep, and the stages are long. There is neither accommodation nor any supplies available during this part of the trek, and you will meet almost no one. It is, however, a beautiful and wild route experienced by very few trekkers.

WHEN TO GO?

This is definitely an autumn or late summer route. In June and July the trail is not accessible, due to high water levels. If you want to go in August, ask the locals in Padum about the state of the rivers in general, and particularly in the area of Thantak (or Shade) and between Thantak and the Stongde La. Something else that might hinder progress (or prevent the trek) is rain or snowfall; at such times the route between Phukthal and Thantak

217

The approach to the Stongde La (Stage 6)

can become very dangerous – the tiny traverses can be very slippery, or even washed away. In late September and October crossing the river would be really painful as the water is freezing cold. Camping in late autumn would be cold too. The author trekked this route in mid-September.

ACCESS

For details on accessing the start point, please refer to the Padum section in the Introduction. The Padum–Zangla bus runs six times a week, via Stongde. The bus leaves Zangla early in the morning, arrives at Stongde about 9am and goes on to Padum.

Start	Padum (3600m)
Finish	Raru (3805m)
Distance	22km
Time	6hrs
Altitude range	3600m (Padum) to 3848m (Mune)

This is a rather boring stage – mainly along the asphalt road to Raru – which may be very hot in summer. Cover your head! There are two interesting monasteries on the way: Bardan and Mune. It's possible to avoid walking on the road – see alternatives below.

Alternatives

- You may skip this and a big part of the next stage by taking a jeep (finding a car to be shared with other people might also be possible). In September 2014 it was possible to go by car as far as Enmu (a village opposite Changpa Tsetan, see Stage 2 for details) and the road may soon go right up to Purni.
- There is an alternative, scenic route on the opposite (right) side of Lungnak (Tsarab Lingti). Go by car to Shilla village, where the road ends. Start the trek by following a clear traverse high above the river, up-valley. It takes about 2hrs to reach Pibcha village, which is opposite Tiyul (Tiengul). There is a fantastic view of Bardan Gompa on the way. Cross the bridge in Pibcha to join the main route.

Water supplies

From Padum you need water for 2hrs; from Takkar take supplies sufficient for 1hr, then from Bardan for another 1hr. In Mune refill your bottles to cover the last 1hr.

Route

From **Padum** the route follows the road to Raru, on the true left bank of the Lungnak River (Tsarab Chu). From the main junction in Padum head towards the upper part of Padum (S) by the main road, which passes the mosque and turns left opposite the Khar Ging Guesthouse, about 150m beyond the mosque. Follow the road that goes around the hill and then upvalley, just above the river. The first settlement on this side of the river is **Takkar** (3643m), about 6km from Padum, where there is one house and a campsite; refill your water bottles.

Bardan Gompa, which is worth visiting, is 2½–3hrs' walk from Padum. Walking on for 30mins, you will pass the tiny settlement of **Tiyul** (Tiengul). Pibcha village is on the opposite side of the river. (If you were walking from Shilla (see alternatives above) you would join the main route here.) It is 6km (1½hrs) further to Mune. **Mune Gompa** (3848m) is left of the road, high above the river. A hotel belonging to the monastery sits just by the road on your right; prices are similar to those in Padum and food is available. Staying here enables you to attend a morning *puja* (prayers) at the monastery.

Follow the road for about 1.5km. A path to the right towards a small hill is a shortcut to Raru. You can either follow it or continue by the road. If on the path, you will reach a small lake where there is a campsite; otherwise walk straight down to **Raru** village. There are a few shop-restaurants and homestay accommodation; ask at one of the shops.

STAGE 2
Raru to Kalbok

Start	Raru (3805m)
Finish	Kalbok (3863m)
Distance	22km
Time	8½hrs
Altitude range	3730m (bridge over Raru Nala) to 3879m (path junction beyond Changpa Tsetan)

The left bank of the Tsarab Chu is followed all day. There are repeated ascents and descents, first by the road then on a dirt path.

Alternatives

- Between Raru and Ichar you could follow the opposite side of the valley. This option will save you from walking on the road, but is much more demanding as well as narrow and precipitous in places. From the Raru Nala Valley, turn left downstream along the left bank and cross the bridge over the Lungnak. Then climb steeply and walk south and then southeast, high above the river. You will reach the high fields of Ichar and descend to a side-valley just beyond them. From there go up to the main part of Ichar and then down towards the road and the bridge on Lungnak. It takes about 3–3½hrs to cover the way from Raru. The road continues along the true right bank of Lungnak from Ichar to Enmu – cross to the left bank and follow the main route as described below.

The solitary house at Kalbok is located on a terrace high above the Lungnak River

- Although not checked by the author, there is also a path from Ichar to the Shingri Valley (a substantial shortcut), crossing a pass high above Ichar. Ask the locals for details.

Water supplies
The road and the path in the latter part of the stage keep high above the valley floor and side-streams are rare. Usually water is only available in the villages.

Route
Leave the road. Take the path passing to the left of the school in **Raru**, heading to a ridge about 500m away towards the S, left of a hill with a *chorten*. The Raru Nala, fed by the glaciers of the Great Himalayas, is in a deep valley on the opposite side of the ridge, and is a tributary of the Lungnak. Cross the ridge to that valley and then go right towards the road bridge and cross it. Take enough water for 2hrs. Follow the road down the Raru Nala and then up the Lungnak River.

Around 1½hrs from Raru, you will arrive at the road bridge over the Tsarab. The road continues for a few more kilometres on the other side of the valley. Follow a path on the true left bank (walking upstream the river will be on your left). There is another bridge 30mins further on; the village on the opposite side is **Ichar**. ◀ Follow the left bank of the Lungnak to come to another bridge in 30mins; **Dorzong** village is on the opposite side, but do not cross the river. At the stream just beyond here, get water supplies for 1½hrs. You will be walking high above the valley floor and there are occasional small side-streams, but they may have dried up late in the season.

Pepula is 4km beyond the Dorzong bridge. It is only open in the high season for camping or accommodation at a small hut. Refill your water bottles and continue on the clear path, walking high above the river for some time, before descending into the deep ravine of a side valley. ◀

Cross the small bridge on the stream and climb the steep slope opposite. High above the Lungnak again, you

Above this settlement is a high pass that the locals use to cross to the Shingri Valley.

Check out the local watermill (the small building with a water channel on the right bank of the side-stream).

will pass above the small settlement of **Changpa Tsetan**. In 15mins reach a *chorten* and a junction with a new road (under construction in September 2014) leading to Surley (right) and a planned bridge on Tsarab Lingti (left). Continue straight, slightly down on a traversing path. (If you reached Enmu by car or walking on the road from Ichar, you can join the main route here by crossing the bridge from Enmu.) You will reach a small side-stream 45mins further on. ▶ Cross it and follow the path straight on for 30mins to **Kalbok**, ascending gradually. The settlement is situated high above the valley on a series of terraces. It's a beautiful place with a campsite and well-organised shop. You may either stay at the family house or camp.

You will pass a steep descent on your right just before the side valley; this path leads to Surley village.

STAGE 3
Kalbok to Phukthal

Start	Kalbok (3863m)
Finish	Phukthal (3922m)
Distance	11.5km
Time	3½hrs
Altitude range	3801m (bridge over the Kargyak Chu in Purni) to 3922m (Phukthal)

This is a short stage. You leave the main route that leads towards the Shinkul La and Darcha along the Kargyak River, and continue along the Tsarab Valley that turns towards the northeast. Phukthal Gompa, at the end of the stage, is perhaps the most extraordinary place in Ladakh!

Alternatives
- For an interesting and rarely chosen route, cross the bridge to Cha village and then go to Phukthal along the right side of the Tsarab Valley, high above the river. The author checked this option in September 2013. It is precipitous and narrow, and might be challenging for some trekkers, but it's probably no

more difficult than the route towards the Stongde pass ahead. You need to climb above the Cha village where the traverse starts. It takes about 2hrs to cover the distance between the main part of Cha and the guesthouse below Phukthal (plus the time needed to reach Cha from the bridge).

- If you continue straight (upstream) from the confluence of the Tsarab and Kargyak rivers, you eventually reach Darcha on the Manali–Leh road. It is a classic, popular and relatively easy route (the reverse of Trek 3).

Water supplies
In Kalbok, stock up with sufficient water for 1½hrs, then do the same in Purni.

Route
Follow the clear path up the Lungnak Valley. You descend steeply to a deep side valley just beyond **Kalbok** and then ascend gradually. Pass a single house 20mins after leaving Kalbok and a bridge on Lungnak just beyond it. **Cha** village is on the opposite side. Continue on the true left bank. The path forks about 15mins further on; take the left branch. Descend gradually, passing the confluence of the Tsarab and Kargyak rivers to reach a bridge over the latter. Cross over; it takes no more than 15mins to

Purni village on the Tsarab Chu, just above its confluence with the Kargyak River

reach the main part of **Purni** village (3833m). There are two houses, a big campsite and a shop-restaurant. ▶

Continue upvalley, passing above the campsite to another house and a campsite in 15mins. This quieter spot is **Khangsar** (3897m). Food is available here and it is a good place for both a stay or a lunchbreak.

From Khangsar, continue on the left bank up the Tsarab Valley on a frequently used path for a little more than 1hr. You come to a bridge on the Tsarab. Cross it. Just beyond it, a long row of *mani* walls and *chortens* begin. **Phukthal Gompa** dazzles in front of you. The new monastery guesthouse is just beyond the bridge, but for a better glimpse of the life of Phukthal, stay at the guest dormitory of the *gompa*. It takes 2hrs to get here from Purni.

Most of the groups taking the Darcha to Padum (or reverse) route stop here for the night and go for a side-trip to Phukthal.

STAGE 4
Phukthal to Niri Valley camp

Start	Phukthal (3922m)
Finish	Niri Valley camp (3912m)
Distance	18.5km
Time	8½hrs
Altitude range	3822m (camp in Tsarab Chu Valley) to 4103m (pass above Yata)

Precipitous paths make this stage very hard. In some places the path is just 30cm wide and in many places it traverses sheer slopes high above the valley floor. Take extreme care. At times parts of the path may be damaged, and you will need to search for another route. However, this trail is quite popular among the locals, as this is the still best and easiest route to Thantak and Shade villages. Normally when the track is damaged, locals will set up other options (see Introduction); look out for signs indicating an alternative path. Do not attempt this route just after serious rain or snowfall! The highlight of the day is the valley itself, especially in autumn when the Tsarab Chu becomes incredibly blue.

The Tsarab Chu and the fields of Yugar village as seen from Phukthal

Alternatives

If you are in need of a rest, or want to spend more time in Phukthal, you can divide the stage into two shorter parts. The best place to camp is in Yata, but other options are possible.

Water supplies

You will be walking high above the valley floor. Water is available from side-streams; see details below.

Route

There is a footpath – or a corridor – in the monastery that leads towards the NE, upstream, high above the Tsarab Chu. Follow it past all the monastery buildings and then climb to a ridge with a *chorten* and prayer flags. Follow the well-defined path with beautiful views; it continues to the left towards a deep side-ravine. (There is a stream where you need to collect sufficient water for 2hrs.) On the other side of the ravine, follow a high traverse. About 45mins from **Phukthal**, the trail forks. The left branch climbs gradually to a ridge and the other continues the traverse: it is fine to take either trail as the two pathways meet further, but it is not necessary to ascend here.

Going straight on, there soon is a steep descent, followed by a traverse 20–30m above the valley a few minutes later. Head down almost to the river, then below rock outcrops for a few minutes before heading on again above the valley floor. You will soon descend once more, then traverse above the river on a clear path. Some 2hrs from Phukthal, there is a green terrace (3882m) – a camping place, as water is available from a stream close by. Continue along the traverse to another side-stream in 20mins (another camping spot).

Almost 4hrs from Phukthal, at a sharp right turn of the valley (E), there is a deep ravine with a small stream on your left. Cross it to reach a fork in the path. Avoid the indistinct and very dangerous traverse straight ahead, and follow a clearer trail that climbs the slope to the left. ▶ When you reach the top of the steep slope, follow the clear path to the right, slightly up, until you get to a pass (4103m) with some prayer flags. It takes 30mins to get here from the ravine.

The local people take the steep ascent as well!

It's a steep descent from the pass towards the valley floor. A series of small camping-terraces and a tiny spring mark the camping place known as **Yata** (3993m). It takes 4½hrs to get here from Phukthal, with a further 3½–4hrs to go. The most difficult challenges are still to come!

Continue downwards, then to the left, to a path roughly 30–40m above the river. Pass a small cave just above the path. Be careful, as the way is very narrow in some places. If you can spot any fresh footprints follow them. About 30mins from Yata you will need to negotiate an old, damaged section of the path: descend steeply and then ascend to pick up the traverse again. There may be more, similar detours. Just over 1hr after leaving Yata the confluence of the Tsarab and Niri rivers is reached. The Tsarab flows from the south-southeast, the Niri from the north-northeast. Follow the Niri Chu upstream, continuing the traverse high above the valley floor and passing a rope bridge over the river: luckily you don't need to cross it! ▶

The bridge marks the beginning of a very demanding and dangerous stage along the Tsarab Chu that finishes on the Manali–Leh road near Sarchu (see Trek 2).

Continue the traverse of the valley's true right slope (with the river on your right as you face ahead). Be careful, as the path is still narrow and precipitous. There is a series of dry terraces high above the valley floor, about 2hrs from Yata. These are good places for camping; from one a quite clear path leads to the river, enabling you to take water. Less than 15mins after the last terrace, while on the traverse again, you will see a solid stone and wood bridge. Although the traverse on the right bank continues, cross to the opposite side. The path traversing the true left slope is more comfortable and safe; additionally, crossing here will save you from fording the river near Thantak.

From the bridge, walk to the right (downstream) first, then climb the slope and continue upstream by a traverse about 20m above the river. It is 2km (45mins) to a river flowing in a ravine from your right (E): this is the Nyalo Kuntse Valley. ◄

The trail from Sarchu and the Morang La via the Nyalo Kuntse and Gotunta passes join here (see Trek 2).

Cross the small bridge on the Nyalo Kuntse, climb the valley's opposite bank and continue up the Niri Chu. You will descend to the valley floor a few minutes further on. There are willow bushes by the river and a perfect place to make camp for many tents. There is another, smaller, place, 15mins later, around 20m above

The elaborately laid bridge over the Niri Chu

the river. The sun warms the second one earlier in the morning, but the spring there may be dry. (It is also possible to find home accommodation in Thantak, a little under 1hr further on; but don't expect anybody to speak English there.)

STAGE 5
Niri Valley camp to Shingri Valley camp

Start	Niri Valley camp (3912m)
Finish	Shingri Valley camp (4195m)
Distance	18km
Time	9hrs
Altitude range	3912m (Niri Valley) to 4251m (Shingri La)

This is a long stage with gradual ascents; in some places the path is precipitous. There are many river crossings towards the end of the day that are never easy. Although brown bears are extremely rare in Ladakh (maybe not more than 100 individuals), sightings are possible: the author has seen fresh prints. These animals stay at high altitude, in fairly open valleys near the snowline in summer, but in autumn descend to lower elevations to feed. The upper part of Zanskar is one of the areas where bears are found, and they may be aggressive. It is a good idea to make a lot of noise while walking through the willow bushes on the valley floors.

Alternatives
- This and Stage 6 can be split into two. Sleep on the terrace between Jingchikmo and the Shingri La on the first night, and then at the Stongde La Base Camp on the second. Cross the pass on the third day.
- If you want to spend an extra day in this area, take a side-trip to a lake up the Nyalo Kuntse Valley about 3hrs' walk from the camp. Return to the last bridge crossed on Stage 4, and follow the side valley upstream.

- If you want go to Shade village (up a side valley beyond Thantak), you could continue over a few passes to Zangla Sumdo and eventually finish in Zangla, Zanskar Valley (unchecked by the author). Ask in Thantak or Shade for details.

Water supplies

The route runs high above the valley floor for the major part of the day and side-streams are rare, so you need to carry water. From the camp or a place just beyond it, take sufficient water for 2½hrs (see also below).

Route

The buildings that can be seen further up the valley are **Thantak** village – two houses and a small monastery – linked to the Phukthal Gompa. Head towards these along a terrace on the valley floor, and then ascend to a small green terrace (an alternative camping place for Stage 4). Continue traversing the slope 20m above the river. If you don't want to visit Thantak pass below it, continuing along the main valley that turns gradually left towards the WNW and distinctly narrows. A clear path continues high above the river.

Birch shrubs as seen from the Shingri La on a late autumn afternoon

Willow shrubs in the Shingri Valley: protection against the cold wind when camping

A deep side-ravine on your right is reached 1½hrs after leaving camp. ▶ Cross the ravine on the bridge (4015m) and follow the main valley, upstream, again above its floor. The path is well defined and the traverse much easier than the one negotiated on Stage 4. Half an hour from the ravine, descend to the riverbank (about 3990m). The valley is wider here with willow bushes along the stream. Ford to the true right bank. After the crossing do not ascend a steep path but continue upstream on a reasonably clear trail just along the river on its true right bank (with the river on your right, facing upstream). A few minutes later there is a small, very steep, green valley on your left.

Ascend here, about 3hrs from the previous night's camp, to **Jingchikmo** (a camp spot at 4030m). Water is in the next side valley, around 100m further on. Continue along the main valley, towards the NW, high above the river. Cross a 30m-deep ravine; beyond it the slopes get sheer again and the traverse precipitous. About 5hrs from the previous night's camp you will reach quite a large, green terrace high above the river, with a small stream flowing through it. There is a simple shepherds' shelter.

The path to Shade leads up this valley.

This is a good place for several tents; stay here if you want to divide the stage.

Further on, the path ascends gradually, traversing the slope and cutting across a number of small, steep, dry side valleys and small ridges. The **Shingri La** (4251m) – a relatively low pass – is at the end of the ascent (6hrs from camp). On the other side of the Shingri La, to the right (northeast) is the confluence of the Niri Chu (flowing from the north) and the Shingri Chu (from the west). A third river, flowing from the northwest and clearly visible from the pass, is the Humlung Togpo. The onward route follows the Shingri Chu upstream (W) en route for Stongde La Base Camp – you will have to cross the river many times.

Descend gradually to the valley floor on a clear path. There is a place to camp just by the riverbank (4100m), but it is not ideal, being cold in the morning. You also have to start the day by fording the stream: not a good idea! Continue for at least 1hr, upstream along the valley floor. The following hour brings at least 10 unavoidable river crossings.

> It is probably **impossible to cross the river** on this section in spring and early summer. Even in mid-September the water was above the author's knees, and the crossings were quite difficult; in autumn too a build-up of algae makes the stones on the bed very slippery. Take care!

After 1hr in the valley floor, nearly 2km from the first river crossing, look for a path ascending the slope on your left (S). Climb 20m or so to a dry terrace (4123m): a perfect place for a camp. However, if you want to cross the pass on the next day, it is recommended that you go on. Continue along the traverse of the true right slope of the valley (with the river on your right) for 30mins and then descend to the river again. Try to keep on the true right bank (on your left) when possible; you will still have to cross the stream a few times. In another 30mins you will come to a place on the true right bank where the path leaves the terrace and starts another traverse of the right slope. The valley turns slightly left beyond this place. Although the ground is stony here, make camp; willow bushes will protect you against the cold wind.

STAGE 6
Shingri Valley camp to Stongde Gompa

Start	Shingri Valley camp (4195m)
Finish	Stongde Gompa (3800m)
Distance	21km
Time	10hrs
Altitude range	3800m (Stongde Gompa) to 5178m (Stongde La)

This is a very hard and long stage, 12km in distance and with 1000m altitude difference between the Shingri Valley camp and the Stongde La! The descent to the monastery is also long.

Alternatives
It is a good idea to divide this stage. The best place to spend the night is Stongde La Base Camp, reached in 4hrs.

The Stongde La is marked by prayer flags and a cairn

Water supplies

Rivers are followed for the first part of the day, so you don't need to carry much water. From Stongde La Base Camp you need water for 3hrs.

Route

From the camp, start traversing the good trail on the true right slope of the valley (with the river on your right as you walk upstream). The valley turns slightly to the left. Walk above the river for about 15mins and then return to the valley floor. There is a side valley and a stream on your left, flowing from the SE (4247m). Cross it. Continue up the main valley for no more than 200m to a fork where two big streams join, just to the right. The Shingri Chu, the one you have to follow, is further to the right, and flows from the west. ◄

The valley ahead, continuing towards the south-southwest, does not lead to the Stongde La. According to maps, the Leshun flows from the glaciers of Cha peak.

Watch out here – it is easy to miss the correct path! There are trails leading in all directions, as local people come to these valleys to collect wood and to graze their animals. Please note that the place might be incorrectly drawn on some maps. Cross the Leshun Chu first, then enter the Shingri Valley (W). Cross the second river. There is a clear path among the willow bushes towards the W on the true left bank of Shingri Chu, upstream. After 15mins you will have to ford the river again, to its true right bank. There is a good place to camp a few minutes further on, then you will reach another fork in the valley where the Ronchil Chu (on your left), comes in from the SW. ◄ This is **Salang Stakda** (4295m).

The path along it probably leads to Ichar in the Lungnak Valley.

Continue along the Shingri Chu (on your right, flowing from the northwest). The path is on the true right bank; follow it for about 1hr, then take water and ascend to the ridge on your left (4376m). The trail is clear. The main valley now turns left (W), and a tributary stream in a deep ravine can be seen from the ridge on the NNW side. Follow the main valley along a gradually ascending traverse. Reach the valley bottom 1hr from the ridge. There is a solid shelter and place for one tent here; there is more room to camp on a terrace further upstream, on the true left bank above the river. This is **Stongde La Base**

Camp (4550m), 4hrs from the previous camp. Sleep here if you want to divide the stage.

It is a tiring climb of 3hrs to the pass and at least another 2½hrs of descent to Stongde Gompa. Take sufficient water for 3hrs, cross the river and follow the clear path traversing the true left slope of the valley. It is a long but not very steep climb. Within 2hrs you will reach a place where a small side valley on your right can be seen; head towards this. The pass is to the NW, 2km away. As the path gets steeper, in 40mins you will arrive at a small stream in the valley (5111m). Take water for 2hrs. Cross the stream and gradually climb the opposite slope of the valley. The **Stongde La** is just ahead, 400m further on. The pass is at 5178m (7½hrs from the camp), and well marked with prayer flags and a big cairn. ▶

The trail is clear from the pass. Drop steeply at first, then continue on a long traverse of the left slope. Stongde Gompa is on the ridge at the end of the valley, and can be seen from the path after the pass; the author took 2½hrs to reach it. It is possible to camp on the way – there is a terrace with a few shepherds' shelters about 1½hrs from the pass called **Stara Doksa** (4355m). There

The Zanskar Valley and the Great Himalayas as seen from Stongde Gompa

Sultanlango Peak is towards the southwest, 3.5km away; from the pass and on the descent there are splendid views of the Great Himalayas to the west, and the Zanskar Valley ahead.

Chortens of Stongde Gompa

should be water in a small spring on the right of the path. Beyond Stara Doksa, continue the traverse of the left slope until you get to the monastery where you can ask for accommodation. There are incredibly beautiful views of Stongde village, the Zanskar Valley and the Himalayas from the monastery.

> **Buses and shared jeeps** leave Stongde village for Padum at about 9am and it takes about 20mins to walk down from the monastery to the road. Consult the locals for details.

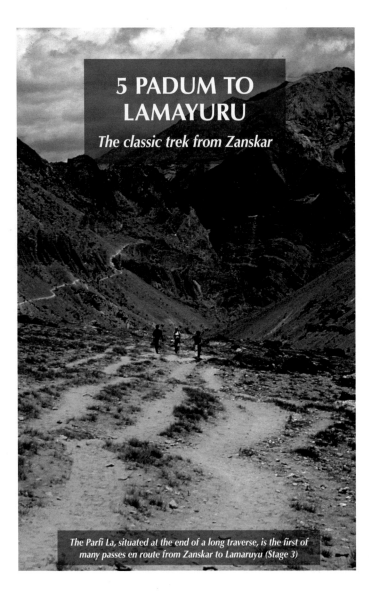

5 PADUM TO LAMAYURU

The classic trek from Zanskar

The Parfi La, situated at the end of a long traverse, is the first of many passes en route from Zanskar to Lamaruyu (Stage 3)

237

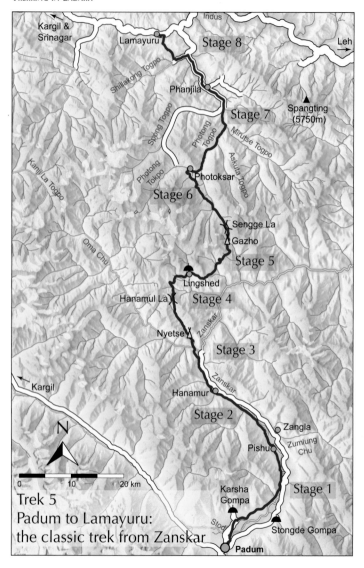

Trek 5
Padum to Lamayuru:
the classic trek from Zanskar

INTRODUCTION

Start	Padum in the Zanskar Valley (3600m); alternatively Zangla, Pishu
Finish	Lamayuru, on the Kargil–Leh road (3491m); alternatively Phanjila, Wanla, Nurla, Mangyu or Alchi
Distance	148km
Time	50hrs (8 days)
Altitude range	3183m (bridge in Wanla) to 4954m (Sengge La)

COMBINATIONS AND ALTERNATIVES

Trek 5 can be used as an extension of Trek 3 (Darcha to Padum: the classic trek to Zanskar) after a few days' rest in Padum. These two trails combined make a classic and very popular route in Ladakh.

Another option is to follow the right bank of the Zanskar River. From Zangla, go down the valley by the road that is planned to link Zanskar and the Indus Valley until you get to Honya village. Cross the Namtse La and the Takti La to Nyeraks and then cross the bridge over the Zanskar to Yulchung to join the main route to Lamayuru (see Stage 5); not checked by the author.

From Lingshed join the Kanji La route via the Barmi La and then follow that route to Lamayuru, or go to Rangdum on the Padum–Kargil road,

The approach to the Hanamul La is long, gradual and laborious; the descent is steep and dramatic (Stage 4)

just at the foot of Nun Kun peaks (see Trek 6 Stage 4). Be aware that this trail is only possible in late summer and autumn.

From Photoksar cross the Sirsir La then the Nyigutse La and join Trek 6 in the valley of the Shillakong Togpo. As there are many river crossings along the way, don't take this route in spring or early summer.

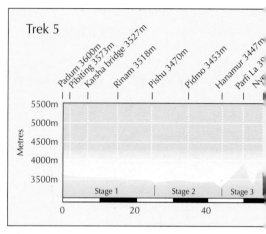

Regardless of the season, another option is to finish Trek 5 by the most common route – from Photoksar to Phanjila via the Sirsir La and Hanupata (a road has been built here, and it is possible to find transport in Photoksar).

While in Phanjila, ascend to the village of Ursi. Cross the Tar La to Tar village and then either descend to Nurla on the Leh–Kargil road or continue over the Hibti and Mangyu passes to Mangyu village and Alchi (see Trek 7).

The descent from the Parfi La to the Oma Valley (Stage 3)

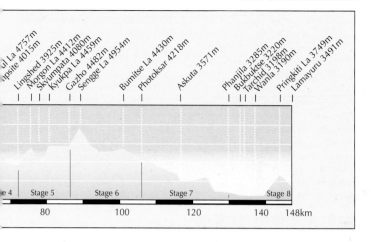

It is probably possible to finish the trek between Lingshed and Photoksar, as the road connecting these two villages with Phanjila further on, as well as Khaltse on the main Srinagar-Leh road, may now be finished. However, do not expect frequent transport here. If you want to finish here, pre-arrange to be picked up before setting off for the trek.

You may also finish in Phanjila, which has a bus connection to Leh.

GENERAL INFORMATION

This is a moderate route. Basic food is available at the end of every stage in season and it is possible to rely on homestay in any village on the way (although you will not stay in a village every night). This is also a very popular route; you will meet other trekkers every day and the trail is

clear. There are no important river crossings, but there are two major passes (the Hanamul La: 4757m and the Sengge La: 4954m) as well as a number of smaller crossings. Some stages are long, and the trek starts with a long, hot, dusty walk along the Zanskar Valley. This is a good route on which to start trekking independently if you are not an experienced hiker. It is interesting and the trail is diverse. Lingshed is, no doubt, one of the most beautiful villages in Ladakh.

The road has extended on this route in recent years. In 2014 the road head was somewhere between Lingshed and Sengge La; soon it will be possible to drive all the way from Lingshed to Leh, making the trek significantly shorter.

The route is very popular with organised groups. In the high season,

241

dust can be a problem. Furthermore, many tourists on this trek seem to be unaware of local customs and sensitivities. Don't be surprised to see trekkers in shorts, or to hear 'One sweet!' from villagers in answer to the customary greeting, 'Julley!' Please don't encourage the local people to beg for sweet, pens, money and the like. Help the local community by employing them for trekking as well as by eating in local restaurants and buying local products.

DIFFICULTY, SUPPLIES AND ACCOMMODATION

There are organised campsites on the way, where you will have to pay a fee. It is rarely possible to wild camp. There are number of small shops and restaurants where you can rest and eat during the day. However, most of these – as well as most campsites – are only open in the high season (mid-July to the end of August). Outside this period, you will need to carry more food.

Homestay accommodation costs per person roughly the price of pitching a tent at a campsite. The price for food and accommodation is usually Rs250–400 per person. You will get a generous evening meal and breakfast; in some places, a 'packed' lunch is included. If you need ponies or horses, it should be not be difficult to arrange them in Zanskar in the high season. Check at campsites in Padum.

WHEN TO GO?

This route is possible from June to October; the high season is July and August. Trekking in June, early July or in September will be quieter. The author trekked in mid-July 2009 and late August 2004 and neither was a good time. Because there are no important river crossings (there are bridges over every major river or stream, including a series of bridges along the Askuta Way), the passes are relatively low, and there are villages en route offering accommodation, it would appear to be a good trail to do in autumn. A few trekkers do it late in the season; while trekking between Padum and the camping place in the Oma Valley in late September, the author met just one small group.

ACCESS

For details on accessing Padum see the Introduction. If you want to skip Stage 1, take a bus to Zangla; there is a Padum–Zangla bus connection six times a week (see below).

Lamayuru, at the end of the route, is on the main Kargil–Leh road. Usually buses pass the village in each direction daily throughout the season; if you leave in the morning, you will reach Leh or Kargil on the same day. However, the road is sometimes closed, in which case the best option is to descend to Khalatse. Build a spare day into your schedule in case you can't leave Lamayuru exactly when you wanted to.

STAGE 1
Padum to Pishu

Start	Padum (3600m)
Finish	Pishu (3435m)
Distance	25.5km
Time	7hrs
Altitude range	3435m (camp in Pishu) to 3600m (Padum)

Most of Stage 1 follows an asphalt road between Padum and Karsha that continues unpaved (and rarely frequented) as far as Pishu. It is a long stage, but there are no major ascents or descents as the trail is relatively flat. Although usually windy, it is hot even in late September, so protect your head and face from the sun.

Alternatives
The monastery in nearby Karsha village is definitely worth visiting; take a day trip from Padum to Karsha before starting this trek. However, it's also possible to visit the *gompa*

Zanskar Valley and the peaks of the Great Himalayas as seen from Karsha

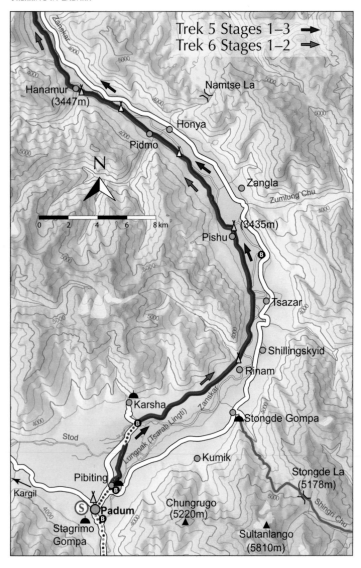

Trek 5 Stages 1–3 ➡
Trek 6 Stages 1–2 ➡

Hanamur
(3447m)

Namtse La

Honya

Pidmo

N

0 2 4 6 8 km

Zangla

Zumlung Chu

(3435m)

Pishu

Tsazar

Shillingskyid

Rinam

Karsha

Stongde Gompa

Lungnak (Tsarab Lingti)

Zanskar

Stod

Kumik

Stongde La
(5178m)

Pibiting

Shingri Chu

Kargil

Chungrugo
(5220m)

Padum

Stagrimo
Gompa

Sultanlango
(5810m)

en route; if you do that, stay in Karsha overnight (there is a campsite and homestay) or continue down the Zanskar Valley to Rinam or Pishu. To skip the stage, take a bus or shared jeep to Zangla and cross the footbridge over the Zanskar River to Pishu (ask the driver to drop you at the bridge). It's also possible to hire a jeep to take you directly to Pishu.

Water supplies

From Pibiting take sufficient water for the trek to Rinam and then for Pishu. In autumn (unless you want to visit the main part of Rinam village, 500m off from the trail), take water from Pibiting for all the way to Pishu. The water of the Stod and Zanskar rivers is not suitable for drinking without filtration (see Stage 2).

Route

From the main crossroads in **Padum** head towards Pibiting, 2km away to the NE. The monastery can be clearly seen on a hill in the middle of the 6km-wide valley. Either follow the road or take a shortcut path that starts 200m from the crossroads and leads through the fields, left of the road.

In **Pibiting** leave the asphalt road and turn right on to a dirt one, heading towards a big school down in the valley (Landom School). From a steep slope before the school, Karsha Gompa can be clearly seen in the distance about 6km ahead, (N). The bridge you need to cross is below it; head towards it on a path through the fields. You join the asphalt road after 3.5km; follow it to the bridge (3527m), 1½hrs from Padum. ▶

Leave the road just beyond the bridge and go to the right, first by a path and then by a dirt road. It takes 2hrs to reach **Rinam**, where there is a campsite and small shop (3520m). Take water for 2hrs. Follow the road until you get to **Pishu** village (3470m), a picturesque place with a few houses offering homestay accommodation. The campsite is a bit beyond the village, just below it, on a vast beautiful terrace (3435m). As the ground is a bit damp, you may feel slightly cold if camping here in autumn.

If you want to visit Karsha, follow the road to the village.

STAGE 2
Pishu to Hanamur

Start	Pishu (3435m)
Finish	Hanamur (3447m)
Distance	16km
Time	5½hrs
Altitude range	3425m (camp between Pidmo and Hanamur) to 3495m (high terrace just beyond Pishu)

Continue down the Zanskar Valley on the left bank. Compared to the following stages, Stage 2 is rather relaxing on a good trail, though is usually hot. The road will eventually be extended beyond Pishu.

Water supplies
There are no good water sources between Pishu and Pidmo (3hrs), or between Pidmo and Hanamur (2hrs), so carry sufficient supplies between the villages.

Route

Chortens at Pidmo village in the Zanskar Valley

Beyond **Pishu**, ascend to a high terrace; follow it then descend to the valley floor. (It is possible to camp, just near the path, 2hrs from Pishu at 3453m.) Water is

available from the Zanskar River. It is not seriously polluted but it does carry a lot of rock flour and certainly requires filtration.

Pidmo village is reached in just under 3hrs, just beyond a deep side ravine. There is a shop-restaurant and home accommodation here. In the village, do not take the clear trail ascending to the slope on the left, but go straight through the fields. Then descend to the terraces of the valley floor, following the Zanskar River. It is possible to camp on a terrace, near a simple shepherds' shelter (3425m) beyond the village. In early summer a tiny spring exists here.

It takes just under 2hrs to cover the distance from Pidmo to **Hanamur**. There are two houses and two big campsites in the village. One of the houses is marked as a guesthouse and has a room for rent; food is available. There is no place to camp between Hanamur and the Oma Valley on the other side of the Parfi La so do not go further unless you are capable of walking for another 5hrs.

STAGE 3
Hanamur to Nyetse

Start	Hannamur (3447m)
Finish	Nyetse (3744m)
Distance	14km
Time	8½hrs
Altitude range	3302m (side valley beyond Hanamur) to 3921m (Parfi La)

Although quite short this stage is not easy; there are two steep ascents and one very steep descent. The path is precipitous in some places; it is usually hot on the way, and there are no water sources. Nyetse is the best place to start the Hanamul La climb on Stage 4. It is not a big campsite; if there are large groups going in the same direction as you, an early start is recommended to find a camping spot. If there is no room at Nyetse, refer to Stage 4 for camping options further on.

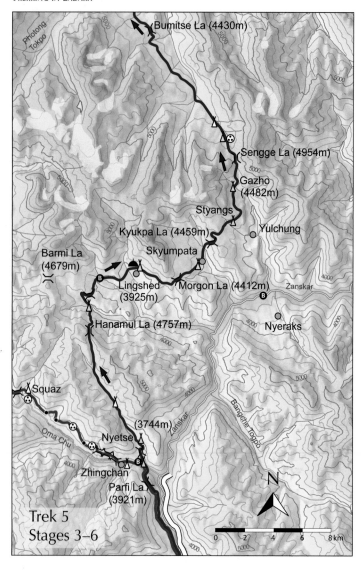

Bumitse La (4430m)

Sengge La (4954m)

Gazho (4482m)

Styangs

Yulchung

Kyukpa La (4459m)

Barmi La (4679m)

Skyumpata

Lingshed (3925m)

Morgon La (4412m)

Zanskar

Hanamul La (4757m)

Nyeraks

Squaz

(3744m)

Oma Chu

Nyetse

Zanskar

Bangchu Togpo

Zhingchan

Parfi La (3921m)

N

Trek 5
Stages 3–6

0   2   4   6   8 km

Alternatives

The route splits at the bridge over the Oma River. The classic route to Lamayuru goes via the Nyetse and Hanamul La; the way via the Kanji La leads upstream, along the Oma Chu (see Trek 6). An interesting option is to combine these two routes. Walk along the Oma Chu up to Lingshed Sumdo and then turn into the side valley towards your right (east). Cross the Barmi La and join the classic route near Lingshed. There are no river crossings on this part of the trail along the Oma so it should be possible throughout the season, and will take three days. Sleep in Zhingchan, then in Skuaz, and on the last night somewhere between Lingshed Sumdo and the pass.

The author crossed the Barmi La once in the opposite direction (detailed description not included in this book); the pass is not difficult, and there is a path. The Oma Chu route is not an easy option.

Water supplies

There is a side-stream 45mins beyond Hanamur. The Oma Chu, beyond the Parfi La, is the next place where you can refill your bottles – it takes 4hrs to get there. Carry sufficient supplies! From the bridge on the Oma Chu you need to take water for 2hrs.

The narrow pathway leading to the Parfi La

Route

Walk high above the valley floor beyond **Hanamur** and then descend to a side-stream (3300m). Take water for 4hrs and continue along the Zanskar, high above the river, on a clear path. Further on, start ascending steeply the left slope of the valley. About 4hrs after leaving Hanamur the **Parfi La** (3921m) is reached. The river in the deep valley on the other side is the Oma; on the opposite side of the valley is the steep onward trail towards Nyetse, Hanamul La and Lingshed. The bridge over the Oma, that you need to cross, is just 1.5km as the crow flies, but 500m below. Descend steeply.

There is a campsite (3379m) and a small shop next to the bridge. It is a nice place, but do not stay here overnight: the next day is much harder and so you need to get further along the trail today. Cross the river by the bridge and climb the opposite slope (N). You come to another pass, 100m lower than the first one (3802m). There is a valley on its opposite side. Do not descend: walk to the left, traversing the slope until you get to a stream and a campsite where there is a small shop in season. This is **Nyetse**.

STAGE 4

Nyetse to Lingshed

Start	Nyetse (3744m)
Finish	Lingshed (3925m)
Distance	17km
Time	9–10hrs
Altitude range	3744m (Nyetse) to 4757m (Hanamur La)

This is a long and tiring stage. The Hanamul La is only moderately high by Ladakhi standards, but from the camp in Nyetse it is a long way in distance, with a significant altitude difference. From the pass a very steep descent leads to the valley, 700m below, followed by a 200m ascent to another pass. Lingshed is a beautifully situated and picturesque settlement.

Alternatives

Beyond the Hanamul La you can leave the classic trek and switch to the route to Lamayuru over the Kanji La. Descend to the valley on the northern side of the pass, stay overnight at the campsite in the valley and then go to the pass – the Barmi La – at the end of the main valley, northwest of the camp. A long descent along the valley leads to Lingshed Sumdo in the Oma Valley. From there pick up Stage 5 of Trek 6.

Water supplies

On the way to the pass look out for the point at which the valley becomes dry. Take water for the remaining ascent and 1½hr descent. From Base Camp, on the northern side of the pass, take water for 1hr and after that from streams for the remaining way to Lingshed.

Route

From **Nyetse** follow the path upstream along the valley floor, switching from side to side as necessary. In order to avoid various small waterfalls and some sheer sections you will need to climb up the slope in places. (It is

The verdant irrigated terraces of Lingshed village contrast sharply with the grey slopes of the surrounding mountains

251

possible to camp 10mins beyond Nyetse among the willow bushes; if you stay here, expect to pay the camping fee.) Another possible camping spot is 2hrs further along the valley floor, although the water sources dry up in the late season.

About 3hrs after leaving Nyetse, climb from the valley floor, traversing its true left slope (on your right as you ascend towards the pass). The path is clear and soon reaches a fork in the valley. The path passes above the fork and enters the branch on your right, then turns slightly to the right (N). Continue along the dry riverbed for some time; about 40mins from the fork, climb to the right to the pass on the ridge. This is the **Hanamul La** (4757m), 5hrs from Nyetse. The terraces of a green oasis, Lingshed village, are visible from the pass towards the northeast (about 5km as the crow flies). The white buildings concentrated on the steep slope above the settlement comprise the monastery; the campsite can be seen just right of the *gompa*. ◄

Descend steeply on a zigzag trail on the northern side of the pass. The descent to the valley takes about 1½hrs, to a stream and a campsite (4015m). Take water for 1hr and climb the ridge on the opposite side of the small valley to another part of the campsite (4040m) with a tent-shop-restaurant. There is no water here. Ignore the path climbing the ridge on your right (NE). Marmots live in this area so proceed gently if you want to see them. Follow the path up the main valley for some 15mins (about 800m), and then climb to a pass on the ridge on your right (E). It is a steep, but thankfully short, ascent (4230m).

From the second pass descend a little and then go left, traversing the slope and cutting across a number of small valleys to the bridge (3990m) at the foot of the steep slope of the main valley. Continue on the very clear traverse E to reach **Lingshed**; it is 3km between the bridge and the *gompa*. Stay at a family house or at the big campsite next to the monastery. There is a shop; dinners and breakfasts are available. Visit the monastery for morning prayers, taking a cup for the tea that is served; everyone is expected to have their own cup or bowl.

The clear path to the right of the village is the path towards Lamayuru that will be followed on Stage 5; the Zanskar Valley is towards the east.

STAGE 5
Lingshed to Sengge La Base Camp (Gazho)

Start	Lingshed (3925m)
Finish	Sengge La Base Camp (4482m)
Distance	14.5km
Time	7hrs
Altitude range	3925m (Lingshed) to 4482m (Sengge La Base Camp)

There are two passes to be crossed on this stage with a climb of 500m to the first, a descent to the valley, then an ascent of over 400m. Both climbs are steep.

Alternatives

- The route over the Kanji La can be joined by crossing the Barmi La (see Stage 4 Alternatives).
- Follow the right bank of the Zanskar River to rejoin the main route of Stage 5, beyond the second pass.
- If you want to return to the Zanskar, cross the Kyukpa La and descend to Yulchung village. Turn right (south)

Yaks carrying firewood from Lingshed Sumdo to Lingshed over the Barmi La on the alternative route to the Oma Valley, Dibling and the Kanji La

downstream, then go high above the river as far as the Zanskar Valley. Cross the bridge over the Zanskar then go on to the Takti La and the Namtse La. Continue to Padum on the right bank of the Zanskar River (unchecked by the author). It is not a popular route, and there are few villages on the way, so be sure to have sufficient food with you.

- If you can find transportation or have pre-arranged it, you can finish the trek at the head of the road that's under construction between Lingshed and Phanjila. In 2014 it had already crossed the Sengge pass, so it may now have reached Lingshed.

Water supplies

From Lingshed take water for 2hrs. From the river before the climb to the second pass, you also need supplies for 2hrs. From Styangs take water for 1hr.

Route

On this stage you will join the road that extends from Phanjila and will eventually connect it with Lingshed.

From **Lingshed**, go towards the ESE, upwards to a clearly visible *chorten* (4319m). Trek on to another *chorten* on a ridge above and head slightly to the left to the first pass. This is the **Morgon La** (4412m) and it takes 1½hrs to climb it. An easy, gradual 30mins of descent will bring you to **Skyumpata**, with a campsite and small shop (4080m). About 1km further on you come to a river (4020m). Another campsite and Gongma village are above, upstream. Do not go there, but cross the river and begin the very steep ascent of the valley's left slope (ENE). It takes almost 1½hrs to climb to the **Kyukpa La** (4459m).

From the pass, traverse the slope on your left, going NNW, then NE, high above Yulchung village. In 30mins you will reach a campsite and a shop, at **Styangs** (4456m). It takes 1hr of gradual ascent to cover the remaining distance to **Gazho** – the Sengge La Base Camp. There is no shop, but a camping fee is collected. The pass is just ahead (N), 500m higher up.

STAGE 6
Gazho to Photoksar

Start	Gazho (4482m)
Finish	Photoksar (4218m)
Distance	19.5km
Time	8hrs
Altitude range	4218m (Photoksar) to 4954m (Sengge La)

Today there is a long, steep climb to the first pass, followed by a lengthy walk along a beautiful, wide, high altitude valley. An ascent to the second pass precedes a descent to the next deep valley. The stage ends at the picturesque village of Photoksar. Road construction is progressing fast here, already stretching towards the passes. If the road has not yet reached Gazho, expect to find it just beyond the first pass.

Water supplies
Take water from the camp for 2hrs. Between the passes you walk along a river, so you don't need much water.

The fertile fields of Photoksar in summer bloom

Refill the bottles before the final ascent to the second pass.

Route

Ascend steeply to the pass. It is not far or very high, and it takes 1½hrs to get to the top; the **Sengge La** (4954m) is the crossing of the main Zanskar Range in the area. From the pass, descend steeply for a short while along the left slope to a shepherds' shelter in the valley floor after 30mins. There is a campsite and a shop-restaurant in a tent (4480m).

Continue downstream on the left bank for 20mins to a tributary stream on the right. The valley floor becomes wider, with a good grassy place for a camp soon reached. 20mins later the path leaves the valley floor and ascends the left slope. Another picturesque side valley is a little further on and another nice camping area (4335m). Take your boots off and ford the side-stream, taking care and using your trekking poles.

Follow the path ascending gradually on the left side of the main valley, passing a small stream 20mins beyond the river crossing. Camping here is not possible; take water for 1½hrs. Continue to the **Bumitse La** (4430m), about 2hrs from the river crossing. ◄ The village of Photoksar is clearly visible on the opposite, sheer slope, 200m below. Follow the distinct trail towards the village NW on a gradual descent to a stream and another potential camp (about 20mins' hike) with 20mins more to the first fields of **Photoksar**. If you want to stay at a family house, descend to the bridge (4145m) and ask at the village (4120m). To make camp follow the traverse upstream above the fields; the campsite, with space for many tents, is by the river, above the western end of the village (4218m). Basic food is available at the small shop.

See map: Trek 5
Stages 6–8

STAGE 7
Photoksar to Phanjila via the Askuta Way

Start	Photoksar (4218m)
Finish	Phanjila (3285m)
Distance	24km
Time	8hrs
Altitude range	3285m (Phanjila) to 4218m (Photoksar)

This is a beautiful stage, encountering a dramatic canyon over 1000m deep. In some sections it is so narrow that the path has been cut out of the rock! This trail is called the Askuta Way, as it passes Askuta village; it is, however, considered dangerous by some guides. It is true that the path is narrow and precipitous in some places but, unless damaged, it is clear and safe; the local people even take this route with pack animals. Unless you suffer from vertigo, fear precipitous paths or have heavily loaded animals with you, it is fine to take this route. You will not need to ford the river, as there are solid bridges on the way.

Alternatives
Until 2009 the most common route went upstream from Photoksar to the Sirsir La then to Hanupata, where the roadhead was. Most organised groups took this route, needing two days to reach Phanjila. However, the road

Beyond Photoksar the Askuta Way follows the Photong Togpo below Askuta village

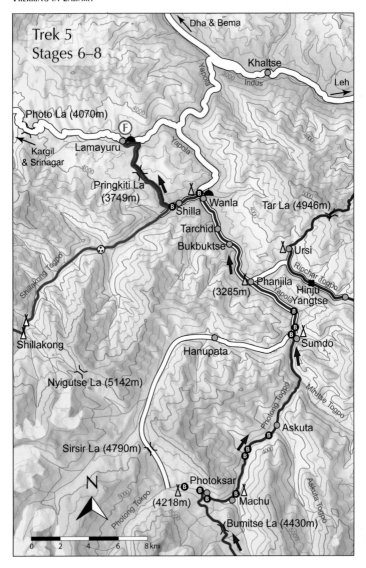

Trek 5
Stages 6–8

Dha & Bema

Khaltse

Indus

Yapola

Leh

Photo La (4070m)

F

Lamayuru

Kargil
& Srinagar

Tapola

Pringkiti La
(3749m)

Shilla

Wanla

Tar La (4946m)

Tarchid

Bukbuktse

Ursi

Ripchar Togpo

Shillakong Togpo

Phanjila

Hinju

(3285m)

Tapola

Yangtse

Shillakong

Sumdo

Hanupata

Mholse Togpo

Nyigutse La (5142m)

Photong Togpo

Askuta

Sirsir La (4790m)

Askuta Togpo

N

Photoksar

Photong Togpo

(4218m)

Machu

Bumitse La (4430m)

0   2   4   6   8 km

is now finished over the Sirsir La and heads above the village, west of Photoksar and the campsite. Transport can be arranged here. If you cross the Sirsir La, you could continue northwest over the Nyigutse La to Shillakong and then descend along the Shillakong Togpo (see Trek 6).

Water supplies
The river is followed all day, but in some places, particularly beyond Askuta, you will be walking some 20m above it so will not have access to water for 1hr or so.

Route
According to many maps, the path down from **Photoksar** follows the left bank of the Photong Togpo. This is wrong! Leave the camp and follow the left bank until you get to the main part of the village (about 12 houses). Descend steeply to the bridge (4070m) and cross to the right bank. ▶ Follow the trail on the right bank, high above the river, downstream. Further on you will cross an irrigation channel that brings water to Machu village and you will descend nearer to the river. Half an hour after crossing the bridge in Photoksar, pass below **Machu** village. One house can be seen.

Don't follow the path on the left bank; it is dangerous and ends a few hundred metres further on.

The valley meets the river flowing from the Sengge La, previously followed. At a bridge (3965m), cross to the left bank and camping place. Continue on the left bank for less than 1hr, then cross to the right bank by a solid bridge (3861m). There is another crossing to the left bank after 5mins. The next bridge is in 30mins; cross here and continue on the right bank. You will see a side valley on your right and pass below **Askuta** village in 15mins.

Further on, the path keeps to the right bank. In some places it ascends above the river; at others it runs just above the water. In some places the river fills the entire river floor and the trail is cut out of the rock wall or elaborately laid with stones and small sticks on a sheer slope – an incredible path! Skirt a side valley and a stream from the right (3580m) a little more than 1hr beyond Askuta. In another hour you will pass below **Sumdo** settlement in the next side valley.

This is the route from Hanupata (the popular alternative from Photoksar).

Follow the main valley; there is a place to camp a bit further on. Continue on to reach quite a big valley (left), with a road. ◄ Cross the river to the left bank by a bridge (3643m) and join the road (you will follow it as far as Wanla on Stage 8). It takes 2hrs to reach Phanjila, walking on the left bank for a short while, then crossing a road bridge to the right side. Where the river flows into a rock tunnel, return to the left side. An hour before reaching Phanjila, you finally cross the bridge to the right bank: a long, rather boring walk on asphalt.

In **Phanjila** there are a few good restaurants, well-supplied shops and a campsite. For accommodation, ask at a restaurant. If you want to finish the trek here there is a regular bus to Leh three times a week.

STAGE 8
Phanjila to Lamayuru

Start	Phanjila (3285m)
Finish	Lamayuru (3491m)
Distance	18km
Time	5hrs
Altitude range	3183m (bridge at Wanla) to 3749m (Pringkiti La)

Unfortunately this stage involves another rather boring walk along an asphalt road to Wanla, then a stretch on a dirt road. The route becomes more interesting along a narrow, labyrinth-like, dry valley to the Pringkiti La. It is not a long or difficult descent to Lamayuru.

Alternatives
- It is said that there is a recently renovated path between Phanjila and Wanla on the left bank of the Yapola River. Ask in Phanjila; if the path really exists and is safe it must be a good alternative to the boring road walk part of this stage.

Lamayuru, dominated by its monastery, clings to the slopes overlooking the valley floor

- If you go up the side valley from Phanjila, you will join Trek 7 and can finish the trek in two to four days, crossing the difficult Tar La.
- You can also end the trek in Phanjila and take a bus or jeep to Leh.

Water supplies

On the way to Wanla, water is available in the villages. Take water for all the way to Lamayuru (3hrs) before turning into the dry valley leading to the Pringkiti La.

Route

It takes 1½hrs to cover the 7km of asphalt road to Wanla. There are two villages on the way: **Bukbuktse** (3220m), 30mins from Phanjila, and **Tarchid** (3198m), 30mins further on; accommodation is available in both.

There is an interesting **monastery** on a hill above Wanla. It is one of the oldest *gompas* in Ladakh, dating back to the time of Rinchen Zangpo (11th century). The Alchi Association has done some conservation work here. To visit it, follow the right ascending branch of the road at the fork between Tarchid and Wanla. To return to the main trail, follow a footpath directly to the village.

In **Wanla**, leave the main road, turn left across the bridge on the Yapola River (3183m), and walk up the side valley of the Shillakong Togpo. There are a few campsites just beyond the bridge. Follow the dirt road.

Shilla village is reached 30mins after crossing the bridge in Wanla. Cross the road bridge (3215m) from the true right to the true left bank of the Shillakong River. No more than 10mins further on there is a dry, quite narrow, side valley on your right leading towards the WNW. ◄ Refill your water bottles and turn into the side valley to enter a magical 'lunar' landscape leading to the pass (no more than 2hrs).

There are chortens at the confluence of the valleys and a clear path in the dry one.

Follow the trail in the valley floor, ascending gradually for long time before a short, steep, final climb to the **Pringkiti La** (3749m). During the last hour of the trek a short steep descent is followed by a gradual downward hike. The valley becomes green as the fields of **Lamayuru** are reached, where a big valley comes in from your left (W). There is a *chorten*, and the village and impressive monastery can be seen.

There are a few restaurants (open in the high season only), small shops and a few guesthouses.

Turn left up the main valley alongside the tiny stream for about 1.3km to reach the village, then go right to the road. ◄ Tharpaling Guest House is recommended: it's a beautiful house some 200m from the restaurants along the road to Kargil on the right. Room standards and prices are variable; food and hot water are available. The same family runs one of the restaurants.

Buses from Kargil to Leh and back arrive at Lamayuru about 9am and are usually packed. Truck drivers can give you a lift (you will need to pay) and it is possible to stop a passing shared jeep-taxi. The drive to Leh takes about 6hrs. Sometimes the road via Lamayuru is closed and vehicles take another road that passes above the settlement. In that case, climb to the junction. If there is no bus in Lamayuru, you could descend to the junction with the road from Wanla and Phanjila, or as far as Indus valley, where an alternative road from Srinagar joins.

6 PADUM TO LAMAYURU VIA THE KANJI LA

The Zanskar Range as seen from Barmi La (Stage 5 alternative); en route from Padum to Lamaruyu a number of ridges in this range are crossed

263

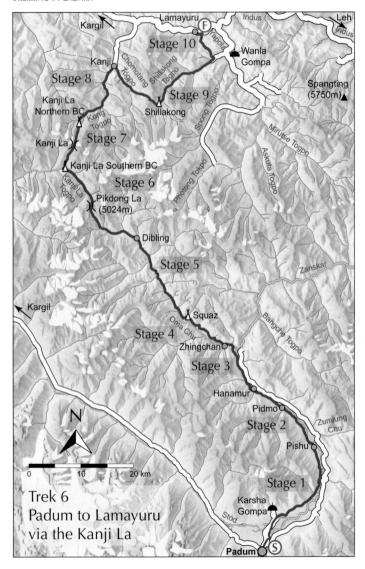

Trek 6
Padum to Lamayuru
via the Kanji La

INTRODUCTION

Start	Padum in the Zanskar Valley (3600m); alternatively Zangla, Pishu or Rangdum
Finish	Lamayuru, on the Kargil–Leh road (3491m); alternatively Wanla, Nurla, Mangyu, Alchi or Rangdum
Distance	169km
Time	75hrs (10 days)
Altitude range	3233m (Shilla) to 5272m (Kanji La)

COMBINATIONS AND ALTERNATIVES

Trek 6 can be linked to Trek 3 (Darcha to Padum); take a few days' rest in Padum and then continue to Lamayuru.

A shorter and easier option for Trek 6 is to start trekking in Rangdum on the Kargil–Padum road and follow the Kanji La Togpo to meet the trail from the Pikdong La (see Stage 6).

To combine the way along the wild valley of the Oma Chu with the route via Lingshed, leave the Oma Valley in Lingshed Sumdo by turning into the side valley. Cross the Barmi La and join Trek 5.

Pishu village (Stage 1)

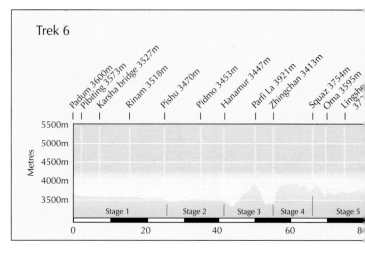

Trek 6

Padum 3600m
Pibiting 3573m
Karsha bridge 3527m
Rinam 3518m
Pishu 3470m
Pidmo 3453m
Hanamur 3447m
Parfi La 3921m
Zhingchan 3413m
Squaz 3754m
Oma 3595m
Lingshe 37...

5500m
5000m
4500m
4000m
3500m

Metres

Stage 1   Stage 2   Stage 3   Stage 4   Stage 5

0   20   40   60   8...

It is also possible to finish the trek in Rangdum (see above). From Pikdong La, walk down the main valley to Rangdum, the first village on the way.

For another option to shorten the trek, continue down the valley from the village of Kanji (Stage 8) until you get to the Kargil–Leh road: a 12km walk on a dirt road.

You can also combine Trek 6 with Trek 5. From the Shillakong camp (Stage 9) cross the Nyigutse La, then the Sirsir La, descend to Photoksar and join Trek 5 to finish the trek by the Askuta Way.

There are even more options if you continue to Wanla from Shilla (Stage 10). You can finish in Wanla and catch a bus there, or continue to Phanjila. From Phanjila ascend the side valley to Ursi and join Trek 7 (the Alchi circuit).

Cross the Tar La to Tar village and then either descend to Nurla on the Leh–Kargil road or continue over the Hibti and Mangyu passes to Mangyu village and Alchi (see Trek 7).

GENERAL INFORMATION

Although easy at the beginning, this is a demanding route. The trail along the Oma Chu is not popular and the path is indistinct and precipitous in some places. This is a great alternative to the classic route from Padum to Lamayuru.

DIFFICULTY, SUPPLIES AND ACCOMMODATION

There are many river crossings on this trek. The Oma Chu, Kanji La Togpo and Kong Togpo have to be forded

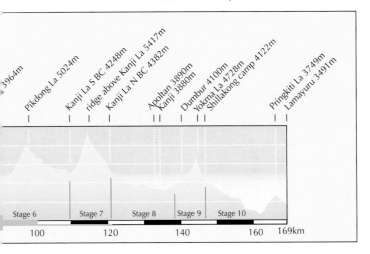

3964m | Pikdong La 5024m | Kanji La S BC 4248m | ridge above Kanji La 5417m | Kanji La N BC 4382m | Apoltan 3890m | Kanji 3880m | Dumbur 4100m | Yokma La 4728m | Shillakong camp 4122m | Pringkiti La 3749m | Lamayuru 3491m

| Stage 6 | Stage 7 | Stage 8 | Stage 9 | Stage 10 |

100   120   140   160   169km

a few times, and the Shillakong frequently. These crossings are not difficult in autumn, but are likely to be very taxing or even impossible in early summer. You definitely need trekking poles on this route!

Both the Pikdong and the Kanji passes are high; ascents to both are

Prayer flags at the Pikdong La, crossed on tiring Stage 6

267

Yaks grazing high above Oma river (Stage 4)

long, steep and tiring. However, the view from the Kanji La is one of the best in Ladakh. If the weather is clear, it is possible to see as far as K2 – the highest peak of the Karakoram, 200km away. On the way to the Kanji La you will see Nun Kun, twin peaks more than 7000m high in the Great Himalaya Range. Although the popularity of this route is increasing, according to local information (Kanji villagers) only about 10–12 groups trek it in a season.

There are no permanently inhabited settlements between Zhingchan and Dibling, or between Dibling and Kanji. No food or accommodation is available and you will probably meet very few people. You need to carry your own provisions all the way from Hanamur to Kanji.

WHEN TO GO?

This is a late summer and autumn trail. Early in the season, in June, there may be too much snow on the Kanji La. In late June and July river levels are high, making the crossings very difficult or impossible. October is fine but cold. September is therefore the best period; the author trekked in late August, and at the end of September/beginning of October.

ACCESS

For information on access to Padum see the Introduction and Trek 5; check the latter for information on getting away from Lamayuru at the end of the trek.

STAGE 1
Padum to Pishu

Start	Padum (3600m)
Finish	Pishu (3435m)
Distance	25.5km
Time	7hrs
Altitude range	3435m (camp in Pishu) to 3600m (Padum)

See Trek 5 Stage 1 for map and route description.

STAGE 2
Pishu to Hanamur

Start	Pishu (3435m)
Finish	Hanamur (3447m)
Distance	16km
Time	5½hrs
Altitude range	3425m (camp between Pidmo and Hannamur) to 3495m (high terrace just beyond Pishu)

See Trek 5 Stage 2 for map and route description.

STAGE 3
Hanamur to Zhingchan

Start	Hanamur (3447m)
Finish	Zhingchan (3413m)
Distance	13.5km
Time	7½hrs
Altitude range	3302m (side valley beyond Hanamur) to 3921m (Parfi La)

Although quite short in distance, the stage is neither easy nor short in time, with a steep ascent and very steep descent. The path is precipitous in some places. It is usually hot on the way and there are no water sources, so you will need to carry water.

Alternatives

The route splits at the bridge over the Oma Chu. Trek 6 via the Kanji La leads upstream, along the river; the classic trek to Lamayuru goes via Nyetse and the Hanamul La. Trek 6 misses the picturesque village of Lingshed with its important monastery, but the two routes can be combined by continuing along the classic route over the Hanamul La to Lingshed (Trek 5). You can then cross the Barmi La to return to the Oma Valley and join Trek 6 in Lingshed Sumdo. The Barmi La is not a difficult pass and there is a clear path all the way between Lingshed and Lingshed Sumdo (the author walked this route in 2004, but details are not included in this book).

Water supplies

There is a side-stream 45mins beyond Hanamur. The Oma Chu, beyond the Parfi La, is the next place where you can refill your bottles. It takes 4hrs to get there. Carry sufficient supplies!

Route

From **Hanamur** walk high above the valley floor and then descend to a side-stream (3302m). Take water for 4hrs and continue along the Zanskar high above the river, along a good path. Further on, start a steep ascent of the left slope of the valley; be careful at any exposed areas. About 4hrs after leaving Hanamur, you will arrive at the **Parfi La** (3921m). On the other side of the pass is the deep valley of the Oma Chu; the steep path across the valley is the trail towards Nyetse, Hanamul La and Lingshed. One of two paths to Zhingchan is also visible from the pass, running towards Nyetse and turning left, traversing the valley's slope.

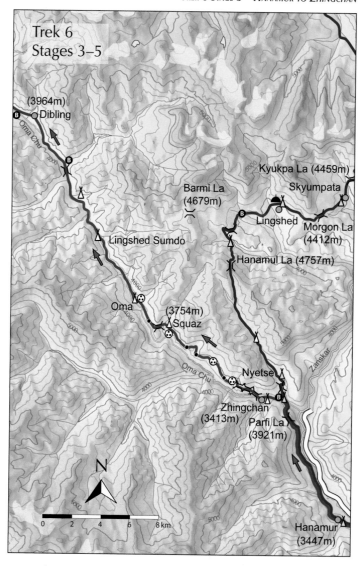

Trek 6
Stages 3–5

(3964m)
Dibling

Oma Chu

Kyukpa La (4459m)

Skyumpata

Barmi La
(4679m)

Lingshed

Morgon La
(4412m)

Lingshed Sumdo

Hanamul La (4757m)

Oma

(3754m)
Squaz

Oma Chu

Nyetse

Zanskar

Zhingchan
(3413m)

Parfi La
(3921m)

N

0   2   4   6   8 km

Hanamur
(3447m)

The Oma bridge is just 1.5km from the pass as the crow flies, but around 500m below. Descend steeply to reach a pleasant and relaxing campsite and small shop. Groups often stay here for the night, as there are not enough suitable camping spaces at Zhingchan. If you have just one or two tents, continue to Zhingchan; sleeping further on makes Stage 4 easier.

> During research in September, it was possible to **walk along the river** from the bridge upstream on the true left bank. However, the slope is sheer, the path indistinct and precipitous, with some really unpleasant steps on exposed rock. This route is not accessible when the water is higher and it is dangerous at any time.

Cross the bridge (3379m) and climb up to the path on the opposite side. Go left, traversing the slope high above the river, upstream (W). The valley is very narrow above the bridge but widens before the settlement of **Zhingchan**, 2km away. There is a small aspen and willow copse in the valley floor. The solitary house is on the true

The solitary house at Zhingchan, the last habitation before two days in the wild valley

left bank of the Oma Chu, before the next narrow section of the main valley, opposite a side valley. This is a picturesque place, especially in autumn when the trees are colourful. Ask the villagers where to camp.

STAGE 4
Zhingchan to Squaz

Start	Zhingchan (3413m)
Finish	Squaz (3754m)
Distance	11km
Time	7hrs
Altitude range	3413m (Zhingchan) to 3946m (ridge above the Oma Chu)

A series of steep ascents at the start of this stage lead to several passes, followed by a long, high and occasionally precipitous traverse above the river. The true left bank of the Oma Chu is followed all day.

Path traversing high above the Oma Chu

273

BROWN BEARS

Although brown bears are extremely rare in Ladakh, opinions on the possibility of meeting one in the Oma Chu Valley vary. I was warned by a man from Hanamur to be very careful in the valley, but the locals in Dibling told me that there were no bears in this area. Bears can be aggressive and dangerous. In autumn the animals certainly descend to the bushy valleys from the high pastures where they usually spend the summers. They always choose quiet places, and the Oma Valley is a tranquil one. Some of these stories must be true, as I have seen very clear and fresh prints left by a bear in a valley north of the Kanji La, just on the main path. It is a good idea to make a lot of noise while walking through the willow bushes in this area, and when descending to any rivers.

Alternatives
There are no alternatives for this stage.

Water supplies
Take water for 2hrs from the camp, then from the stream under a waterfall for 4hrs.

Route
Take the path towards the NW, which starts just behind the sole house of **Zhingchan** and climbs the slope of a narrow side valley: precipitous traverses of the sheer slope are encountered on the way. Cross the tiny stream and climb steeply (WSW), zigzagging up the opposite slope. At the indistinct fork, keep on climbing the slope (WSW), instead of following the traverse into the valley. You will arrive at a pass (3622m); continue steeply upwards, cutting across a dry side valley, to another pass (3744m). Climb the next pass just ahead (3848m) and then ascend more gently, traversing through three dry side valleys, to the fourth pass (3895m).

Continue upwards for 25mins more to the ridge (3902m) left of a solid shepherds' shelter. From here you traverse the valley's slope, 300–400m above the Oma Chu. The ridge that can be clearly seen ahead, 1.5km away, is your next destination. To reach it, take the traverse to the right, to the side valley with a small water-fall. There are several indistinct paths, so take the one that does not descend too much. At the stream, take supplies of water for 4hrs.

Continue ascending gently past a shepherds' shelter and cut across several dry side valleys. About 3hrs after leaving Zhingchan a big ridge (3946m) is reached and the valley turns slightly to the right. There is a big tributary stream on the opposite side, in a relatively big valley. ▶ **Continue the traverse. Do not take any path downwards!**

Head towards an orange rock, almost 2.5km further up the valley; next to this is a pass that you need to cross. On the way, about 30mins from the last ridge and just after a relatively big, dry side valley, you will pass two simple shelters. The path, which has been clear, forks and becomes indistinct. Arrive at the second, lower shelter, where there is a quite obvious trail leading steeply downwards. **Don't follow it! Do not descend towards the valley floor here!** There is also a tiny but clear path to the right, ascending very gently: follow this one.

This is a dangerous section, so take care. Pass rocks in a side valley and then continue the traverse towards the orange rock near the pass. The way crosses the ridge (3924m) slightly above the pass. It takes about 40mins to get here from the traverse through the rocks (about 5hrs from Zhingchan). There is a deep, side valley on the other side of the ridge and another ridge on its opposite side. Go to the right, descending to the valley axis (dry in September) and then descend for about 15m. Continue traversing the loose slope – the path is generally clear, although it disappears briefly in places.

Next is a ridge or indistinct pass. Looking straight ahead along the Oma Chu Valley (NW), you will see a reddish-brown pass (Stage 5) 2.5km away as the crow flies. Continue the traverse by a quite distinct, although not frequently used, path. **Do not descend towards the valley floor!** In 40mins there is a small side valley with a tiny spring; after a further 30mins a big, deep valley

According to maps, there is a trail down in that valley, leading over the Ralakung La to Phe village by the Stod River on the Kargil–Padum road.

with a stream is reached. The ruins of houses mark the place known as **Squaz**. Make camp here; the spot has a generally open aspect, so the sun warms it relatively early.

STAGE 5
Squaz to Dibling

Start	Squaz (3754m)
Finish	Dibling (3964m)
Distance	20km
Time	8½hrs
Altitude range	3596m (Oma) to 3964m (Dibling)

This long stage goes high above the valley and then along the Oma Chu. Beyond Lingshed Sumdo it is easier, on a good, frequently used trail with a few summer shelters. The river has to be forded a few times, which is easier in autumn. Dibling is a beautiful and untouched place, inhabited by friendly, hospitable people. Watch out for brown bears.

Alternatives

- To join Trek 5 (classic trek from Zanskar) leave the Oma Chu Valley in Lingshed Sumdo by turning right into the side valley (east). Camp before the Barmi La in preparation for the next day. Beyond the pass, descend to Lingshed on a fairly frequently used trail.
- If you have time, it is a good idea to divide this and the following two stages into three shorter sections. Make a camp in Lingshed Sumdo or further on, somewhere on the way to Dibling, for the first night. Ascend to the last place suitable for a camp before the Pikdong La the following day, then cross the pass and descend to Kanji La Base Camp.

Water supplies

Take water for 3hrs from the camp at Squaz. At Oma take water for 1hr, after which water can be taken along the river.

Route

Before leaving **Squaz**, note the pass about 150m above the opposite slope of the side valley – the clearly visible trail you need heads over the steepest part of the slope. Cross the stream. Descend a few metres and then start the traverse, ascending quite steeply at first. Continue rather more gently, high above the valley floor, over the sheer, potentially dangerous slope. From the pass (3911m), about 40mins from the camp, traverse to a clearly visible ridge (3886m), 15mins further on. Next follow a long, gradual descent to a relatively large, dry terrace on the floor of the Oma Valley. This spot, which is visible from the ridge, is **Oma** (2hrs from Squaz). There are a few shepherds' shelters and it is a suitable camping place (3595m).

Cross the side-stream (true left tributary) that joins the Oma Chu, then find a clear, wide path, which climbs rock debris and traverses the slope some 30m above the river (still on the true left bank). After a bit less than 1hr,

Remote, quaint and very hospitable Dibling village

you come to a place where two side valleys join. Cross the left tributary (3660m) and continue the traverse lower than before on a clear path along the true left bank (with the river left, facing upstream). Follow the traverse – now generally 20–30m above the river – descending occasionally to the valley floor. Further on, the trail is higher, about 100m above the river. Descend once again to reach **Lingshed Sumdo** (3731m), about 4hrs after leaving Squaz, at a spot where a left tributary (on your right) joins the Oma Chu. ◄

There is a good path on the true right bank of the side valley to Lingshed.

Continue up the main valley, keeping to the true left bank on a clear path for 15mins before fording the river. The clear path continues along the true right bank. An hour beyond Lingshed Sumdo pass a big right tributary river (on your left, SW). Continue up the main valley towards the N. About 10mins further on the Oma flows through a very narrow section and turns sharply a few times. You will need to cross the river three times.

Continue on the true left (E) bank for 15mins. At another sharp turn of the valley the trail becomes narrow, precipitous and potentially dangerous. If you want to avoid a few risky steps, choose a route across the river, twice cutting the meander. Further on, following the true left bank of the Oma, pass another side valley on your right (a left tributary) with terraces divided by small stone walls; this is a nice place to camp (3750m), 2hrs from Lingshed Sumdo. Continue along the river on the same bank. Around 15mins later you pass a big right tributary (on the opposite side of the valley). Keep straight on (NNW), generally a few metres above the valley bottom.

According to maps, there is a trail to Lingshed along the right side of this stream, crossing the Marpo and Skyerse passes.

A small pass (3813m) is reached roughly 2½hrs from Lingshed Sumdo. There is another side-stream beyond it, on your right. ◄ Cross the small bridge (it's possible to make a camp here) and continue up the main valley on the true left bank towards the NW. After 15mins the river snakes a little and the path climbs steeply. To avoid this climb ford the river a few times instead. The trail continues above the left bank of the Oma Chu to **Dibling** (about 4hrs from Lingshed Sumdo).

Dibling is one of the author's favourite villages in Zanskar; it is a picturesque place situated on the alluvial fan of a side-stream. People are friendly, hospitable and you can find accommodation here. There is a small monastery in the village, where a young *lama* speaks English. If you prefer to sleep in your tent, continue up the main valley for about 30mins and make camp there.

STAGE 6
Dibling to Kanji La Southern Base Camp

Start	Dibling (3964m)
Finish	Kanji La Southern Base Camp (4248m)
Distance	24km
Time	11hrs
Altitude range	3913m (trail near the bridge, 15min beyond Dibling) to 5024m (Pikdong La)

This is a very long stage: it is more than 12km to the Pikdong La, with over 1000m of altitude gain. The descent is also long and tiring, with two serious river crossings. It is possible to miss the turn towards Kanji La Base Camp at the end of this stage, so read the directions carefully. If you started the trek in Rangdum, note that you need to leave the main valley where it turns at the river's northernmost extremity, turning into a side valley which leads to the Kanji La. Nonetheless, it is a beautiful stage, hiking through picturesque, wild, high altitude surroundings.

Locals frequently use this trail, because it is the shortest way from Dibling to any road, and the path is clear all the way. The villagers of Dibling claim that it usually takes 2hrs to get to the pass, although some trekkers can take up to 4hrs. They also claim that it is possible to reach Rangdum (over 15km beyond Kanji La Base Camp) in one day! Maybe, but walking with a heavy rucksack it took the author 6½hrs to reach the pass from Dibling.

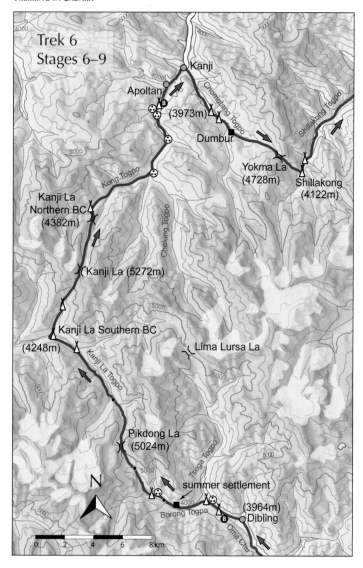

Trek 6
Stages 6–9

Kanji

Apoltan

(3973m)

Chomlang Togpo

Dumbur

Shillakong Togpo

Yokma La
(4728m)

Shillakong
(4122m)

Kong Togpo

Chelung Togpo

Kanji La
Northern BC
(4382m)

Kanji La (5272m)

Kanji La Southern BC

(4248m)

Kanji La Togpo

Lima Lursa La

Pikdong La
(5024m)

Tsega Togpo

summer settlement

Borong Togpo

Dibling

(3964m)

Oma Chu

N

0   2   4   6   8 km

Alternatives

- According to maps, there is an alternative route to the Kanji La Togpo Valley. Where the valley forks, 45mins beyond Dibling, it heads straight towards the north-northwest, along the Tsega Togpo. It then crosses the Lima Lursa La and joins the Kanji La Togpo Valley just 2km before Kanji La Base Camp. This way is longer and less frequented, so ask the locals in Dibling for details.
- If you want to divide the stage, camp near a solid shelter 3hrs from Dibling and cross the pass the next day.
- To finish the trek in Rangdum, pass above Kanji La Base Camp, continuing the traverse. You will arrive at a big side valley on the left in no more than 1hr. Camp here and continue down the valley to Rangdum the next day.

Water supplies

You don't need to carry much water initially, but it is important to restock before starting the main ascent of the pass. On the descent you can find water most of the way, except in one section (see details below).

Route

From **Dibling** village follow the true left bank of the main valley (NW), passing near a bridge 15mins beyond the village. Do not cross this bridge, but follow the clear path straight on (good places to camp a bit further on). About 45mins from Dibling the valley forks (3915m). There are shepherds' shelters and camping options here. The river on your right, flowing from the NNW, is the Tsega Togpo. Ford it and continue WSW, along the true left bank of the second of the two streams, the Borong Togpo. The path is clearer further on.

Pass a summer settlement situated on an alluvial fan 45mins' walk beyond the confluence (4025m). The valley turns here to your right (WNW). After 30mins climb a small ridge (4139m) before descending to a wide terrace, then head towards a clear valley fork (WNW). Before you

Looking back from the final steps of the approach to the Pikdong La

reach it, pass a narrow but quite big ravine on your right. Just beyond it, 20mins from the ridge and about 3hrs from Dibling, you come to a solid shelter (4140m). This is the last camping place before the Pikdong La.

Keep on walking to the valley fork. Leave the valley that is on your left and continue straight towards the NW. The path becomes indistinct for a moment but continues on the true right bank of the valley (on your left as you walk up it). The riverbed will be dry in the autumn, but there is a stream further on. Traverse the slope, ascending gradually, and 1hr from the shelter (4hrs from Dibling) you will reach the valley bottom (4357m). The valley turns slightly left here (WNW). Take water reserves for 3½hrs, cross the stream and start the steep climb of the massive slope in front, towards the NW. It is more than 650m of ascent to the pass.

About 1½hrs later you should reach the ridge (4750m). The pass is to the NNW, still 1.5km away. Continue to the right, steeply along the ridge, which becomes easier for a while; then ascend a steep section of rock debris. The trail is clear and ascends gently on the right side, then more steeply again to another section of stony debris. The **Pikdong La** (5024m) is about 300m further on, marked by two medium-sized stone cairns and prayer flags.

From the pass, descend steeply to the valley ahead (there is water here). Go to the right, gently down the valley on its left slope. About 30mins from the pass, you go past a major valley on the right, then 10mins later descend to the riverbed for a short while. Keeping on the left, follow the short traverse above the stream and then along the stony riverbed again. The path becomes indistinct; follow the valley floor downwards. One hour from the pass is another major valley on the right. The path gets clearer here and then, after a few minutes, climbs the left slope to a ridge (4601m). From the top, there are breathtaking views of the mountain peaks and glaciers.

Descend to the side valley and cross the glacier river (4522m). Even in autumn, the stream is not very easy to ford; it is fast and very cold. Beyond the stream, take a route leading to the main valley; you will walk high above its floor. About 30mins from the river crossing reach another, smaller valley on the left (4451m). Take water for 2hrs. A third major valley appears on the right after another 45mins. There is a simple shelter below the path and a place to camp. However, it's better to continue, as Stage 7 (the Kanji La) is tough. Expect a further 1hr to Kanji La Base Camp from here.

Continue high above the river as the valley turns gradually left (roughly WNW). In just under 1hr from the third valley on the right, where the river turns to the WSW, pass a very narrow, rocky ravine (the fourth major tributary) on the right. There may be prayer flags across the walls of this valley, and there are a few one-tent platforms at the head of the valley, over 50m below. This is the Kanji La Southern Base Camp, and the ravine leads towards the Kanji La.

Continue along the main valley for a short while and search for a very clear path descending steeply to the valley floor. Leave the main trail (it leads to Rangdum) and walk downwards. ▶ Cross the main river to the **Kanji La Southern Base Camp**, cold and dusty place with room for two to three tents. Luckily the sun hits the camp area early in the morning.

The peaks visible towards the west are Nun Kun, over 7000m high, part of the Great Himalaya Range.

STAGE 7

Kanji La Southern Base Camp to
Kanji La Northern Base Camp

Start	Kanji La Southern Base Camp (4248m)
Finish	Kanji La Northern Base Camp (4382m)
Distance	11km
Time	8½hrs
Altitude range	4248m (Kanji La Southern Base Camp) to 5272m (Kanji La); 5417m (optional ridge above the pass)

The height gain on this stage is in excess of 1000m. It is a rather steep and long ascent, starting from a stony, dried-up riverbed. The incredible views of the Himalayas and Karakoram peaks from the pass and from the ridge above it more than compensate for the tough ascent. Take care on the 5km descent alongside a glacier.

Alternatives

If you need to finish the trek, return to the path leading down the main valley and follow it until you get to Rangdum on the Kargil–Padum road (see Stage 6).

Water supplies

There should be water at the start of the valley leading to the pass, but the major part of this valley is dry. The stream may continue for only 2km or so beyond the camp in summer, but is even shorter in autumn. Keep an eye on it and fill your bottles before it disappears. Take water for the whole day, as far as the Northern Base Camp – there are no other water sources before the end of the stage.

Route

From the camp, enter the narrow ravine towards the N. Keep to the valley floor and do not ascend. There is no clear path; just follow the stony riverbed. Remember

to take generous supplies of water before leaving the stream! 30mins from the camp there should be a path on the slope on your right (true left slope). The main valley then turns slightly to your right and a relatively big side valley can be seen on the left. Follow the path for 15mins before crossing to the true right side of the valley.

About 500m further on there are two notable height gains (step-like) in the valley, with a large side valley on the right at the second one. Two small terraces, about 200m beyond the side valley (approximately 4530m), provide good spots for tents, but staying here is probably possible only in summer; by autumn the valley is dry. Follow the clear path along the valley floor, climbing more step-like sections and occasionally changing from one side of the valley to the other. About 2½hrs from Base Camp, at around 4830m, you will pass a big valley on your right. (Be prepared for another 2hrs to reach the top of the Kanji La.)

Continue by the main valley (NE). Next the route negotiates a substantial steep, massive, step-like section (150m or so) of fallen rock debris. A similar section, by a side valley on your left, also has to be crossed. You are

The Zanskar Mountains and the Great Himalayas as seen from the Kanji La

285

at an altitude of over 5000m already, but there is still another 200m to be climbed and over 600m to be covered. Continue climbing rough, dry terrain all the way to the top of the obvious pass at the end of the valley. This is the famed **Kanji La** (5272m). It took the author 4½hrs to reach it from the Base Camp.

WARNING

Siân Pritchard-Jones and Bob Gibbons crossed this pass in July 1983, when the route from Base Camp was almost all covered with snow. They had to start the long climb before dawn in order to reach the top before the sun's intense heat caused the snow to become soft and exceedingly difficult to trek over. Needless to say, before dawn the snow is quite icy. If you find such snowy conditions, extreme care will be needed to reach the summit. This pass is no picnic for ill-equipped trekkers and even for anyone well kitted out, especially earlier in the season – so check its condition before any attempt.

There are marvellous views from the pass! To the south are stunning glacier-covered peaks and, far below, the Kanji La Togpo Valley through which you have already trekked. Towards the north is the barren, jagged Ladakh Range and, in the far distance, the chiselled spires of the Karakoram. On a clear day, K2, the second highest mountain in the world, is visible roughly 200km away.

> For even **better views** of the Himalayas, including Nun Kun, the Zanskar Range and the surrounding peaks of the Pikdong La, climb the ridge to the left (west) of the pass. The ridge is about 150m higher and the round trip takes about 1hr.

You don't need to descend to the glacier from the pass or cross the patches of permanent snow. Do not start descending here; a clear path starts a few metres left (W) of the pass, a bit higher along the ridge, next to a boulder. Follow this, descending steeply about 70m, then traverse over the sheer slope of potentially dangerous loose stones

above the glacier. **Be careful: there is ice under the stones.**

The trail heads to moraines left of the glacier about 1hr from the pass. After reaching the moraines (at 4930m), the walking is more pleasant and the way clear. 15mins later you traverse the left slope again, cross a small pass and then descend steeply, still on the clear traverse along the left slope of the valley.

The clear traverse will bring you to the pass (4596m) atop the left slope, about 2hrs after leaving the Kanji La. Cross it and descend steeply to the floor of the valley on the other side. The whole way ahead is now clear downstream in the valley. Follow it for about 100m to a large camp spot on the first terrace on the left bank, about 2½hrs from the Kanji La. It is cold here at night, and the sun does not rise very early in the morning.

The Kanji La as seen from the ridge above

STAGE 8
*Kanji La Northern Base Camp to
Chomotang Togpo Valley*

Start	Kanji La Northern Base Camp (4382m)
Finish	Chomotang Togpo Valley (3973m)
Distance	17.5km
Time	6½hrs
Altitude range	3841m (Kanji) to 4382m (Kanji La Northern Base Camp)

Despite the beautiful, peaceful scenery, the ground underfoot along a stony riverbed can be unpleasant and tiresome. There are many river crossings on this stage, easy in autumn but probably very difficult in early summer. Look out for brown bears; the author has seen clear bearprints on this stage. Bears may be dangerous, so make a noise while walking to deter one from approaching.

Alternatives
If you want to end the trek on this stage keep following the road that starts in Kanji village; it might be possible to find transportation. It is 12km from Kanji to the main Kargil–Leh road.

Water supplies
Rivers are followed all day.

Route
Trek down the valley, ignoring a path that climbs the left side, and continue until you meet the valley from the Kanji La (the one left at the end of Stage 7). From the confluence (4230m) continue downstream in the stony riverbed, with occasional respite along the banks. The way is mostly clear, marked by tiny cairns. About 1½hrs from the camp is a confluence with a huge valley on the right. There are shepherds' shelters (4017m) where villagers spend the summers, grazing goats, sheep and yaks.

The valley of the Kong Togpo

It's possible to camp in these beautiful surroundings. Continue down the valley with more river crossings in 30mins; even in early October you will need to take off your boots. A clear path appears on the right bank soon before the valley narrows.

There are more shelters by another big right tributary and a left turn (NNW) of the main valley. If the water in the river is high, it is better to take the path that traverses the right side. Otherwise, it is fine to follow the path along low terraces on the right bank. ▸

There is a right turn of the valley and shelters 40mins from the last turn in the valley. Suitable places to camp can be found 10mins further on, with a bridge just beyond them. Cross the bridge (3895m) to the left bank. About 20mins later a big tributary on the left is reached, with fields and a house; this is **Apoltan** village (3890m).

Follow the main valley downstream on the left bank on a clear path through the fields. Pass a rocky, narrow section of the valley; the big village of **Kanji** (3880m) is just beyond it. There are about 40 houses, a *gompa*, a big school and a campsite with food supplies. It is 20mins' walk from Apoltan to Kanji village, roughly 5hrs from the previous

Note the beautiful rock face on the opposite side of the river, which looks like a paradise for climbers.

night's camp. The Yokma La is towards the southeast, at the end of the valley opposite the village, 9km away.

If you want to finish the trek follow the road that starts here and runs along the main valley downstream to reach the main Kargil–Leh road after about 12km; or ask about transportation in Kanji.

Cross the bridge (3840m) to the right side of the main valley and enter the valley of a side-stream known as Chomotang Togpo. Follow its true left bank (on your right, facing upstream, SE). Don't cross the bridge on the Chomotang Togpo, and ignore the valley on your left – the clear pass at its top is *not* the Yokma La! Head SE through the fields to a narrow section of the valley with a rock face on your left. Pass it and continue upstream on the true left bank. A single house near another valley on the right appears, and you continue up the main valley.

There is another substantial valley on your right in another 10mins (3950m). Ignore a path ascending its alluvial fan and hike on along the main stream on its true left bank for about 800m until you reach a slight left turn of the valley and a side valley on the left, with some stone walls on its alluvial fan. Make camp opposite here. The best place is to the right, a few metres from the path. You will need to walk a distance to fetch water, but the ground is dry, it is less windy than camping by the river, and the sunshine arrives earlier in the morning.

STAGE 9
Chomotang Togpo Valley to Shillakong

Start	Chomotang Togpo Valley (3973m)
Finish	Shillakong (4122m)
Distance	8.5km
Time	4½hrs
Altitude range	3973m (Chomotang Togpo Valley) to 4728m (Yokma La)

This is a much more relaxing stage. The way to the Yokma La is quite steep, but it is not very high; the descent is steep but short. There is a beautiful camp in a wild valley at the end. It is very easy to be confused about the correct way to the Yokma La, and possible to cross another pass, south of the correct one, by accident. Read the detailed directions carefully!

Alternatives

If you want to cross the alternative pass rather than the Yokma La, you need to go right of the peak that is clearly visible up the main valley. There are paths, but they are used mostly by animals. The pass can be clearly distinguished and there is a cairn and prayer flags on its summit. On the other side descend steeply to the narrow gorge of the Shillakong Togpo. Follow the river downstream (not easy) to reach the Shillakong camp.

Water supplies

The valley is dry in its upper part. While going upstream take sufficient water supplies for the rest of the trek to Shillakong, before leaving the stream behind.

Route

The main pass is visible from the camp towards the ESE, almost 6km away as the crow flies, at the end of the valley and left of the clearly distinguishable peak. It appears

Independent camp at Shillakong

too steep to be climbed (and is very steep indeed!). The path follows the valley almost as far as the foot of the sheer slope, which it eventually traverses.

From the camp continue along the river upstream, on the true left bank. There is a side valley in 15mins on your left and a good, green place to camp. The confluence with a big valley on the right comes next, in another 15mins (4080m). There is unlikely to be water from here on, so fill your bottles. Continue straight on, beside the stone-walled fields on your right. A solitary house, **Dumbur** (4100m), is passed a little further on.

The valley turns slightly to the left here, and in 15mins you pass a wide valley on your right. Hike close to the riverbed, along the main valley, which continues its slight left turn. Ignore the trail that leads into the side valley and on to its right slope and ridge. ◄ Arrive at the slight, right turn of the valley (towards the ESE). The path disappears in some places and is narrow but mostly distinct as you follow the riverbed from here for about 1hr. Pass another wide valley on your right and then, still in the riverbed, turn sharply left and then right a bit further on.

From here you can see the final climb, with an enticing view of the summit prayer flags on the pass. You can see the clear path that traverses the sheer slope just right of the pass – the final ascent. Follow the riverbed until it gets narrow and very steep. Leave the riverbed and walk along the right of it (facing the pass) for about 20mins. The path becomes indistinct. When almost at the foot of the sheer slope, turn sharply to the right, heading to the obvious pathway that crosses the sheer slope straight towards the pass. The **Yokma La** (4728m) is about 3hrs from the previous night's camp.

Descend steeply from the pass, following the axis of the valley. You need to get to the main valley, 600m below the pass. The Shillakong Togpo flows from the right (S) to the left (N). ◄ The **Shillakong** camp is in the main valley on the right bank, just opposite the way from the pass at a confluence with a tributary stream. There are a number of small platforms for tents. Sadly, the place is sometimes littered.

Take one of these paths if you want to go to the alternative pass that is to the right (south) of the peak ahead.

Another clear pathway descends gently from the pass, to the right, but do not take this: it leads up the Shillakong Togpo to pastures high in this valley.

Start	Shillakong (4122m)
Finish	Lamayuru (3491m)
Distance	23km
Time	8hrs
Altitude range	3233m (head of the dry tributary valley near Shilla) to 4122m (Shillakong)

Although this is a long and tough stage, it is definitely worth the effort. The Shillakong Togpo Valley is one of the most extraordinary and beautiful canyons in Ladakh. Its narrow and vertical, rocky walls are a few hundred metres high. The time required to cover the distance to the Shilla settlement, where you turn towards the Pringkiti La and Lamayuru, depends on the height of the Shillakong Togpo; there will be many river crossings. At the beginning of October, when the level was so low that fording the river did not require taking off boots, it took the author 5hrs; in early August, when river levels are much higher, it might take 8hrs or even more. The 8.5km between Shilla and Lamayuru takes 3hrs to cover.

Alternatives

- There is a possible option over the Nyigutse La at the end of the tributary stream that flows from the southeast and joins the main valley in Shillakong. If you cross it, you can join the Photoksar–Hanupata route (part of the most popular route from Zanskar to Lamayuru) in the valley on the opposite side of the pass. If you head towards the southeast over the Sirsir La, you will reach Photoksar and can descend to Phanjila by the Askuta Way (see Trek 5). Both possibilities avoid river crossings.
- For an alternative finish: in Shilla do not turn into the side valley to Lamayuru, but continue downstream to Wanla, where you can find accommodation and catch a bus to Leh.

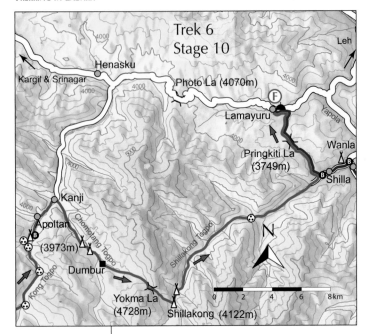

Water supplies

You will not need to carry water while walking along the Shillakong Togpo. However, a dry valley is followed from the turn at Shilla over the Pringkiti La to Lamayuru, so you need supplies sufficient for 3hrs.

Route

Walk downstream.

> There is a **good place to camp** 15mins below Shillakong, by a tributary on the right. It is less littered but probably colder here – there is space for just two or three tents. During the first hour of walking, you pass places for a single-tent camp. Later the ground is too stony.

Just over 2hrs from the camp, pass two impressive perpendicular rock faces on each side of the valley. The canyon narrows even more and the river passes through a rock 'gate' (3640m).

Reach a simple, stone shelter at the foot of a rock face on the left bank, 3hrs after leaving Shillakong (another possible camp, 3625m). It takes at least 2hrs to Shilla and it is another 3hrs from there to Lamayuru. There are no good places to camp further on. 30mins beyond the shelter, pass a big valley on your right (3415m) and about 1hr later come the first bridges where river crossings are required. Soon you reach a road and some ugly buildings on the left bank (3296m) – the public baths, utilising the waters of a hot spring.

Follow the road along the Shillakong Valley, which becomes wider and greener. Reach a dry tributary valley (3233m) on the left 20mins beyond the baths just before **Shilla** settlement; there are prayer flags and small *chortens (stupas)* marking the way in. ▶ Take water for 3hrs and turn left into the dry valley on a very frequently used trail. Follow this to the pass; it should take just under 2hrs

Interesting rock formations high above the Shillakong Togpo

Note If you reach the road bridge, you have gone too far.

295

Lamayuru Gompa

through a magical, moonlike landscape. Ascend gradually for a long time before a short, steep final climb to the **Pringkiti La** (3749m).

From the pass there is a short, steep descent, followed by a gradual descent to the valley floor, which gets greener. You come to the fields of **Lamayuru** and a big valley coming from your left (W); there is a *chorten*. The village and the impressive monastery appear like a fairytale dream. Turn left and follow the main valley up and along the tiny stream for about 1.3km to get to the village. Then go to the right, to the road.

Lamayuru has a few restaurants (high season only), small shops and a few guesthouses; Tharpaling Guest House is about 200m from the restaurants along the road towards Kargil on the right. Room standards and prices are variable; food and hot water are available. The same family runs one of the restaurants. For information on leaving Lamayuru please refer to the end of Trek 5.

7 ALCHI

A circuit over five passes

A number of small, beautiful and wild valleys are followed on Trek 7: the Sumdha Valley in autumn (Stage 3)

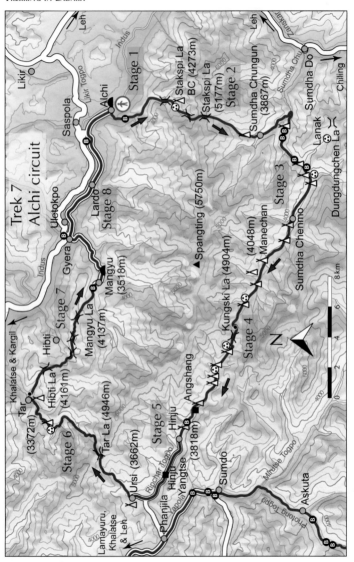

INTRODUCTION

Start	Alchi in the Indus Valley (3121m); alternatively Sumdha Do
Finish	Alchi (3121m); alternatively Sumdha Do, Chiling, Hinju, Phanjila, Wanla, Lamayuru, Nurla or Mangyu
Distance	98km
Time	47hrs (8 days)
Altitude range	3090m (Gyera) to 5177m (Stakspi La)

COMBINATIONS AND ALTERNATIVES

An easier three-day option would be to start the trek in Alchi, cross the Stakspi La, descend to Sumdha Chungun and then follow the Sumdha Chu Valley downstream. You will reach Sumdha Do on the banks of the Zanskar River, from where there is a road connection to Nyemo and Leh.

This trek can also be started from Sumdha Do. From Leh go to the village by bus or jeep, and then walk up the Sumdha Chu until you join the route from Sumdha Chungun. This is recommended if you are not acclimatised.

Approaching Sumdha Chenmo (Stage 3)

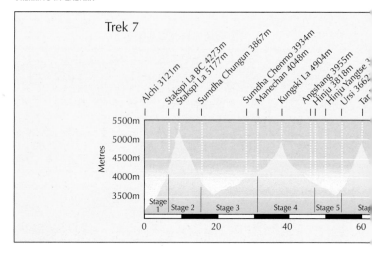

Another possibility is to follow the trail almost as far as Lasgo in the Sumdha Chu Valley (Stage 3) and then turn left towards the Dungdungchen La. Cross it and descend to Chiling, from where you can return to Leh by bus or jeep. You could also continue the trek along the Markha Valley: from Chiling, follow the road along the Zanskar River upvalley to the new road bridge on Zanskar. Cross it, continue on the road to Kaya and then follow on the pathway to Skyu where you will join Trek 8.

The trek can also be finished in Hinju or Phanjila. Both villages have a bus connection with Leh at least once a week.

From Alchi follow the route as far as Hinju then descend to Phanjila, and continue to Lamayuru according to Trek 5. This way, you would avoid

one of two major passes on Trek 7: the Tar La.

To shorten the trek, continue down the main valley from Tar village until you get to Nurla on the main Leh–Kargil road.

GENERAL INFORMATION

Overall this is a relatively easy route, with clear route-finding. However, the trail climbs steeply at the beginning, with an ascent to 5177m on the second day: a big test for your body. You must be well acclimatised to do it safely. If you are not certain of your acclimatisation, start the trek in Sumdha Do. Trek 7 is a beautiful, diverse trek through deep valleys characterised by willow shrubs as well as high altitude Ladakhi meadows. The landscape is dominated by

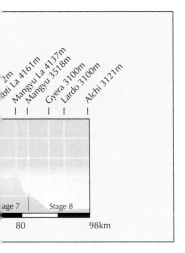

alpine scenery with high, glacier-covered peaks. Wild animals are likely to be encountered on this trail: blue sheep, marmots, many birds and, if you are lucky, other Ladakhi animals. The path from the Kungski La is where the author saw a snow leopard in late autumn 2009.

DIFFICULTY, SUPPLIES AND ACCOMMODATION

Most of the stages are relatively short, and there are many options for shortening the trek too. However, both the Stakspi La and the Tar La are high and steep, and the Kungski La is not much easier. The trail climbs as high as 5177m and drops as low as 3090m, with many ups and downs. The route is less popular and slightly harder than the Markha Valley trek, and is a good alternative if you want to trek in the Indus Valley area.

There are villages where you can rely on homestay accommodation and food, so you don't need to carry much. However, if trekking independently you might need a tent on a couple of nights unless you can manage the very long and hard stages all the way from Alchi to Sumdha Chungun in one day, and can cross the Kungski La, starting from Sumdha Chenmo. Both options are possible.

WHEN TO GO?

The route becomes accessible as soon as the passes are free of snow, normally in June or maybe even in late May. There are bridges across all the major streams, so no river has to be forded, making it accessible all summer. In late autumn (mid-October) the route is very cold. The author stayed in local houses on most nights but it was still cold; the locals keep just one room – the kitchen – warm, so the sleeping room for guests is usually as cold as a tent.

September is the recommended time, when it is not so cold and the landscape has already taken on the magical colours of autumn. This trek is also a good choice for early summer, when many other routes are not accessible due to high river levels, and when the most popular routes are busy.

An autumn view of fields at Ursi (Stage 5)

ACCESS

There are two direct buses from Leh to Alchi each day, leaving at about 8am and 3pm. The same buses return from Alchi at more-or-less the same time. Although there are a few guesthouses in Alchi, all are of a high standard and expensive. Therefore, it is a good idea to arrive here about noon and start on trek on the same day, and at the end of the trek leave Mangyu early to catch the afternoon bus.

Alternatively, you can get off any bus going from Leh to Khalatse (or anywhere further in the direction of Kargil and Srinagar) at the bridge on the Indus River just west of Saspola village, and walk to Alchi from there. On the way back, walk to this bridge and try to catch transportation on the main road. There may also be an occasional shared jeep connection between Alchi and Saspola or Khalatse. If you want to start the trek in Sumdha Do, take a bus to Chiling from Leh and get off in Sumdha Do. From the village, follow the Sumdha Chu upstream until you join the route on Stage 3.

STAGE 1
Alchi to Stakspi La Base Camp

Start	Alchi (3121m)
Finish	Stakspi La Base Camp (4273m)
Distance	6.5km
Time	4hrs
Altitude range	3121m (Alchi) to 4273m (Stakspi La Base Camp)

Although the locals can walk from Alchi to Sumdha Chungun over the Stakspi La in one day, the path is tough, and it is better to divide it into two stages. Stage 1 reaches the Base Camp, over 1000m above Alchi, but still almost 1000m below the pass. Although short, it is not easy – it's a steep and laborious climb.

The camping place at the end of this stage is small: there is a summer shelter and space for two tents. A more convenient place is passed about 45mins before it. However, big groups need to cross the pass in one day and go almost as far as Sumdha Chungun village. In this case, leaving Alchi early is essential.

WARNING

According to some maps of the region, there are two passes: the Stakspi and the Sminopi. Be aware, however, that the location of the Stakspi La on those maps can be incorrect (where it is marked at the actual location of the Sminopi La). The maps show a path that leaves the main valley and turns towards the west-southwest, along a side-stream, and eventually reaches this incorrectly marked Stakspi La. The path *does* exist and it is very clear, but it does *not* lead to the Stakspi La! It is easy to confuse it with the correct way (as the author discovered – painfully – on his first time on this route in 2004). Nevertheless, the main route from Alchi to Sumdha Chungun used by the locals is as described below. Please read the information carefully.

Bear in mind that you will be ascending very fast on this stage and on Stage 2. Unless you are well acclimatised, there is a risk of altitude sickness. Do not ignore any symptoms.

Camp below the Stakspi La

Alternatives
Leave Alchi early and cover Stages 1 and 2 in one day. This avoids the need to sleep in a tent, but will make the day very hard, with a steep 2000m climb from Alchi to the pass.

Water supplies
You don't need to carry much water; a stream is followed all day.

Route
Alchi village is situated on the left bank of the Indus on an alluvial fan formed from a tributary flowing from the SW; the way to the Stakspi La leads along this stream. ◀

Alchi Gompa, one of Ladakh's major attractions, is situated in the southeastern part of the village, below a small square where the buses stop and the road ends.

From the square follow the road towards the NW with the Indus on your right for about 300m, and then turn left on to a path. The side valley you need is clear, but the path wanders through the fields to reach it. Go upwards until you get into the side valley. Follow a road for a short while, then leave it and follow the stream up its true right bank. As you walk further into the valley, it turns left; the river flows from the S.

About 30mins after leaving Alchi, cross to the true left bank via a bridge (3285m). Continue upstream on a good trail above the valley floor. Reach the left tributary stream (on your right) about 20mins beyond the bridge. ▶

Keep straight on up the main valley, on the true left bank of the stream, SSE at first and then ESE, crossing to the true right bank about 400m beyond the tributary. A little under 1hr after passing the tributary a clear right turn of the valley (S) is reached. Following the valley, cross the stream twice more and come to a fork near some stone walls in another 30mins (about 3880m). Head off on the true left slope of the side valley on your left (SE) for 10mins. Leave the valley, climb S towards the ridge on your right (3991m) and then go upwards to reach a pass (4002m). ▶ On the other side there's a place to camp in the valley. It's probably more convenient than the Base Camp, but it's further to the Stakspi La from there.

From the pass descend gently for just a few metres then walk gradually upwards by a clear path traversing the true right slope of the valley (on your left). Around 15mins after leaving the pass go past a side valley on your left (4120m) and then, some 350m further on, cross the main stream to the true left bank. Climb to the small ridge about 15m above the stream and walk along it to the solid shepherds' shelter. This is **Stakspi La Base Camp**.

A very clear path leads into this side valley, but this is not the correct way to the Stakspi La!

The green oasis visible from the pass down towards the north, on the opposite side of the Indus, is Likir.

STAGE 2
Stakspi La Base Camp to Sumdha Chungun

Start	Stakspi La Base Camp (4273m)
Finish	Sumdha Chungun (3867m)
Distance	9km
Time	6hrs
Altitude range	3867m (Sumdha Chungun) to 5177m (Stakspi La)

A sheer slope and a 5000m-high mountain ridge block the valley from the south-southwest side. The Stakspi La is on the left side of this ridge, 900m above the camp. The path to the pass climbs the sheer slope. The ascent takes 3½hrs and is only one of the difficulties of this stage; the descent is steep and quite long.

Alternatives
If you want to camp at the end of the stage instead of staying at a family house, there are a number of small places for a single tent beyond the village, in the willow bushes.

Water supplies
There are no streams on the upper, sheer part of the slope along the approach to the pass, and the other side of the ridge is dry. Before leaving the stream behind take water for the ascent and for 1½hrs of descent.

Route
From the camp near the shelter continue upstream along the main valley, towards the SW. There is a clear although narrow path on the small rise between the two streams, in the middle of the valley. Pass a side valley on your left. The main valley may be dry further up, so take water.

Further on reach a fork at the foot of the sheer slope (4550m), almost 300m (1hr) above the camp. Turn into the valley on your left, towards the S. The pass is visible

in the same direction, 600m higher. The path, which is quite distinct all the way, does not go straight to the pass. Follow it along the valley on its true left bank for about 20mins and then, before another clear fork, turn sharply right and start climbing the steep slope.

Reach a small pass (4755m) 20mins later. Continue upwards, first along the ridge and then slightly to the left of it. 15mins after crossing the small pass, turn sharply left, toward the S, to some rocks and huge stones. Here climb steeply uphill, very slightly to the left. When the trail is above the sheer part of the slope, go to the left (SSE). Traverse the slope above an almost vertical valley to a place under a clear pass. Over 100m of steep climb remain; ascend directly to the **Stakspi La** (5177m), marked by prayer flags, cairns and small stone piles. ▶

Descend steeply from the pass towards the valley (roughly S), 500m directly below the pass. You will be zigzagging on a sheer slope of small, loose stones. When you reach the valley floor, follow its dry riverbed downwards on a clear path. About 1½hrs from the pass is a solitary house and fields (4235m). In autumn the water starts flowing just before this; continue down the stream

The recently renovated gompa in Sumdha Chungun is one of the oldest in Ladakh

To the north are countless peaks and ranges and, 2000m below, the Indus Valley; south and east the ridges, peaks and valleys of Central Ladakh and Zanskar are visible.

on its left bank. There is a quite good place to camp by the stream, 10mins onwards (4118m).

Continue the descent on the left, then on the right, side of the stream. **Sumdha Chungun** (3867m) is about 2hrs' walk from the pass, at the confluence with a big right tributary stream. There are fields, a small monastery and a few houses. Ask for accommodation; the author slept in a fairly new house with a nice family at the north-west end of the settlement, 200m up the tributary valley (excellent food).

> There is an interesting **12th-century gompa** in the village. It has been recently renovated by a team from the World Monuments Fund and their project won the UNESCO award for Cultural Heritage Conservation in 2011.

STAGE 3
Sumdha Chungun to Manechan

Start	Sumdha Chungun (3867m)
Finish	Manechan (4048m)
Distance	15.5km
Time	6hrs
Altitude range	3453m (confluence with the Sumdha Chu) to 4048m (Manechan)

This stage follows deep, beautiful and narrow valleys with no major ascents. There is a gradual descent at the beginning, and a gradual ascent later in the day.

Alternatives
- If you want to finish the trek early, turn left at the confluence with the Sumdha Chu. Walk downstream along a clear path to Sumdha Do village on the bank

The colourful Sumdha Valley

of the Zanskar River (about 1hr). The Nyemo–Padum road is under construction; the Nyemo–Chiling section has been completed, and buses link with Leh a few times a week.

- If you want to go to Chiling (where you can either finish the trek or continue to the Markha Valley), walk along the trail for 2½hrs, then turn left to Lanak. Cross the Dungdungchen La the next day.
- If you do not want to camp, you can find accommodation in Sumdha Chenmo, 1hr before Manechan.

Water supplies
Although the route follows rivers all day, you will be above the valley floor in some places, so will need to carry some water. See below.

Route
From **Sumdha Chungun**, continue descending along the left bank of the river. There are camps in the willows further downvalley, before the confluence with the Sumdha Chu. Beyond the village, cross a bridge (3651m) to the right bank after 15mins, then return to the left side of the stream a few minutes further on by another bridge.

About 40mins after leaving the village, the deep, main valley of the Sumdha Chu is reached. The river flows from right (W) to left (E). Unless you want to go to Sumdha Do, turn right and walk up the Sumdha Chu on its true left bank, traversing the slope about 20m above the valley floor.

You will descend to a terrace in the valley floor 20mins later. There is a bridge and camping spot here (3538m). Cross to the true right bank, and then in just 3mins return to the left bank by another bridge. Beyond a sharp turn of the valley to your left (SW), you will pass through a rock gate (roughly 30mins past the bridge). 10mins later, still on the true left bank, you will go past a relatively big side valley and a stream on your right (3594m).

About 100m further on, the path forks. An old and damaged path leads straight ahead, and a clear, new one descends to the left. Follow the latter. Another 150m on, at the bottom of the ravine, cross the bridge to the true right bank, and then, shortly, return to the left one.

Climb steeply to a high traverse. After 20mins pass a ruined bridge beside wine-coloured rocks. ▶ Follow the left bank for 70m to the valley floor, where a new bridge (3661m) is found. Cross it and continue on the true right bank for 15mins. Reach a relatively large valley with a stream on your left, flowing from the SE, and see a narrow, tributary valley on the opposite side of the Sumdha Chu. It is a nice camp; probably a campsite with a shop and tent-restaurant in the high season (3710m).

This elaborate bridge was once an impressive construction of wood and stones. It was in use when the author was here for the first time in 2004.

A path towards the southeast, on the left bank of the tributary valley, leads to Chiling over the **Dungdungchen La**. If you choose this route, you can camp further along in this valley, just before the final ascent to the pass at Lanak, near the shelter where a few herders stay in summer. ▶

Follow the main valley, along the Sumdha Chu. Cross a bridge to the true left bank just beyond the campsite and continue in the valley floor. You will pass a good camp 10mins later. Within another 10mins you will come to another big side valley on your left, and a sharp right turn in the valley (W). The valley widens here, with huge mountains all around. There is a nice campsite in the valley in a small copse (3680m). ▶

Continue up the Sumdha Chu on a good wide trail on the true left slope, high above the valley. You will reach **Sumdha Chenmo** village in 1hr. Continue through the settlement high above the river. A campsite (3990m) is found in the second part of the settlement, next to a side-stream and small *gompa*. Homestay is available. It takes 5hrs to get here from Sumdha Chungun.

Do not cross the bridge here. The path on the other side of the river leads towards the east. It crosses a pass and joins the way to the Dungdungchen La.

From the village, follow a clear path along the main valley, upstream. Pass a small restaurant just beyond the settlement and then descend to the valley bottom. (There is a good place to camp on a terrace 15mins' walk from the village.) Ignore the bridge here and continue on the true left bank until you get to a relatively big valley on your left 10mins later. Cross the stream to the true right bank (3965m). Next you need to follow a path that traverses the true right slope of the valley, with the river on the right (facing upstream) about 20m below. Pass a *chorten* beside the path as the valley turns. Make your camp on a dry terrace, high above the valley about 15mins later, opposite a large true left tributary valley. This place is **Manechan**, and it is apparently warmer at night here than in any other part of the valley. Descend to the river to fetch water.

STAGE 4
Manechan to Hinju

Start	Manechan (4048m)
Finish	Hinju (3818m)
Distance	16km
Time	7½hrs
Altitude range	3802m (lower part of Hinju) to 4904 (Kungski La)

The ascent to the pass is long – the pass is 900m higher than Manechan. The descent to Hinju is also long, but the trail is clear all day, through multi-coloured landscapes of barren mountains.

Alternatives
There are no alternatives for this stage.

Water supplies
Fill up with water before you enter the dry section of the valley for the remaining ascent and 1hr of descent. Further down towards Hinju take supplies for 1hr before you start the traverse above the valley floor.

Route
Beyond the camp, traverse high on the valley's right slope for 30mins. Then descend to the riverbank (4133m).

Pass a big side valley on your right about 40mins after leaving the camp. (It is possible to camp here, above the main valley on the alluvial fan of the tributary valley.) 10mins further on, just after passing a tributary on your left, the valley forks. Continue straight on along the floor of the main valley (W). A bit further, 1hr after leaving Manechan, you will pass quite a big camp (possibly a campsite in high season). The valley forks again just beyond it – take the valley on your right, flowing from the NW. Keeping on the true left bank of the stream, enter a beautiful, green valley.

There will be a shepherds' shelter in 30mins or so and another valley fork (4355m). This is the last place where it's possible to make camp; it takes 2hrs more to the pass. Ignore the valley that is on your right and continue straight on towards the WNW. Watch the stream carefully, because it soon becomes dry and there is no water further on. Pass a side valley on your right and then, 45mins from the shepherds' shelter, reach another valley fork (4525m). Go to your right, towards the NW. At the next fork (4590m) in 15mins, go left towards (W); it takes 1hr to reach the pass from here.

A beautiful autumn view from the ascent to the Kungski La

Follow the valley floor until you have covered half the distance to another fork, roughly 200m. Leave the valley and start the steep climb of the slope on your left, following a clear path. After making a couple of zigzags, you come to a ridge (4744m). Continue up, quite steeply, along the ridge to where it flattens (4875m). Traverse the slope to an indistinct pass, marked with prayer flags and a cairn, on the ridge on your right. This is the **Kungski La** (4904m), 4hrs from Manechan (and 3hrs' descent to Hinju). It is usually windy and cold here.

The colourful mountain behind (northeast) is **Spangting** (5750m). Faraway towards the northeast there is the 6000m-high Stok Range. Glacier-covered peaks are visible towards the south-south-west. There are countless barren mountains ahead (northwest), and a wide valley.

Morning view looking east towards the Kungski La from Hinju village

Descend steeply to the valley (4520m) and then follow its dried-up riverbed. Just under 1hr from the pass, you will reach a large left tributary valley where there is a basic shelter (4475m). If any water flows here, it is possible to make camp (two tents). Continue down the

valley to reach a point where two large tributary valleys join the main one. (Good places for camps are just before the confluence and after, next to solid shepherds' shelters that may be inhabited in summer: 4285m.)

Take water for about 1hr and follow the path, first on the terrace a few metres above the valley and then along the traverse. There are more good places to camp (below the path), further on before the valley turns, while 15mins later you will pass abandoned fields. The fields and houses ahead are **Angshang** (3955m), which is not permanently inhabited. (There is a campsite just before it, below the path.) Continue high above the river to pass Angshang. Cross a bridge in a side valley (3853m), pass above a campsite and arrive at **Hinju** (45mins from Angshang), which is quite a big settlement. Ask the locals for details of accommodation.

STAGE 5
Hinju to Ursi

Start	Hinju (3818m)
Finish	Ursi (3662m)
Distance	7.5km
Time	2½hrs
Altitude range	3487m (road junction below Hinju and Ursi) to 3818m (Hinju)

This is a short and easy stage along a dirt road with a gradual descent to the confluence of two valleys, followed by a short, steep ascent to Ursi. Ursi is a beautiful, green village at the day's end. Rest well here, because crossing the Tar La on Stage 6 is tough.

Alternatives
- It is possible to finish the trek at Hinju; if you are lucky, you might arrange transport from there, but

The Ripchar Togpo Valley below Hinju

Phanjila is a better option. Follow the road down for 2½hrs; there are shops, restaurants and guesthouses in Phanjila. The settlement has a regular bus connection with Leh and it is possible to catch a taxi, as many tourists come there to start the trek to Padum.

• If you want to go to Lamayuru, follow the road to Phanjila, where you can join Trek 5 (Padum to Lamayuru). It is possible to cover the distance from Hinju to Lamaruyu in one day. Wanla Gompa is on the way – one of the oldest Ladakhi *gompas* and well worth seeing.

Water supplies
The route runs high above the valley floor, so you need to carry water for the whole day.

Route
Follow the dirt road on the right downstream along the valley. There are places to camp in bushes by the river, below the road. You will reach fields and houses 30mins after leaving the village. This is **Hinju Yangtse** (3669m); people only stay here in summer. Continue along the

road to a deep, big valley that runs from right (NNE) to left (SW). Ursi is the beautiful, green oasis on your right, with houses in its upper part. ▶

When the road forks, go upwards to the right. Although it is possible to take a shortcut through the fields, it is easier to continue along the road as far as the houses of **Ursi**. There is a campsite at the top of the village, and a few houses offer accommodation.

The Tar La is on the summit of the huge ridge that closes the valley from the northeast.

STAGE 6
Ursi to Tar

Start	Ursi (3662m)
Finish	Tar (3372m)
Distance	15.5km
Time	7½hrs
Altitude range	3372m (Tar) to 4946m (Tar La)

This is a demanding stage. The trail to the Tar La is about 5.5km long and the pass is almost 1300m higher than Ursi, giving an average gradient of 23 per cent for the path – and it is 32 per cent in some place! The descent is even steeper at the beginning, and then is long and tiresome – a drop of over 1500m from the Tar La to Tar village. Be careful: it is possible to miss the way to the Tar La. Furthermore, the path for this stage is marked incorrectly on one of the maps available, which shows that there is a ridge to cross on the way down from the pass. This is incorrect – just follow the main valley downstream until you get to Tar village.

Alternatives
Descend to Phanjila to join Trek 5 (see Stage 5) or to go to Leh by bus.

Water supplies
You need to take water from Ursi, or from just beyond it to cover the trek to the pass and for at least 1hr of the

descent (supplies for about 6hrs). You will follow a stream further on.

Route

◀ Leave **Ursi** and go up the main valley (NE), to the foot of a rock just above the village. The valley forks here, forming two ravines. There is some wording on the slope, made up of small stones, that reads 'Welcome to Ursi'. Enter the ravine on your right, leaving the notice on your left. Follow the stony, dried-up riverbed – it's quite a steep climb. Ignore the path ascending the slope on your right that you will reach about 40mins after the fork.

Continue along the riverbed of the main valley to where it turns distinctly right (E), just over 1hr from Ursi, widens and becomes much steeper. The clear trail continues along the floor of the main valley, but you need to find another path that turns left (N) into a side ravine; the first important side valley on your left from Ursi. To enter it you need to climb a steep scree slope next to a rock. The path forms a clearly visible zigzag here. **Be careful, because it is easy to miss the correct route here.**

Follow the side valley, heading N at the beginning and NE just beyond the scree slope, from where you will hike in a dry, stony riverbed. There is a clear path all the way, passing a sheer side valley on your left and a smaller one on your right. Follow the main valley, which becomes steeper and steeper, eventually turning right towards the ENE. About 1hr along this valley there is a fork (4535m). (It is still more than 1hr to the pass and more than 400m of altitude gain.) Continue steeply upwards along the floor of the valley on your right, towards the E.

It gets very steep. You will reach another valley fork (4745m) 30mins later. Both sheer valleys finish shortly, at the ridge 200m above. The Tar La is at the steep end of the valley on the left, but the path does not follow the valley. Continue climbing in the floor of the sheer valley on your right, for about 10mins. Then, leave it and go to the ridge on your right (S). When you get there (4811m), continue upwards along the ridge (E). Continue left of the rocks

The Tar La is to the northeast of the village on a high ridge. The path is clear, but it forks in places and it is quite easy to miss the correct way: take care.

Looking North from the Tar La

and, when past them, turn left (NNE). Follow the traverse to the pass, above the sheer valleys that you left earlier. It takes 4hrs to climb to the **Tar La** (4946m) from Ursi; it is 10km down to Tar village and will take 3hrs.

Descend to a ridge on your left, 100m below the pass, and then go to the left to a very steep valley. The route descends very steeply across masses of loose, small stones. Further on the valley joins another larger one on the right (4580m). Turn left here and go on down the valley towards the ENE and then NNE. It is no less steep here – you will be happy that you are not going in the opposite direction! At some point on the way you should see a stream flowing. About 1½hrs from the pass reach a confluence with a tributary stream on the right (3905m). ▶ Continue down the valley by a clear path on one or other side of the stream, switching sides when you have to.

Reach a big, tributary stream on the left (3660m) 40mins after passing the first confluence. There is a place to camp for a single tent; it takes 1hr more to Tar. After about 10mins there is another left tributary (flowing in almost the opposite direction), and the ravine turns sharply right (N). Just beyond this confluence, you will pass a ruined building that makes a good place to

Although according to some maps a ridge should be crossed, do not ascend anywhere!

Tar village as seen from the way to the Hibti La (Stage 7)

camp (3586m). Another 15mins later, the trail leaves the valley floor and follows a traverse of the right slope, some 20m above the river. Pass another tributary valley to the left and another sharp, right turn of the valley. Head E for 500m and join another big valley with a stream flowing from your right; fields and some buildings are passed.

Descend to the valley floor and continue along the river on a good trail (15mins to the village). You will need to cross the river a few times, but it's easy (there is a camp by the river, before the main part of the village.) **Tar** is a quiet and beautiful small settlement of just four families. Homestay is available at a new house on the left bank, about 100m from the river.

Start	Tar (3372m)
Finish	Mangyu (3518m)
Distance	12km
Time	7hrs
Altitude range	3372m (Tar) to 4161m (Hibti La)

Although the Hibti La is just 4161m, it is still 800m above Tar village and the ascent is very steep. From there the route goes on a long traverse to another pass of similar altitude before descending to Mangyu village on a good trail. The monastery in Mangyu is reputedly one of the oldest in Ladakh, dating from the same period as the Alchi complex.

Alternatives

The trek can be shortened by following the main valley downstream from Tar to Nurla village (3.5km) on the Indus River by the main Kargil–Leh road. It is normally possible to catch a bus to Leh there.

Water supplies

Take water from the Tar for the whole day. Although there may be a tiny stream at the beginning of the ascent to

Hibti village as seen from the way to the Mangyu La

the Hibti La in early summer, there is certainly no water further on, all the way to Mangyu village. It may be hot and dry on this trail in summer.

Route

The Hibti La is SE of Tar village, and you follow a side valley that heads in that direction. From the main part of **Tar** village, take a path that climbs steeply to a 25m-high ridge. After crossing it, reach the side valley. Follow the riverbed upstream, ascending gradually. You will pass a valley on your right. An hour after leaving the village the valley becomes steeper and narrower. It takes another 1hr to get to the pass from here, with over 500m of height gained.

Ascend, following a clear, zigzagging path, slightly to the right, then slightly to the left, along the main valley. The valley widens further on, passing a side valley on the left, then another on the right. Go straight towards the SE, passing between small rocks, then head slightly to the right until you get to the obvious **Hibti La** (4161m). It's 2½hrs from Tar and has a wonderful view of the Indus Valley.

Do not descend from the Hibti La. You need to continue to another pass of similar altitude – the Mangyu La. It is clearly visible in the distance, roughly 4km towards the SE. Follow a long traverse on your right, cutting across a few valleys and crossing two minor passes. There is a distinct path all the way. Below there are great views of Hibti village.

A steep ascent remains before the trail reaches the **Mangyu La** (4137m), over 2hrs from the Hibti La. Across the pass, down in the valley, Mangyu village is clearly visible. Descend along an obvious path until you get to the main valley, then follow the left bank to the road and a bridge (3486m). It takes a little more than 1hr to get here from the pass. The main part of **Mangyu** village is 30m above, 500m along the road to the right. There are also some houses further along the main valley. Go to the right and ask about accommodation in one of the shops. It is surprisingly expensive here.

STAGE 8
Mangyu to Alchi

Start	Mangyu (3518m)
Finish	Alchi (3121m)
Distance	16.5km
Time	4hrs
Altitude range	3090m (Gyera) to 3518m (Mangyu)

This can be a tiresome stage along a dirt track and asphalt road. A bicycle would be great; however, the route does have its attractions. The Indus Valley is worth more than just a look out of the window of a bus. During the author's trek here in mid-October the waters of the Indus were grey with glacial flour; a week later, on the return to Alchi on Stage 8, he was surprised to see the river had become incredibly clear, and a beautiful blue. It gets hot and windy on this route.

Alternatives
The trek can be ended here; there is a bus from Mangyu to Leh once a week, and it is also possible to arrange a taxi. You can also walk down the valley to Gyera, and cross a pedestrian bridge on the Indus to the main Kargil–Leh road to pick up a bus, taxi or truck in either direction.

Water supplies
No water is available between Gyera and Lardo or between Lardo and Alchi. It is usually hot along the Indus Valley!

Route
Return to the bridge at **Mangyu** and follow the road downvalley on the true left bank (no camps) to reach **Gyera** (3100m) at the confluence with the Indus in 1½hrs. Take water for 1hr before turning right into the Indus Valley. Follow it upstream on its left bank, by the road. ▶ Further on you reach **Lardo** village (3100m),

There is a well-intentioned but unsuccessful farm here based on a large-scale irrigation project.

323

The clear blue Indus River between Gyera and Lardo – an autumn view

where there is accommodation. Collect water for 1hr and continue by the road along the Indus.

Pass a road bridge on the Indus 45mins after leaving the village. ◄ Follow the road along the true left bank of the Indus. It is 20mins' walk to Alchi. You will need to ascend a 20m-high steep slope and pass a school on your left. A *chorten* marks the start of **Alchi** village. At the road fork go straight; do not go up to the right. Follow the road until you get to the small square where the buses stop. There are a few shops and a restaurant. The famous Alchi Gompa is to the left, towards the Indus, below the square, and should not be missed.

Cross the bridge for the main Kargil–Leh road. The green oasis 1.5km east from the bridge is Saspola village; all the buses stop there.

> **Buses to Leh** leave around 8am and about 3pm and arrive in Leh on the same day. There are a number of guesthouses in the village, but all of them are expensive.

8 MARKHA VALLEY

An independent trekker approaching the Kanda La –
the first of two passes on Trek 8 (Stage 3)

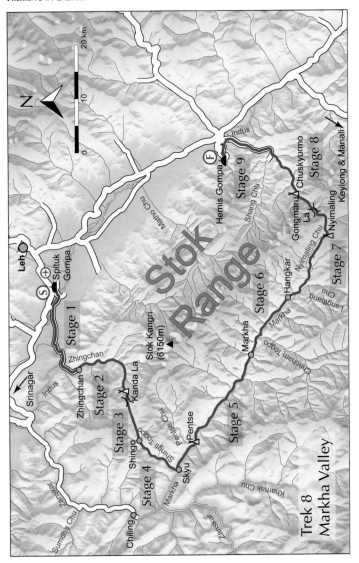

INTRODUCTION

Start	Spituk (3214m), southwest of Leh; alternatively Zhingchan, Stok, Kaya or near to Chiling
Finish	Hemis (3649m) near the Indus Valley, southeast of Leh; alternatively Shang Sumdo, Kharu, Lhatho, Pang, Zangla or Padum
Distance	113km
Time	55hrs (9 days)
Altitude range	3190m (road junction just beyond bridge over the Indus River) to 5287m (Gongmaru La)

COMBINATIONS AND ALTERNATIVES

It is possible to skip Stage 1 by going to Zhingchan by car. Do not do this unless you are well acclimatised because there is over 1000m of altitude gain on Stage 2 culminating in an overnight stay at 4400m.

The trek can also be started near to Chiling on the western bank of the Zanskar River, on the road that will link the Indus Valley with Padum or even in Kaya, which is the first village in the Markha Valley and can be reached by a new road bridge (for both Chiling and Kaya take a bus or taxi from Leh).

Spituk village and the Indus Valley as seen from Spituk Gompa (Stage 1)

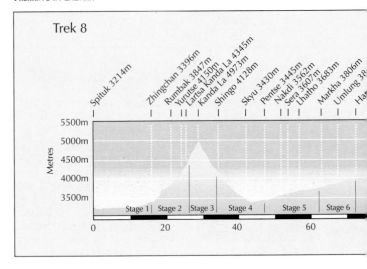

Trek 8

You can also walk to Chiling, starting either in Alchi (see Trek 7), Phanjila or Lamaruyu (for both reverse Trek 7). If you start in Chiling, follow the road up the Zanskar Valley to the new bridge on Zanskar. Cross it and continue on the road towards Kaya. It climbs a bit at the beginning then traverses the true-right bank of Markha river, which comes to your view on your right after a while. From Kaya continue on the path to Skyu (it takes about 3hrs to get here from the bridge), where you can join Trek 8 at Stage 4. Starting in Chiling makes the trek significantly easier, and is recommended if you are not properly acclimatised to cross the Kanda La. You do eventually cross a 5000m-high pass, but trekking along the Markha River will give you enough time to get properly acclimatised.

You can also start the trek in Stok via the steep Stok or Namlung passes (about 4850m) and join Stage 2 of Trek 8 in Rumbak (not researched by the author, but popular).

The trek can be reduced to four days and finished in Chiling; a good plan if you are short of time. From Skyu (Stage 4) go down the Markha Valley along its right bank to Kaya village. Continue on the road to the bridge on the Zanskar River and then follow down the valley to Chiling. There is a bus connection between Chiling and Leh, but check the details before setting out.

If you go from Skyu to Chiling, you can continue northwest to the Sumdha Valley, where there is an option to join Trek 7 and go to Alchi over the Kungski and Tar passes.

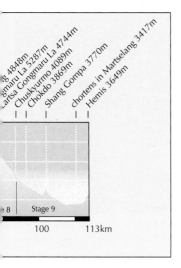

To finish this trek in Zanskar, leave the Markha Valley between Markha and Umlung villages (see Stage 6), and walk south along the Chacham Togpo to Rabrang La. After a few days with many river crossings, the route crosses the Charchar La and eventually reaches Zangla in the Zanskar Valley. This is a long and demanding trek across remote areas. Because of the high level of water in spring and early summer, this trek is best in the late summer and autumn.

Another option is to join the Kharnak trek (Trek 1), either by turning into the Langthang Chu beyond Hangkar (Stage 7) or by crossing the Kongka Ngonpo from Nyimaling. The route can either be finished in Pang or combined with the Tsarab Chu trek (Trek 2), eventually reaching Padum.

Both options make for a long, remote and demanding trek; both are late summer or autumn alternatives.

You can also trek southeast from Nyimaling (Stage 8) up the main valley to finish in Lhatho, on the main Leh–Keylong road (untested by the author, but it would seem to be a nice, if unpopular, option). After crossing two passes, the trail descends along a beautiful valley, which local people use frequently.

Instead of walking along the road from Shang Sumdo to Hemis (Stage 9), you might go up the valley to Shang and then reach Hemis by crossing one more pass, north of Shang; ask in Shang for details.

Part of the last stage can be skipped by taking a bus from Shang Sumdo.

You could also miss a bit of walking by descending to Kharu instead of ascending to Hemis at the end of the route.

GENERAL INFORMATION

The Markha Valley trek is a very popular and relatively easy route. The path is clear, so you are unlikely to lose your way. There are villages where you can rely on homestay accommodation and food, so carrying much in the way of supplies is not necessary. Most of the stages are relatively short and there are many options to divide the route into stages according to your liking. On every stage you will meet many people,

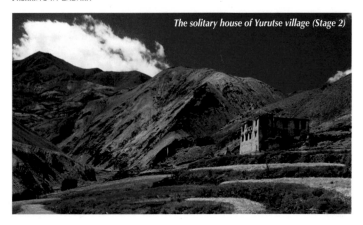

The solitary house of Yurutse village (Stage 2)

both locals and other trekkers; commercial trekking companies particularly favour this route.

DIFFICULTY, SUPPLIES AND ACCOMMODATION

Although relatively easy overall, the first pass is quite hard: the trail climbs to almost 5000m in just three days. There are a few Markha River crossings that might be difficult in early summer. The trail follows a number of precipitous paths, especially beyond the Gongmaru La, which might be challenging. Beware of altitude sickness on the early stages.

Most trekkers on Trek 8 travel in big, organised groups. At the campsites the staff start work early in the morning and finish late at night, and horses' bells are noisy all night long. This may be disturbing at some small campsites, which do not have separate areas for animals. If you need horses or ponies to carry your luggage, pick them up in Leh.

Homestay accommodation is available in most of the villages on the way. Although going without a tent and supplies of food is not recommended, the number of camps can be limited to four or five. There is also at least a tent-shop in every village and at every campsite in summer. However, in many of them don't expect to buy much more than biscuits and sweets, or to be served food other then instant noodle soup or tea. On this route in particular, staying at family houses is a more tranquil option than camping in high season.

WHEN TO GO?

In spring the route becomes accessible as soon as the passes are free

Zhingchan valley (Stage 2)

of snow in June, or even in May. Trekking here is normally possible until mid-October, depending on snowfall. However, in late June and early July, the level of the Markha River is higher but this need not prevent crossings – use trekking poles. In summer the trail is usually packed, and it is probably better to choose Trek 7 during this period.

As for all routes described, September is the best time. It is quieter than summer and the beauty of autumn can be experienced. Regardless of the season, it will probably be hot along the route and cold in Nyimaling. When the author was there in mid-June, the side-stream froze at night; in late August there was slight snowfall, and in the morning it was really cold.

It's possible to do at least part of the trail in winter. The author spent 10 beautiful days in the valley in January 2014, trekking village-to-village from Chiling to Hangkar and back, seeing no other people but the locals.

ACCESS

Spituk is just a few kilometres from central Leh and buses go there every 15mins during the day. It is also easy to get to any of the alternative starting points. Hemis or Kharu at the end of the trek have good bus connections with Leh. If you only have a short time in Ladakh there is no need to build in extra days to get to the start and finish points of this trek. There is no accommodation in Spituk; to start the trek, leave Leh early by one of the first buses (around 8am) and walk to Zhingchan on the same day. At the end, stay overnight in Hemis to visit the monastery and its museum. There is a bus to Leh about 8am and in the early afternoon, about 1pm.

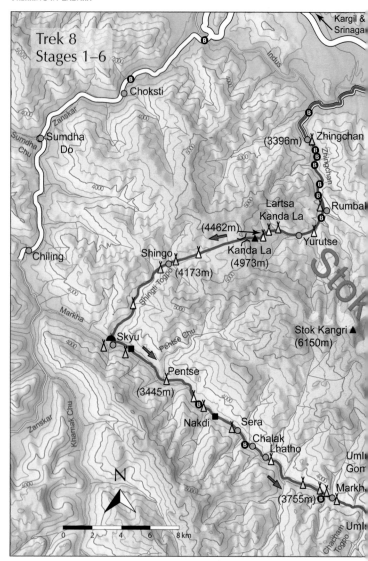

Trek 8
Stages 1–6

Kargil &
Srinaga

B

B Choksti

Zanskar

Sumdha
Chu

Sumdha
Do

Indus

(3396m) B Zhingchan

B
B
B

B Zhingchan

B

B Rumbak

Chiling

Lartsa
Kanda La

(4462m) Kanda La
(4973m)

Shingo

(4173m)

Shingti Togpo

Markha

Yurutse

Stok

Stok Kangri
(6150m)

Skyu

Pentse Chu

Pentse
(3445m)

Kharnak Chu

Zanskar

Nakdi

B

Sera

Chalak
Lhatho

Umlu
Gon

Markh.
(3755m) B

N

0   2   4   6   8 km

Chacham Togpo

Umlu

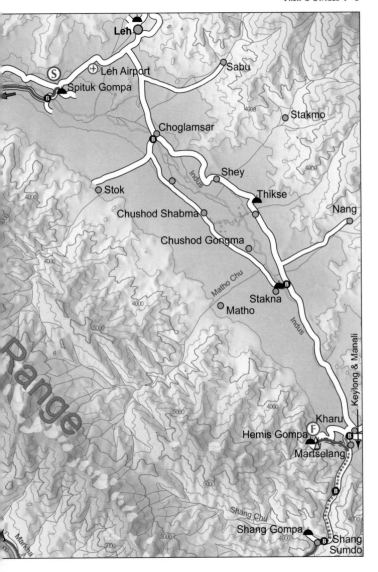

STAGE 1
Spituk to Zhingchan

Start	Spituk (3214m)
Finish	Zhingchan (3396m)
Distance	16km
Time	5½hrs
Altitude range	3190m (road junction just beyond bridge over the Indus River) to 3396m (Zhingchan)

Stage 1 is quite a long hot walk on a dusty road in a wide valley so early starts are important. Zhingchan, in a side valley at the end of the stage, is not a particularly interesting place.

Alternatives

Footbridge over the Indus River at Spituk

- Most organised groups skip the first stage, going to Zhingchan by jeep. If you do this check the minibus connection (there may be a bus once a week) or hire a taxi. Stay at the Zhingchan campsite. However, walking on this stage aids acclimatisation.

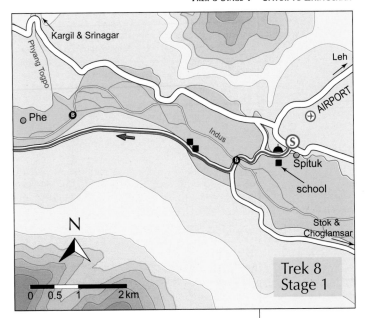

- You can start in Stok (see Combinations and alternatives), saving a road walk, but you need to cross an additional pass.

Water supplies

There are no water sources en route, so it is best to take water for the first 3hrs from Leh. Along the side valley to Zhingchan you can take water from the stream.

Route

▶ Start from Leh; take a morning bus (every 30mins from 7.30am). Get off at the junction east of the monastery hill, next to a number of *chortens* about 600m from the main road. (If you go by taxi, ask the driver to drop you at the bridge on the Indus.)

From the junction next to the *chortens* follow a short road (SW), with the monastery above right, then a paved

Spituk is definitely worth visiting, but make a separate trip to visit the monastery.

335

way (SW) alongside *chortens* before heading W at the southern foot of the monastery hill. After walking about 700m (about 15mins) you will reach a dirt road. Follow it left (SW) until you get to the bridge on the Indus, another 700m further (3205m). Cross it. The road forks a few minutes beyond the bridge; go right (WNW), and pass the last houses of **Spituk** 30mins later.

Follow the dirt road through deserted surroundings, high above the Indus River where the planes make incredible turns just before landing or after take-off. Pass above the village of **Phe** on the opposite side of the Indus, and note the green oasis to the north: Phyang village and monastery, around 7km away. Further on, the valley narrows and the river meanders, flowing S, then W and finally NW. ◄

This section of the Indus is popular for whitewater rafting.

About 3hrs (almost 13km) after starting out reach the valley of the left (SW) tributary stream. The road turns into this valley, following its true right bank. After 15mins a road bridge is reached (3254m); cross to the other bank. There is a tent-restaurant just beyond the bridge at a confluence with a small side-stream. Follow the road for 45mins more to reach **Zhingchan**. There are normally one or two campsites in the village, a small shop and a restaurant, but don't expect to find much. The campsite(s) are usually busy, so it is not very tranquil. Try to make camp away from where the horses are kept.

STAGE 2

Zhingchan to camp below Kanda La

Start	Zhingchan (3396m)
Finish	Camp below Kanda La (4462m)
Distance	10.5km
Time	7½hrs
Altitude range	3383m (bridge near Zhingchan) to 4462m (camp before Kanda La)

This is a tough stage with more than 1000m of altitude gain. If you experience any serious symptoms of altitude sickness, descend and make camp. Rest and drink a lot of water. If you are fine the next day, continue the ascent. Read the advice about the dangers of ignoring the symptoms on the Introduction.

Early in the stage, where the beautiful valley is narrow, look for *bharals* (blue sheep) jumping on the sheer slopes. Be wary of stones falling from above while walking through narrow sections. There is a clear, frequently used path all the way.

Alternatives

If you start to feel any symptoms of altitude sickness on the way, divide the stage by sleeping at Rumbak or Yurutse, or near villages where camping is possible.

A trekker heading towards the Lartsa Kanda La

Water supplies

Initially the river is followed so water can be sourced when necessary. Beyond Rumbak the trail runs above the river, so you need to carry supplies.

Route

Continue along the main valley upstream on the true left bank. The road finishes just beyond the camp. A little further on is the Hemis National Park building where an entrance fee used to be collected.

Cross a bridge (3383m) to the true right bank of the river 20mins beyond camp and then cross back a few minutes later. 10mins beyond the second bridge, the path forks. If the water is low, go either way; in early summer, however, follow the path traversing the slope on your right. Return to the valley floor and, 15mins later, cross a bridge. Just under 1½hrs after leaving Zhingchan, pass *chortens* and prayer flags (a possible camp). Go past a big dry side valley on your left in 10mins and a few fields. Follow the true right bank for another 10mins. Reach a small bridge; cross over and continue on the other side for 15mins, then cross the bridge back to the true right bank (3772m). Take water and continue upstream.

The valley widens, with the glacier-covered peak of Stok Kangri in view ahead. The path keeps above the riverbed to fields with a big side valley on your left and campsite; there is a small shop-restaurant (3847m). ◀ This is **Rumbak**, about 3hrs (5.5km and 450m higher than the camp) from Zhingchan; the main part of the village is up the side valley.

Continue up the main valley towards the S on the true right bank for 15mins, then cross the bridge. Follow the path on the opposite side of the stream. The valley forks about 30mins (1.7km) beyond Rumbak; follow a clear path to your right (WSW). The path leaves the valley floor just beyond the turn and climbs to a traverse of the true left slope. Camping is possible a little further on, below the path. Take water for 3hrs and follow the traverse.

The trail from Stok joins the main route here via the side valley.

Yurutse (4150m) is a solitary house and fields 1½hrs after leaving Rumbak (with accommodation). Continue walking straight along the traverse, with a second valley fork occurring about 20mins further on. Follow the valley on your right again, towards the W and NW further on, continuing the traverse of the true left slope.

Just over 1½hrs after leaving Yurutse the first of the Kanda La Base Camps is reached (**Lartsa Kanda La** 4345m). There is a small shop-restaurant and a camping fee, regardless of where you stay. This campsite is usually full of groups, so it's better to go further (and continuing now makes Stage 3 easier).

The valley forks again here. Follow the valley on your left towards the W, traversing the true right slope above the valley floor. Advance Base Camp is about 40mins further, at the next fork. There are small places for single tents between the campsites here, below the path. Water can be taken from a tiny spring. It is a perfect place to watch hares in the morning!

STAGE 3

Camp below Kanda La to Shingo

Start	Camp below Kanda La (4462m)
Finish	Shingo (4173m)
Distance	7.5km
Time	5½hrs
Altitude range	4173m (Shingo) to 4973m (Kanda La)

The pass is 500m above the camp but the ascent is not relaxing; it takes 3hrs to climb to the top. The 5km descent is tiring, but the trail is clear.

Alternatives

There are no alternatives on this stage.

Shingti Valley and the Zanskar Range – the view from the Kanda La

Water supplies

On the way up, before leaving the valley, take water sufficient for 3½hrs.

Route

The pass is WSW of the camp, behind a hill; the trail follows the valley on your left, climbs to the hill and traverses to the pass. Leave the camp and return to the path crossing the true right slope of the valley (the valley and path fork just above the camp). Take the left trail into a steep valley on your left, heading WSW and SSW further on. The path heads upstream on the true left side of the valley to where it flattens and turns towards the SW, some 40mins from camp. It's possible to camp here (4610m). This is the last place to refill your water bottles!

For about 30mins, continue upwards along the valley floor towards the SW, to reach another valley fork (4695m). The pass is above the steep, dry valley on your right. You need to make a loop here, heading towards the ridge (N) across this valley. Go NW for a short while, then steeply up towards the N. When you get to the ridge (4765m), follow it upwards (W) to the top of the hill (4826m). The pass is clearly visible towards the

W now. ▶ Follow the clear short traverse, which ends steeply. The **Kanda La** is 150m higher than the hill, a little over 30mins away.

From the pass (4973m) the Zanskar Range is seen S and SW. The wide Shingti Togpo Valley is ahead and Shingo village is visible in the distance. It takes 2hrs to reach the first campsite in Shingo. Follow a clear path from the pass down to the valley. Move quietly here and you may see marmots.

There is a confluence with a right tributary valley 40mins after leaving the pass by a shelter (4640m). If the riverbed is not dry, camping is possible here.

Continue down the valley to a tributary valley on the left 30mins further on. There is a campsite with a toilet and usually a shop-restaurant. It may be closed in late August, and the stream may be dry. Continue down along the valley on the right bank towards **Shingo** village (4128m). There are two campsites; one smaller area is just before the settlement (4173m), and another noisier, bigger one 15mins beyond. Homestay and food are also available here.

Stok Kangri (6150m) can be seen towards the southeast, 9.5km away.

STAGE 4
Shingo to Pentse

Start	Shingo (4173m)
Finish	Pentse (3445m)
Distance	13km
Time	5hrs
Altitude range	3387m (homestay between Skyu and Pentse) to 4173m (Shingo)

The Shingti Togpo is followed to the Markha Valley with easy river crossings where the path changes sides. Blue sheep are common, but watch out above for dislodged stones. At the confluence of the rivers in Skyu start a long, gradual ascent along the Markha River.

Alternatives

If you turn right in Skyu, and follow the Markha downstream, you reach the Zanskar River. There is Kaya village on the way. The road begins here. Following it, you will cross the bridge on Zanskar; then turn right to reach Chiling. It is about 3hrs between Skyu and the bridge. Accommodation is available in Kaya. From Chiling you can also continue to Lamayuru or Alchi (see Trek 7 Combinations and alternatives).

Water supplies

Initially you will be near the stream. However, the riverbed is dry before Skyu in late summer, so keep an eye on it and take some water in advance. In Skyu, take water for the whole route to Pentse (2hrs), as the route runs high above the Markha with no more sources.

Route

From the first campsite in **Shingo** (4173m), cross to the left bank just below the camp. At the main part of the village (4128m), return to the right bank for a short while and then recross. Follow a clear path through willow bushes and pass the second campsite 10mins after leaving the village (4075m). (Over the next 15mins camping is possible for free.) Pass a ruined house; the valley narrows further on, becoming stony, and the path follows it. Cross to the right bank 40mins beyond Shingo and some 20mins later reach the riverbed. Cross to the left for a short while, and then back to the right.

About 1½hrs from Shingo the trail returns to the left bank again, with more camping spots. Cross the river a few more times further on. About 2hrs from Shingo is a tent-shop (3537m) and restaurants with biscuits and some local products. Take water, because the riverbed dries up beyond here in the late season.

Skyu (3430m) with a small monastery, a campsite, a guesthouse and a number of tent-restaurants is 30mins further on. The Markha River is below the village. Turn left and continue up the valley on the true right bank (with the river right, facing upstream) high above the valley

The gompa in Skyu

floor, so carry water. There is a solitary house (3387m) 20mins after Skyu; the family offers accommodation and food. There is also a campsite (3387m). Continue some 40mins to where the path forks. The left branch ascends and the right follows the valley floor. Unless the river is high, take either fork, as they join in 250m. A similar divide comes a few minutes later.

From Skyu to Pentse takes up to 2hrs; **Pentse** is not a village but just a campsite. There is a side-stream flowing from the N. The shop here does not offer meals; however, local products are on sale.

> Don't miss the dried apricots, apricot juice and local biscuits: *pulli*. You should also try (although you will probably not be a fan) the **seabuckthorn juice**. It is a drink made from the berries of seabuckthorn – a shrub found in abundance in the lower riverbeds of Ladakh.

The campsite, on a beautiful, green terrace, is in the riverbed, below the alluvial fan of the side valley. It might be cold at night, because the ground is moist here.

STAGE 5
Pentse to Markha

Start	Pentse (3445m)
Finish	Markha (3755m)
Distance	15km
Time	7hrs
Altitude range	3431m (spring 15mins beyond camp) to 3755m (Markha)

Continue along the Markha Valley on a clear path passing a few villages during the day. Campsites and shop-restaurants are found almost every hour on the way. The Markha River must be forded once.

Alternatives
There are no alternatives on this stage.

Water supplies
There is a spring 15mins beyond the camp and you will be able to refill bottles at campsites on the way.

Route
From camp follow the valley on its true right bank, above the valley floor. Pass a spring 15mins later, just next to the path. In just under 1hr there is a dusty place with willow bushes, where making camp is possible. There is another one 600m further on before a bridge over the Markha (3527m). Cross it to the true left bank to reach a campsite in **Nakdi** (3532m) in a few minutes. The actual settlement (3562m) is 15mins further on; despite a few buildings and fields no one seems to live here permanently. **Sera** village (3607m) is 30mins (2km) onwards with one house that offers homestay, a campsite and a shop.

After 30mins cross to the true right bank of the Markha by another bridge (3612m) and arrive at **Chalak** village, situated at the confluence of the Markha and a large tributary. There is a shop-restaurant (mainly local

products) in a place called **Lhatho** (3683m), 30mins beyond Chalak, with a side-stream flowing directly from the foot of Stok Kangri. (Camping is possible 10mins later and again 30mins further, on a terrace near a sharp turn of the valley.) Further along on the terrace, high above the valley floor, pass some *chortens*. From the terrace – where the valley turns – note a solitary house clinging to a cliff on your left. Descend to the valley floor and go past the house, where accommodation is available and there is a campsite (1½hrs from Lhatho).

About 10mins beyond the house is a ford across the Markha River to its true left bank. In early summer the water might be high and the crossing difficult. If it looks dangerous, camp or return to the house and try crossing early the next morning, when the meltwater will be less intense and the level should be lower. There is a campsite and shop just beyond the ford. It takes about 30mins from here to the main part of **Markha** village (3806m) with campsites and homestay. A clean and well-organised campsite (3755m), where horses are separated from tents, is just before the bridge in Markha, on the true left bank of the river, right of the path.

The Markha River needs to be forded on Stage 5

STAGE 6
Markha to Hangkar

Start	Markha (3755m)
Finish	Hangkar (3990m)
Distance	10.5km
Time	5hrs
Altitude range	3755m (Markha) to 3990m (Hangkar)

Continue upstream along the Markha, crossing the river at least twice. The diverse landscape offers views of Kang Yaze peak and the incredible Techa Gompa.

Alternatives
The trail to and from Zanskar over the Rabrang La joins the Markha Valley on this stage. See Combinations and alternatives above, and information below.

Water supplies
Water is plentiful at campsites and from streams.

Route
Cross the bridge to the true right bank of the river. Pass two more campsites before reaching the foot of a hill. If you don't want to visit the monastery, you can skirt it. Beyond the hill is the main part of **Markha** village (3806m); a big side-stream flows from the peaks of Pyramide and Shuku Kangri here. Continue along the main valley on the true right bank (with the river right, facing upstream), above the floor, soon passing one more campsite. Places to wild camp are a bit further on, in bushes on a terrace.

There is a fork in the path nearly 30mins after the main part of Markha. The left branch traverses a sheer slope, which is precipitous and requires care. The right one is safer, but requires two crossings of the Markha River.

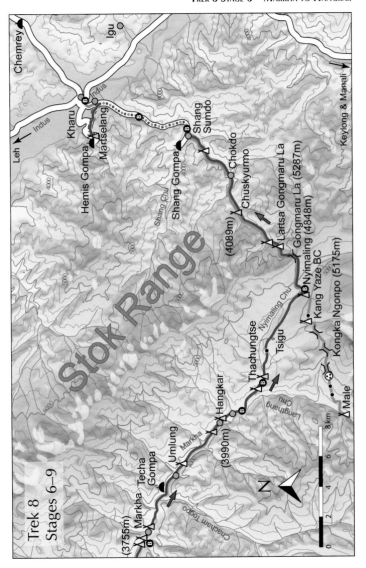

Trek 8
Stages 6–9

One of several campsites in Markha

- If you want to take the left one, make sure there are fresh footprints, and double-check that you don't confuse this traverse with the next one.
- If you take the right option, cross to the left bank and return to the right 300m further on.

The two trails join again just beyond the second ford. Go past a tributary ravine on your left; another ravine on your right comes into view. There is a path that traverses the true right, sheer slope of the Markha Valley, but it is clearly damaged and cannot be used.

The stream is the Chacham Togpo, and the path along it leads to the Rabrang La (not tested by the author).

Instead of following the damaged traverse cross the Markha before reaching the ravine on your right; there is a needle-like rock at its end. ◀ Continue along the Markha Valley through the terraces on the true left bank, passing a cold camping place (3845m). About 500m beyond the side-stream, return to the true right bank, fording the river again. The valley turns sharply left (E).

> **Techa Gompa** is high above the river, an unbelievable construction clinging to a vertical mountainside on the right bank. There is a clear, very steep path to it, but be aware that the *gompa* is often closed.

Continue on the true right bank to reach **Umlung** village (3890m) in 30mins (still 1½hrs/around 5km to Hangkar). There is no campsite here, but there are two tent-shops where you can drink tea and buy local products. (Homestay is available 600m beyond the main part of Umlung, and camps are possible a little further on.) Continue along a terrace on the valley floor with occasional places to camp.

> **Seabuckthorn shrubs** grow beside the trail. Their small orange berries ripen in autumn and are the main ingredient of the seabuckthorn juice and jam sold locally (see Stage 4).

▶ Just over 30mins beyond Umlung cross a tributary stream on your left (3976m). No more than 30mins further on you will reach the first campsite of **Hangkar**. It takes 10mins to reach the village. A few years ago the settlement suffered a heavy flood caused by the side-stream that joins the Markha in the village. There are two small campsites in this part of the village (Hangkar Yokma or Lower Hangkar) and accommodation is on offer.

The glacier-covered mountain that appears towards the south-southeast is Kang Yaze (6400m), 16km away as the crow flies (you will pass to the left of it on Stage 7).

STAGE 7
Hangkar to Nyimaling

Start	Hangkar (3990m)
Finish	Nyimaling (4848m)
Distance	11km
Time	7½hrs
Altitude range	3990m (Hangkar) to 4848m (Nyimaling)

This is a hard stage, with the gentle ascent along the Markha Valley largely behind you. There is a nearly 900m-altitude gain to negotiate. Nyimaling is a beautiful pasture in a wide valley at the foot of Kang Yaze peak. Villagers come here in the summer to graze their yaks, sheep and goats.

It's very crucial that you do not have any altitude sickness symptoms when leaving Hangkar, as you gain altitude quickly and sleep very high on this stage.

A lone trekker passing Hangkar

Alternatives

If you go up the Langthang Valley – one of the two streams that form the Markha River beyond Hangkar – you will join Trek 1 (Kharnak) on the same day. You can either finish in Pang on the Manali–Leh road or in Zanskar; both are demanding options. It is wise to divide the stage if you are not well acclimatized (this particularly applies to trekkers who started in Chiling or Kaya). You can sleep in Thachungtse on the first night and continue to Nyimaling on the second day.

Water supplies

Although the route follows the river beyond Hangkar, it's safer not to drink its water unless you purify it. Carry supplies between the latter part of Hangkar village and Thachungtse.

Route

Continue along the Markha Valley upstream along a clear path. Just beyond the village climb steeply to a hill below the ruins of a monastery. There are a few *chortens* and *mani* walls. The second part of **Hangkar** is on the other side of the hill, below it – Hangkar Gongma or Upper Hangkar (4048m). Descend to it; there's no campsite, but homestay is available. Pass the village and continue along the main valley on the true right bank, above the fields. 20mins from the houses, beyond the last fields, a confluence of two rivers is reached at a clear turn in the valley. The left tributary (on your right, facing upstream) is the Langthang Chu and generally flows from the south, from the Zalung Karpo La; the true right tributary (on your left) is the Nyimaling Chu. A narrow, 30m-high ridge separates the two rivers.

Do not cross the bridge near the confluence but follow the Nyimaling Chu on your left – on its true right bank. Pass a rock gate 500m further on, after which the valley is wider and green. Soon you come to the fields cultivated by the villagers of Hangkar. Pass next to a camp 1½hrs after starting the stage. There is a bridge 10mins ahead (4259m); cross it and continue along the valley on the true left bank for another 15mins to **Thachungtse** (4250m). This open pasture has a campsite, plus a tent-shop in season. Stay here if you feel any altitude sickness symptoms. It will take almost 5hrs to Nyimaling from here.

Continue on the left bank by a good path, up the main valley, at a gradually increasing distance from the river. Cross a side-stream flowing in a green, steep valley, 10mins after passing the Thachungtse campsite. About 10mins later reach another green side valley. Follow this steeply up, towards the SE and E further on, on its true left bank, leaving the Nyimaling Chu behind (possible camp in this valley, at a flat part further on). Continue up the valley, taking water before the river dries up. After 30mins, cross to the true right bank and then climb steeply (ENE) to a ridge on the top of its right slope (4559m) – 1½hrs from Thachungtse.

The Gongmaru La can be seen steeply towards the east-southeast, 6.5km from the ridge. ▶ There are fantastic views of the Stok Range towards the north-northwest. Continue ascending towards the ESE, slightly left of the ridge but basically along it. Follow a tiny stream a little further on and come to a small lake, **Tsigu** (4690m), in 30mins. There is another lake slightly higher (not on the way to Nyimaling) with a good camping spot on its

Another pass, visible towards the south, is the Kongka Ngonpo – this is between Nyimaling and the Zalung Karpo La on Trek 1.

The path to Kang Yaze Base Camp starts there.

bank. ▶ A small stream connects the two lakes. It will take roughly 1½hrs to reach **Nyimaling**, so take water for the whole way and continue ascending towards the ESE from the first lake. There is a clear path.

NYIMALING

Nyimaling is a beautiful place in this wide valley, with shepherds' shelters and a tent-shop. In 2009, sleeping in a tent-dormitory was possible. You need to pay a fee wherever you camp here.

Nyimaling is sometimes littered and the water in the main river could be contaminated, especially in late season, so take it from a small side-stream on the true left bank and camp here. In late season when the stream may have dried up, it's a good idea to camp above the others, further upstream. Do not drink water from the main river without boiling or purifying it. Watch for marmots around the meadows. Try some fresh local dairy products; visit the shepherds and ask for *labo*, a cottage cheese, or *zho*, a yoghurt.

STAGE 8
Nyimaling to Chuskyurmo

Start	Nyimaling (4848m)
Finish	Chuskyurmo (4089m)
Distance	10km
Time	6½hrs
Altitude range	4089m (Chuskyurmo) to 5287m (Gongmaru La)

The ascent to the pass is not very hard and consists of two steep parts divided by quite a long, gentle trek along a plateau. However, the altitude is significant as it is over 400m higher than the camp. The descent is very steep and the following path precipitous in places, so be careful. Fortunately the trail is clear, but avoid less obvious tracks. Do not follow the riverbed of the ravine through its very steep sections or through cascades. There is a path on one of the slopes (see below).

Alternatives

- From Nyimaling go west-southwest, following the way to Pang or to Zanskar on Trek 1.
- Continue upstream along the Nyimaling Chu; cross the Lhalung and Chaktsang passes and finish the trek in Lhatho village on the Manali–Leh road (not tested by the author).
- Spend an additional night in Nyimaling. Walk to Kang Yaze Base Camp (see Trek 1), then descend to Tsigu and return to Nyimaling.

Water supplies

From Nyimaling take water for 3½hrs. On the way down from the pass, take some water before starting each of the traverses.

Route

Cross the bridge to the true right bank of the Nyimaling Chu to find a clear path that starts behind the animal shelter. Climb the steep slope (NNE) and, after 30mins, come to a point where the path is gentler and turns right, towards the clearly visible pass to the E. A little further

The Gongmaru La

on the trail becomes almost flat. Head towards the pass, through beautiful high altitude pasture, until you get to the foot of a sheer slope a little over 100m below the **Gongmaru La**. This final, steep and tiring climb to the pass (5287m) on a good trail takes some 40mins.

> There are **great views from the pass**. Northeast is the Indus Valley, and beyond the Ladakh Range. To the southwest are the meadows of Nyimaling with Kang Yaze peak (6400m) above, on the other side of the valley, some 1000m higher than the pass. A pass to the right of Kang Yaze, on its ridge, marks the way to the Langthang Chu and the Zalung Karpo La – one of many crossings on Trek 1.

It takes 3½hrs to Chuskyurmo from the pass. First descend steeply by a zigzagging path and then, by a long traverse of a sheer slope, to a valley on the left. This valley leads steeply down. Follow it and in 1hr reach a confluence with a small valley coming from the right. Making camp is possible here: this is Gongmaru La Base Camp (4744m: **Lartsa Gongmaru La**).

A bit further down, the valley meets another one coming from the right. Cross the stream and follow the valley downwards on the right bank, to pass near a waterfall and a possible camping spot (one tent). Follow the path traversing the right slope. The valley turns right and the path descends to its floor. Continue along the stony riverbed for a few minutes and then climb steeply to a traverse of the right, sheer slope. There is a clear but narrow and precipitous path. While on the traverse, there is a side valley. Descend along it, back to the main ravine and follow it downwards along the riverbed. **Don't take the old, damaged path traversing the left slope!**

The valley is just a few metres wide here with sheer and high sides. Watch out for animals that might dislodge stones from above. Search for another traverse on the right slope that should start about 15mins along the riverbed; the path is precipitous and narrow again, but clear. Descend to the floor one more time after 10mins, cross the stream and ascend to an 800m-long traverse of the left slope. At its end, descend steeply to the riverbed before a clear right turn in the valley (NE).

It takes about 15mins to the **Chuskyurmo** campsite. Cross the stream and follow the right bank for a few minutes, then cross to the left. There are two parts to the campsite, with places for tents just by the trail and above, on a hill. Homestay accommodation is down the valley in Chokdo village.

STAGE 9
Chuskyurmo to Hemis

Start	Chuskyurmo (4089m)
Finish	Hemis (3649m)
Distance	20km
Time	6hrs
Altitude range	3394m (road bridge over the Shang Chu) to 4089m (Chuskyurmo)

Compared to the previous stage, this is rather relaxing. The descent to Shang Sumdo is easy, and then you follow a road. At the end there is a tiring walk along the dry terrain of the Indus Valley.

Alternatives
- You can finish in Shang Sumdo with its daily bus connection with Leh; the bus arrives at Shang about 5pm and leaves about 8am the next morning.
- From Shang Sumdo go to Shang and then follow a stream towards the north, to a pass. Cross it and descend to Hemis. Ask for details in Shang Sumdo, as this has not been checked by the author.
- If you don't want to visit Hemis, you can finish the trek in Kharu. Follow the road from Shang Sumdo until you get to the bridge on the Indus. There is a

small shop; a bus to Leh should stop there a few times each day. You can also try to catch a bus on the main Manali–Leh road, which passes Kharu.

Water supplies

Before leaving the river at Chokdo, take water for 1hr. Carry water between Shang Sumdo and the bridge 4.5km beyond it. At the bridge, refill bottles again for 2hrs.

Route

From camp go down the valley, on the left side of the stream, by a clear path. A riverbed is reached after a few minutes. Continue downwards, crossing the stream frequently. The path might be indistinct at the beginning of the season – just follow the stream. **Chokdo** village, with accommodation, is 20mins after leaving the camp. A left tributary joins the stream here (3985m) and the valley turns right towards the ESE. Continue along the riverbed, crossing the stream a few times for 10mins. Then, before the sharp left turn in the valley, leave the floor and follow the path on the left bank, about 15m above the river.

From the last house of Chokdo 15mins later, just beyond where the valley turns, it takes more than 1hr to reach Shang Sumdo. A dirt road begins somewhere beyond Chokdo. It follows the left bank on a high traverse, descending occasionally to the valley floor as far as **Shang Sumdo**. There is a campsite and a tent shop-restaurant and homestays in the village. The stream joins the dominant Shang Chu flowing from left (WNW) to right (E then N). There is a dirt road along it. ◀

To visit Shang Gompa, follow the road upstream for 1km; a round-trip from Shang Sumdo takes about 1hr.

From Shang Sumdo, follow the road downstream, on the right bank at first and on the left further on. The Indus Valley and **Martselang** village are reached in about 2hrs from Shang Sumdo and 3km beyond the road bridge on the Shang Chu, which is crossed on the way. ◀ As soon as you get there, still high above the river, leave the main road and turn left (NW) on to a dirt road. The turn is near some large *chortens* and *mani* walls. Hemis is in the next valley on the left and it takes 1½hrs to get there. From the

See the map in Trek 1 Stage 1.

chortens, follow a dirt road along the big *mani* walls and a path further on.

A good trail leads to the surfaced road connecting Kharu and Hemis, over 1.5km from the *chortens*. Follow the road for about 150m, then the route continues on a path along the true left bank of the stream (1.4km to Hemis Gompa). Meet the road again and the main part of the village. A campsite and accommodation is found at a solitary house on the true right side of the stream, opposite the main part of **Hemis**. The monastery has a guesthouse and restaurant; it is more expensive than in the village.

When planning your visit to the monastery and its museum note that buses leave Hemis for Leh (2hrs) at around 8am and 1pm.

Hemis Gompa, one of the most famous monasteries in Ladakh, is well worth a visit

357

APPENDIX A
Treks overview table

Trek	Start	Finish	Duration (days)	Time (hrs)	Distance (km)	Walking time/day	km/day	Max altitude (m)	Camps (no supplies)	Season	Difficulty	Page
1	Kharu (3345m)	Pang (4514m)	10	73	148	7h20	14.8	5287	7	Early June, late Aug–late Sept	Very demanding	108
2	Pang (4514m)	Padum (3600m)	12	75½	174	6h20	14.5	5355	8	Late Aug–late Sept	Demanding	147
3	Darcha (3378m)	Padum (3600m)	9	60	135	6h40	15	5054	1–2	Mid-June–mid-Oct	Relatively easy	190
4	Padum (3600m)	Stongde Gompa (3800m)	6	45½	112	7h40	18.7	5178	2	Late Aug–late Sept	Demanding	212
5	Padum (3600m)	Lamayuru (3491m)	8	50	148	6h15	18.5	4954	1–2	mid-June–mid-Oct	Moderate	237
6	Padum (3600m)	Lamayuru (3491m)	10	75	169	7h30	16.9	5272	5	Late Aug–mid-Oct	Demanding	263
7	Alchi (3121m)	Alchi (3121m)	8	47	98	6h	12.2	5177	1	June–Oct	Moderate	297
8	Spituk (3214m)	Hemis (3649m)	9	55	113	6h	12.6	5287	1	June–Oct	Relatively easy	335

The number of camps where no food supplies are available does not equal the minimum number of days where you will have to rely on your own supplies: it implies that some shops have very simple provisions insufficient for preparing an adequate meal. Some shops may be closed periodically, even in the peak season.

Stage summaries

Stage	Start	Finish	Distance (km)	Time (hrs)	Minimum altitude (m)	Maximum altitude (m)	Page
1 Kharnak							**108**
1	Kharu (3345m)	Camp beyond Shang Sumdo (3742m)	14	5	3345	3770	**114**
2	Camp beyond Shang Sumdo (3742m)	Waterfall camp (4621m)	11	8	3742	4621	**118**
3	Waterfall camp (4621m)	Nyimaling (4848m)	6.5	5½	4621	5287	**120**
4	Nyimaling (4848m)	Langthang Valley (4552m)	13.5	8½	4379	5175	**123**
5	Langthang Valley (4552m)	Gunlus Valley (4460m)	14	9	4460	5197	**127**
6	Gunlus Valley (4460m)	Near Dat village, Kharnak Valley (4299m)	19.5	9	4200 (approx)	4460	**131**
7	Near Dat village, Kharnak Valley (4299m)	Camp near Lungmoche (4743m)	23	9½	4299	4954	**134**
8	Camp near Lungmoche (4743m)	Zara Valley camp (4310m)	23	6½	4310	4743	**139**
9	Zara Valley camp (4310m)	Toze Valley camp (4360m)	10	5	4268	4360	**141**
10	Toze Valley camp (4360m)	Pang (4514m)	15	7	4360	4514	**145**

Stage	Start	Finish	Distance (km)	Time (hrs)	Minimum altitude (m)	Maximum altitude (m)	Page
2 Tsarab Chu							147
1	Pang (4514m)	Toze Valley camp (4431m)	9	3	4431	4514	**153**
2	Toze Valley camp (4431m)	Camp beyond Lung (4275m)	19	7½	4275	4431	**156**
3	Camp beyond Lung (4275m)	Morang La Advance Base Camp (4636m)	12	6½	4275	4669	**159**
4	Morang La Advance Base Camp (4636m)	Tsokmitsik (4095m)	11.5	7	4095	5355	**162**
5	Tsokmitsik (4095m)	Satak (4013m)	15.5	7½	4013	4402	**164**
6	Satak (4013m)	Hormoche (3963m)	15.5	6½	3925	4076	**168**
7	Hormoche (3963m)	Nyalo Kuntse La Base Camp (4406m)	16.5	9½	3963	5148	**171**
8	Nyalo Kuntse La Base Camp (4406m)	Yata (3993m)	10.5	4½	3896	4406	**173**
9	Yata (3993m)	Phukthal (3922m)	10.5	4½	3822	4103	**176**
10	Phukthal (3922m)	Pepula (3749m)	20	7½	3749	3922	**179**
11	Pepula (3749m)	Mune (3848m)	17	6	3730	3848	**184**
12	Mune (3848m)	Padum (3600m)	18	5½	3600	3848	**187**

Stage	Start	Finish	Distance (km)	Time (hrs)	Minimum altitude (m)	Maximum altitude (m)	Page
3 Darcha to Padum							**190**
1	Darcha (3378m)	Zanskar Sumdo (3932m)	13.5	7½	3378	3932	**196**
2	Zanskar Sumdo (3932m)	Chumik Nakpo (4652m)	12	7–8	3932	4652	**199**
3	Chumik Nakpo (4652m)	Lhakhang Sumdo (4477m)	10	6½	4477	5054	**201**
4	Lhakhang Sumdo (4477m)	Kargyak (4135m)	15.5	5–6	4135	4477	**203**
5	Kargyak (4135m)	Testha (3991m)	16	5	3991	4135	**205**
6	Testha (3991m)	Purni (3897m)	8.5	3½	3801	3991	**207**
7	Purni (3897m)	Pepula (3749m)	15	5½	3749	3897	**209**
8	Pepula (3749m)	Mune (3848m)	17	6	3730	3848	**211**
9	Mune (3848m)	Padum (3600m)	18	5½	3600	3848	**211**
4 Round Sultanlango							**212**
1	Padum (3600m)	Raru (3805m)	22	6	3600	3848	**219**
2	Raru (3805m)	Kalbok (3863m)	22	8½	3730	3879	**220**
3	Kalbok (3863m)	Phukthal (3922m)	11.5	3½	3801	3922	**223**
4	Phukthal (3922m)	Niri Valley camp (3912m)	18.5	8½	3822	4103	**225**
5	Niri Valley camp (3912m)	Shingri Valley camp (4195m)	18	9	3912	4251	**229**
6	Shingri Valley camp (4195m)	Stongde Gompa (3800m)	21	10	3800	5178	**233**

Stage	Start	Finish	Distance (km)	Time (hrs)	Minimum altitude (m)	Maximum altitude (m)	Page
5 Padum to Lamayuru							237
1	Padum (3600m)	Pishu (3435m)	25.5	7	3435	3600	243
2	Pishu (3435m)	Hanamur (3447m)	16	5½	3425	3495	246
3	Hanamur (3447m)	Nyetse (3744m)	14	8½	3302	3921	247
4	Nyetse (3744m)	Lingshed (3925m)	17	9–10	3744	4757	250
5	Lingshed (3925m)	Sengge La Base Camp (Gazho) (4482m)	14.5	7	3925	4482	253
6	Gazho (4482m)	Photoksar (4218m)	19.5	8	4218	4954	255
7	Photoksar (4218m)	Phanjila via the Askuta Way (3285m)	24	8	3285	4218	257
8	Phanjila (3285m)	Lamayuru (3491m)	18	5	3183	3749	260
6 Padum to Lamayuru via the Kanji La							263
1	Padum (3600m)	Pishu (3435m)	25.5	7	3435	3600	269
2	Pishu (3435m)	Hanamur (3447m)	16	5½	3425	3495	269
3	Hanamur (3447m)	Zhingchan (3413m)	13.5	7½	3302	3921	269
4	Zhingchan (3413m)	Squaz (3754m)	11	7	3413	3946	273
5	Squaz (3754m)	Dibling (3964m)	20	8½	3596	3964	276
6	Dibling (3964m)	Kanji La Southern Base Camp (4248m)	24	11	3913	5024	279

Stage	Start	Finish	Distance (km)	Time (hrs)	Minimum altitude (m)	Maximum altitude (m)	Page
7	(4248m)	Kanji La Northern Base Camp (4382m)	11	8½	4248	5272	284
8	Kanji La Northern Base Camp (4382m)	Chomotang Togpo Valley (3973m)	17.5	6½	3841	4382	288
9	Chomotang Togpo Valley (3973m)	Shillakong (4122m)	8.5	4½	3973	4728	290
10	Shillakong (4122m)	Lamayuru (3491m)	23	8	3233	4122	293
7 Alchi							297
1	Alchi (3121m)	Stakspi La Base Camp (4273m)	6.5	4	3121	4273	303
2	Stakspi La Base Camp (4273m)	Sumdha Chungun (3867m)	9	6	3867	5177	306
3	Sumdha Chungun (3867m)	Manechan (4048m)	15.5	6	3453	4048	308
4	Manechan (4048m)	Hinju (3818m)	16	7½	3802	4904	312
5	Hinju (3818m)	Ursi (3662m)	7.5	2½	3487	3818	315
6	Ursi (3662m)	Tar (3372m)	15.5	7½	3372	4946	317
7	Tar (3372m)	Mangyu (3518m)	12	7	3372	4161	321
8	Mangyu (3518m)	Alchi (3121m)	16.5	4	3090	3518	323

Stage	Start	Finish	Distance (km)	Time (hrs)	Minimum altitude (m)	Maximum altitude (m)	Page
8 Markha Valley							325
1	Spituk (3214m)	Zhingchan (3396m)	16	5½	3190	3396	334
2	Zhingchan (3396m)	Camp below Kanda La (4462m)	10.5	7½	3383	4462	337
3	Camp below Kanda La (4462m)	Shingo (4173m)	7.5	5½	4173	4973	339
4	Shingo (4173m)	Pentse (3445m)	13	5	3387	4173	341
5	Pentse (3445m)	Markha (3755m)	15	7	3431	3755	344
6	Markha (3755m)	Hangkar (3990m)	10.5	5	3755	3990	346
7	Hangkar (3990m)	Nyimaling (4848m)	11	7½	3990	4848	349
8	Nyimaling (4848m)	Chuskyurmo (4089m)	10	6½	4089	5287	352
9	Chuskyurmo (4089m)	Hemis (3649m)	20	6	3394	4089	355

APPENDIX C
Some Ladakhi language words and phrases

Basics

Hello, good morning, good bye, thank you	*julley*
How are you?	*Khamzang-le?*
I'm fine	*Khamzang*
Yes	*O*
Yes, thanks	*O, julley*
No	*Man*
No, thank you	*Man, julley*
is (there is)	*duk*
is not (there is no)	*mi-duk*
a little	*tsapik*
enough	*dik*

Food and drink

bread	*tagi*
cottage cheese	*labo*
dried cheese	*churpe, chura*
rice	*dass*
soup	*tukpa*
yoghurt	*zho*
local 'beer'	*chang*
milk	*oma*
tea	*cha*
black tea	*cha nakpo*
milk tea (sweet)	*cha ngarmo*
salty, butter tea	*gurgur cha*
water (also river)	*chu*
boiling (hot) water	*chu skol*

Landmarks

base camp	*lartsa*
bridge	*zampa*
cairn (often on a mountain pass)	*lhato*
confluence	*sumdo*
lake	*tso*
mani wall	*ma-ne*
monastery	*gompa*
mountain	*ri*
mountain pass	*la*
river	*chu*
shepherds' hut	*pulu*
stream	*togpo*

Directions

left	*yoma*
right	*yaspa*
straight	*katang*
downhill	*thur*
uphill	*gyen*
far	*takring*
near	*nyemo*
How far to Padum?	*Padum-a tsam-zhig takring yot?*

Addressing people

In Ladakh it is common to use family titles when addressing people. You should add *-le* to the end of the relevant word to express respect. You will certainly hear people calling each other *ama-le*, *aba-le* and so on, and you should use *acho-le* or other as appropriate.

mother	*ama*
father	*aba*
younger sister	*no-*
older sister	*ache*
younger brother	*no-no*
older brother	*acho*
aunt	*a-ne*
uncle	*agu*

APPENDIX D
Glossary

arhat	Being who has managed to become free from the cycle of existence (samsara). Arhats are not often seen as icons, but when they are, their faces have moustaches and beards. The 16 arhats are the original disciples of Buddha.
bharal	Species of blue sheep.
bodhisattva	An enlightened being who has delayed the attainment of Nirvana and has remained to teach.
Bon	Pre-Buddhist religion of Tibet.
cham	Dances performed by monks during festivals; religious dance/dramas with colourful costumes and masks.
chorten	Similar in shape to a small stupa (see below); do not normally contain relics. They are mostly found in high Buddhist mountain country and are seen in profusion across Ladakh.
dharma	Teachings of Buddhism as a whole; the path to enlightenment; a way to alleviate suffering.
dorje/vajra	Thunderbolt that destroys ignorance; a metal object found at many temples and shrines. In Hinduism it is the symbol of Indra.
drubkhang	Hermitage for meditation.
dukhang	Main assembly hall of the monastery, where monks come to offer prayer and meditation.
gompa	Monastery, usually consisting of one or a few temples, an assembly hall and monks' houses.
gonkhang	Small chamber devoted to the protecting deities. Often dark and somewhat forbidding, this room may house the images of Yamantaka, Mahakala and Palden Lhamo, among others.
Hinayana	The 'Lesser vehicle' of Buddhism, in which one is concerned with one's own liberation, and not that of the greater world of all sentient beings.
khang	House or building, sometimes used as an abbreviation of lhakhang.
lama (Sanskrit guru)	Religious teacher and guide; can be male or female. Very few monks and even fewer nuns are considered to be lamas.
lhato	Cairn or small mound (of rocks) often built on mountain passes or some special place en route.
lhakhang	Temple within a monastery.
Losar	Tibetan New Year festival.
Mahayana	The 'Greater vehicle' of Buddhism. Practitioners are dedicated to serving the welfare of all sentient beings, not only themselves.
mandala	A circular pattern made of many colours, often a square or squares within a circle. Represents 'the divine abode of an enlightened being visualised during Tantric practices'.

mani stone	(Usually large) rock engraved with Buddhist mantras, sometimes painted.
mani wall	Long wall made of flat stones engraved with Buddhist mantras; may also contain prayer wheels. These should always be passed clockwise, with the wall on the right.
mantra	Series of Sanskrit syllables, not always words with an absolute meaning. Chanting these sounds is thought to create particular effects in the minds of the practitioner and others.
mudra	Hand position indicating a particular attitude in a Buddha or bodhisattva.
prayer flags	Set of colourful rectangular pieces of cloth inscribed with Buddhist symbols and texts usually strung across mountain passes, at peaks, and on roofs of houses and monasteries. It is believed that the message of the Buddha is blown by the wind and spread across the country for the benefit of all sentient beings. Hanging the flags is also considered a beneficial act for those who hang them.
prayer wheel	Metal wheel engraved with Tibetan script and containing prayers; may either be large and fixed into a wall, or hand held and spun while walking. The action of spinning the wheel activates the prayers.
puja	Ceremony offering prayers, usually for a specific purpose, for example blessing a house.
reincarnated lama	New human form taken by a lama after a previous human life has ended.
samsara	Cycle of birth, death and rebirth; ordinary reality, an endless cycle of frustration and suffering, is the result of karma.
sangha	The community of Buddhists; one of the 'three jewels' of Buddhism. Sometimes used to refer to only monks and nuns, it can also mean all Buddhist practitioners.
stupa	Large monument, usually with a square base, a dome and a pointed spire on top. The spire represents the levels towards enlightenment. A stupa might host the remains of a revered lama or teacher.
sutra	A teaching of Sakyamuni Buddha.
Tangyur	The part of the Buddhist 'bible' which contains Indian treatises or commentaries on the Buddha's teachings, as opposed to the Kangyur, made up of tantras and sutras, Buddha's own teachings.
thangka/tangka	Religious painting, usually on silk fabric; seen in all monasteries hanging on the walls or pillars.
tsampa	Roasted barley; Tibetan staple food. Mixed with butter tea, it is made into a sort of porridge and eaten with the fingers.
tulku	A lama, usually one of high rank, who is considered to be a reincarnation of a lama who was living in the past.
Tushita	Often referred to as Tushita heaven; the place where the future Buddha Maitreya now lives.
vajra	See dorje.
zimchung	Head lama's chamber, often on the roof area.

Significant Tibetan/Ladakhi Buddhist Deities

The following icons are commonly seen in Ladakh's monasteries. The names are given in both Sanskrit and Tibetan/Ladakhi.

Sakyamuni (Sakya Tukpa)

The pure image of the mortal Buddha, Gautama Siddhartha, born in Nepal. He has blue hair, a golden body and holds a bowl in his lap in most depictions.

The Dhyani Buddhas

These face the four cardinal directions, meditating, and are abstract images encompassing the universe. These mystical Buddhas are found in the Mahayana form of Buddhism that developed over the subcontinent.

Vairocana The first Dhyani Buddha and resides in the *stupa* sanctum. Vairocana is the illuminator to light the way and is a very common image in Ladakh.

Akshobhya The Dhyani Buddha who sits facing east. He is regarded as the second Dhyani and his right palm faces inwards. Akshobhya has various wrathful forms, including Heruka.

Amitabha The oldest of the Dhyani Buddhas, who faces west. The Amitabha is linked to Sakyamuni, the earthly Buddha.

Amoghasiddhi The Dhyani Buddha who always faces north. When on a *stupa* or *chorten* a serpent with seven heads usually stands behind him. He is linked to the future Buddha, Maitreya.

Ratna Sambhava The Dhyani Buddha who faces south; his right palm faces outwards.

Vajrasattva The sixth Dhyani Buddha; he is the priest for the other five, and is only found separately from his disciples.

Chenresig (Avalokiteshvara)

A popular *bodhisattva* who renounced Nirvana, the end of the cycle of rebirth. He embodies compassion (*karuna*) and remains on earth to counter distress and suffering. Chenresig in one aspect is seen with 11 heads. The Dalai Lama is considered to be his earthly representative.

Vajrapani (Channa Dorje)

A spiritual son of Akshobhya. He carries a *dorje* and is a powerful and wrathful protector in Ladakh. He has monstrous Tantric powers and wears a snake around his neck.

Manjushri (Jampelyang)

The *bodhisattva* of divine wisdom. He carries the sword to cut through ignorance, and according to tradition is a Chinese saint. To worship Manjushri gives intellect and intelligence.

Yamantaka (Dorje Jigje)
The 'slayer of death', a wrathful emanation of Manjushri. He is the one who can destroy Yama, the guardian at the gates of heaven and hell. Yama is the deity who holds the wheel of life in his jaws.

Tara (Drolma or Dolma)
The Sanskrit Tara who is sacred to both Buddhists and Hindus. She represents the maternal aspect, symbolising fertility, purity and compassion. Tara can appear in different colours: red, green, white, gold and dark blue, each representing a different aspect of her nature. There are considered to be 21 aspects or forms of Tara.

Palden Lhamo
A protectress of the Gelug-pa. A backdrop of peacock feathers sits behind her and she holds a corpse in her mouth.

Maitreya Buddha (Chamba/Jampa)
The future Buddha, who appears in a number of monasteries. His colour is yellow or gold and he is preparing to come to earth. He usually stands, or sits with legs pointing downwards. Maitreya is found in abundance in Ladakh.

Mahakala
One of the eight aspects of terror, depicted as exceedingly ugly and ferocious in art. He often tramples on bodies or corpses. In Ladakh he is known as Gonpo, the great black one. Mahakala is always black or dark blue; he has three eyes that represent the past, present and future. His ghostly crown of skulls or gruesome heads represents the five delusions that poison a soul: ignorance, anger, desire, jealousy and pride.

Padma Sambhava/Guru Rinpoche
The Tantric master who established Vajrayana Buddhism in Tibet in the eighth–ninth centuries. He hid various important teachings in Tibet, Nepal and Bhutan, in order that they may be revealed for future generations in years to come.

Tsong Khapa
Founder of the Gelug-pa sect. He usually wears a yellow pointed hat, and often sits between two similar Buddha figures (his disciples).

Milarepa
Tibet's poet saint, an historical figure associated with many legends.

The Four Harmonious Brothers
In many Buddhist monasteries are paintings depicting four animals, one on top of the other: the Elephant, the Monkey, the Rabbit and the Bird (on top) who represent the harmony that can inspire peace and remove conflict.

The Four Guardians
Known as the Lokapalas, there are the deities seen at the entrance to most monasteries.

APPENDIX E
Embassies and consulates

Foreign missions in India
There are no foreign embassies or consulates in Ladakh; in the case of most countries the nearest mission is located in Delhi. The list below is not exclusive; emergency phone numbers, email addresses and websites have been given. For the embassies not listed please check www.india.gov.in (go to Overseas, Embassies & Consulates). If you are an EU citizen, and your own country has no embassy or consulate, you are entitled to help from that of any other EU Member State.

Australia
Australian High Commission
1/50-G Shantipath
Chanakyapuri
New Delhi 110 021
Tel. +91 (11) 4139 9900
Email AHC.NewDelhi@dfat.gov.au
www.india.embassy.gov.au

Canada
Canadian High Commission
7/8 Shantipath
Chanakyapuri
New Delhi 110 021
Tel. +91 (11) 4178 2000
Email delhi@international.gc.ca
www.canadainternational.gc.ca/
india-inde

New Zealand
New Zealand High Commission
Sir Edmund Hilary Marg
Chanakyapuri
New Delhi 110 021
Tel. +91 (11) 4688 3170
Email nzhc@airtelmail.in
www.nzembassy.com/india

United Kingdom
British High Commission
Chanakyapuri
New Delhi 110 021
Tel. +91 (11) 2419 2100
Email web.newdelhi@fco.gov.uk
www.ukinindia.fco.gov.uk

United States of America
US Embassy
Shantipath
New Delhi 110 021
Tel. +91 (11) 2419 8000
Email acsnd@state.gov
http://newdelhi.usembassy.gov/

Indian missions abroad
For contact information for an Indian Embassy or Consulate in your home country please check the list at www.india.gov.in, as above.

APPENDIX F
Further reading

Recommendations

Gibbons, Bob and Pritchard-Jones, Siân *Ladakh: Land of Magical Monasteries* Pilgrims Publishing (2006) – For detailed description of monasteries as well as religious and cultural background.

Norberg-Hodge, Helena *Ancient Futures – Learning from Ladakh*
Oxford University Press (1991) – A legendary book on the Ladakhi culture and changes in the face of increased tourism. A 'must read' for anybody wanting to travel in Ladakh conscientiously and responsibly.

Norman, Rebecca *Getting started in Ladakhi*
Melong Publications of Ladakh (2001) – A popular phrasebook.

Rizvi, Janet *Ladakh: Crossroads of High Asia*
Oxford University Press (2007) – Probably the best monograph on Ladakh; refer to it for geographical, historical and cultural information.

Bibliography

Ahmed, Monisha and Harris, Clare (eds) *Ladakh Culture at the Crossroads*
Marg Publications (Mumbai, 2005)

Allen, Charles *The Search for Shangrila* Little, Brown and Company (London, 1999)

Cunningham, Alexander *Ladak, Physical, Statistical and Historical* (1853, reprinted by Pilgrims 2005)

Dalai Lama *An Introduction to Buddhism and Tantric Meditation* Paljor Publications (1996)

Francke, Rev AH *A History of Western Tibet* (1907, reprinted by Pilgrims 1998)

Genoud, Charles and Inoue, Takao *Buddhist Wall Painting of Ladakh* Editions Olizane (Geneva, 1981)

Govinda, Lama Anagarika *The Way of the White Clouds* Rider and Company (London, 1966)

Kapur, Brigadier Teg Bahadur *Ladakh the Wonderland* Mittal Publications (Delhi 1984)

Kaul, Shridhar & Kaul, HN *Ladakh Through the Ages* Indus (Delhi 1992)

Khosla, Romi *Buddhist Monasteries in the Western Himalaya* Ratna (1979)

Kohn, Michael *The Shambhala Dictionary of Buddhism and Zen* Shambhala (Boston, 1991)

Kumar Das, Pradeep and Tashi Phunchok *Insight Ladakh* Ratna Voyages Publications (Leh, 2009)

Shyam, Menon G *'Two sides to Ladakh tourism'* www.thehindubusinessline.com 1 December, 2011

Pal, Pradapaditya *A Buddhist Paradise: The Murals of Alchi* Visual Dharma Publications (Hong Kong, 1982)

Pallis, Marco *Peaks and Lamas* (1939, reprinted Book Faith India 1995)

Pfister, Otto *Birds and Mammals of Ladakh* Oxford University Press (New Delhi, 2004)

Powers, John *Introduction to Tibetan Buddhism* Snow Lion Publications (Ithaca, New York 1995)

Prophet, Elizabeth Clare *The Lost Years of Jesus* Book Faith India (1994)

Roerich, George *Tibetan Paintings* Gyan Publishing House (1997)

Roerich, Nicholas *Altai Himalaya* (1929, reprinted by Book Faith India 1996)

Singh Jina, Prem *Some monasteries of the Drigung-pa order in Central Ladakh* Sri Satguru (Delhi, 1999)

Singh Jina, Prem *Religious History of Ladakh* Sri Satguru (Delhi, 2001)

Snellgrove, David *Buddhist Himalaya* Himalayan Booksellers (1995, Asia edition from 1957 edition by Bruno Cassirer)

Tashi Ldawa Thsangspa, *Ladakh Book of Records* Ladakh Study Group (Leh, 2008)

Tchekhoff, Genevieve and Comolli, Yvan *Buddhist Sanctuaries of Ladakh* White Orchid Books (Bangkok, 1987)

Thupstan Paldan *The guide of the Buddhist monasteries and royal castles of Ladakh* Dorjee Tsering (Delhi, 2008)

Tucci, Giuseppe *Shrines of a Thousand Buddhas* Pilgrims (Varanasi, 2008)

Tucci, Giuseppe and Ghersi, E. *Secrets of Tibet* Cosmo Publications (India, 1996) (Asia edition) © Genesis Publishing Pvt Ltd, 24B Ansari Road, Daryaganj, New Delhi, India

Tucci, Giuseppe, *Transhimalaya* Nagel Publishers (Geneva, 1973)

INDEX OF MAPS

INDEX OF PLACE NAMES

LISTING OF CICERONE GUIDES

Walking – Trekking – Mountaineering – Climbing – Cycling

Over 40 years, Cicerone have built up an outstanding collection of over 300 guides, inspiring all sorts of amazing adventures.

Every guide comes from extensive exploration and research by our expert authors, all with a passion for their subjects. They are frequently praised, endorsed and used by clubs, instructors and outdoor organisations.

All our titles can now be bought as **e-books**, **ePubs** and **Kindle** files and we also have an online magazine – **Cicerone Extra** – with features to help cyclists, climbers, walkers and trekkers choose their next adventure, at home or abroad.

Our website shows any **new information** we've had in since a book was published. Please do let us know if you find anything has changed, so that we can publish the latest details. On our **website** you'll also find great ideas and lots of detailed information about what's inside every guide and you can buy **individual routes** from many of them online.

It's easy to keep in touch with what's going on at Cicerone by getting our monthly **free e-newsletter**, which is full of offers, competitions, up-to-date information and topical articles. You can subscribe on our home page and also follow us on **Facebook** and **Twitter** or dip into our **blog**.

Cicerone – the very best guides for exploring the world.

CICERONE

2 Police Square Milnthorpe Cumbria LA7 7PY
Tel: 015395 62069 info@cicerone.co.uk
www.cicerone.co.uk and **www.cicerone-extra.com**